Young Adult Literature in the Composition Classroom

Young Adult Literature in the Composition Classroom

Essays on Practical Application

Edited by TAMARA GIRARDI and
ABIGAIL G. SCHEG

McFarland & Company, Inc., Publishers
Jefferson, North Carolina

ISBN (print) 978-1-4766-6995-3
ISBN (ebook) 978-1-4766-3348-0

LIBRARY OF CONGRESS CATALOGUING DATA ARE AVAILABLE

BRITISH LIBRARY CATALOGUING DATA ARE AVAILABLE

Front cover image © 2018 eclipse_images/iStock

Printed in the United States of America

*McFarland & Company, Inc., Publishers
Box 611, Jefferson, North Carolina 28640
www.mcfarlandpub.com*

Table of Contents

Introduction

TAMARA GIRARDI *and*
ABIGAIL G. SCHEG

In hosting a young adult literature (YAL) conference, Louisiana State University noted that YAL "has never been more popular or prevalent in this country" (LSU). The School of Education at the university planned the event because of its benefits for students enrolled in their programs. Over the last ten years, YAL has continued to grow in the publishing and academic communities. In 2012, the children's book market topped $3.3 billion, according to *Publisher's Weekly*; roughly 55 percent of sales are attributed to adult, not young adult, readers (Milliot). In other words, YAL is a powerful literary category rich with diverse genres and cross-generational appeal, especially in the last few years.

While the category of literature has received heavy criticism for "frequently featur(ing) protagonists who are white, able-bodied, cisgender, and heterosexual," several groups, such as the We Need Diverse Books campaign, Disability in Kidlit, and the Diversity in YA organization have argued openly for greater diversity in the texts (Baumbach). The organizations are not only advocating for diversity, but they also promote diverse texts and track data on the topic. In other words, YAL is popular, and at the least moving toward greater inclusivity. For this reason and many others discussed in this text, we argue that composition instructors should embrace the power of YAL in their classrooms to engage students in academic writing, which might otherwise be foreign to them. It is not just because of the popularity of YAL that it should be included in the composition classroom setting; YAL, like composition, is interdisciplinary, and serves as a unique opportunity to facilitate discussions on innumerable topics.

The prominent composition textbook *They Say, I Say: The Moves That Matter in Academic Writing* by Gerald Graff and Cathy Birkenstein, which we have used successfully in our composition courses, references Kenneth Burke's Burkean Parlor metaphor that defines academic writing as an ongoing conversation. Students join this conversation after much has already been said, while much remains to be discussed. The metaphor often empowers students to accept their academic writing is not meant to regurgitate what others have written on a subject, but to offer insights that only they could present with their unique worldview and interpretation of what "they say." We reference this text because we believe in the power of such a post-process revelation. Students *should* read, research, and write to find their own voices, but beyond that they must understand that their writing is valuable to an audience only when relevant in a larger context (i.e., the Burkean Parlor). Fortunately for composition instructions, in its popularity, YAL possesses the power to intrigue, inspire, and empower students in this way.

To further the discussion, we must consider the audience of first-year composition courses. Publishers regularly identify the young adult audience as ages 12–18, with middle grade texts targeting younger readers (ages 8–12) and the more recently created concept of new adult literature (NAL) targeting older readers (college-aged to mid-twenty-somethings). As this text demonstrates, young adult texts carry significant value for composition students, but by definition, YAL is not targeted to college students; therefore, some discussion on the concept of adults reading YAL is certainly relevant to the conversation.

First of all, as the aforementioned age categories demonstrate, traditional college students fall into the target audience of NAL. While some critics of the NAL genre wrongly assume that new adult "is basically a young adult book with sex and cursing thrown in" (Sarner), primarily for the reason that young adult texts also feature sex and cursing, the truth is that while YAL consists of a fully developed age category of literature, new adult has not grown to fill those shoes. More specifically, while YAL is comprised of several different genres (fantasy, science fiction, dystopian, contemporary, etc.), NAL has not grown as much as some publishers would probably have liked and instead really is more of a genre (primarily romance) than an age category at present. It should be noted, however, that several authors and publishers of NAL hope to broaden the genre beyond romance into others such as fantasy, science fiction, and so on. Nevertheless, the central point here is that while NAL is aiming to grow and develop, YAL has become the publishing power it is from decades of development and refinement.

The variation between YAL and NAL is imperative to this discussion because critics of employing YAL in the classroom might instead argue that NAL texts could be more relevant to our student audience. On the contrary, NAL, as a genre, would require significantly more development to provide instructors the opportunity to select appropriate texts for analysis and discussion in the academic context. The proliferation of YAL in the last decade-plus has led to the market being "flooded with both quality and trash … just as with adult publishing" (Cole 57). Nevertheless, the "quality" is "some of the best in contemporary literature" (Cole 57). "[I]n the last several years, an increasing number of books with multiple, complex themes have found their way onto young adult bookshelves" (Cole 60). In other words, while NAL might be appropriate for the age category of college students on the surface, deeper analysis would demonstrate that YAL provides instructors more options for high-quality writing and stories that can resonate with students and influence them to think deeply about the composition tasks set before them during the semester. That argument aside, more importantly, YAL possesses crossover appeal that will not only attract traditional college students who might still be actively reading YAL but also non-traditional adult students as well.

As Judith A. Hayn, Jeffrey S. Kaplan, and Amanda L. Nolen postulate, "Capturing the imagination of adolescents is no easy task. Young people—especially those more eager to watch than to read—are always transfixed by the here and now" (176). That said, the authors also argue that adolescents enjoy reading contemporary texts, perhaps more than writing academic ones. For most first-year composition students, academic writing is a secondary discourse. In other words, the kinds of academic writing required in colleges and universities proves difficult and foreign to students. "Struggling writers, especially those whose home discourses differ significantly from those of the academy, can learn to see themselves beyond the lens of failure and deficiency" (Fernsten and Reda 181). If academic writing is in fact a variant of the students' home discourses, as many scholars have argued (Bartholomae; Heath; Perl; Wallace and Ewald), then what can be done to bridge the gap between the required academic writing they must conquer to succeed in higher education and their primary discourse with which they're comfortable?

In this text, we recommend composition instructors also employ the contemporary texts with which first-year composition students tend to be most familiar, thus already intertwined with their identity development, those of YAL. After all, students' "home discourses" include the literature they read "for fun" on weekends and school breaks. If, then, first-year composition students are indeed familiar with, or beyond that, fond of such works as Suzanne Collins' *The Hunger Games*, Veronica Roth's *Divergent* series, or Stephen Chbosky's *The Perks of Being a Wallflower*, to name a few, wouldn't it be beneficial to incorporate such literary works in the curriculum? Would doing so perhaps validate the students' personal literary selections, building common ground between the reading they love and the dreaded academic writing they're required to complete?

To state it simply, the popularity of YAL and the realization that many high school and college students read the texts mentioned in this collection for pleasure suggest it's logical to connect composition classroom strategies to works of literature students are *choosing* to read (Monseau and Salvner; Elliot and Dupuis). Of course the prevalence and popularity of YAL among our student writers is not the only argument for its inclusion in our composition classrooms, as many of the authors in this collection further demonstrate with their own contributions. Nevertheless, while students struggle to understand essay structure, strong thesis and paragraph development, supporting evidence, and documentation methods, they can benefit from topics and discussions that engage their interests. However, research to support such claims is limited: "Educators who believe in the use of YAL, and seek to implement its inclusion in school curriculum, need validation for their stance in a solid body of research drawn from the field" (Hayn, Kaplan, and Nolen 177). While the authors were referring to secondary school educators, quite often post-secondary educators are challenged on what scholarship exists to support their pedagogical choices. In agreeing with Hayn, Kaplan, and Nolen, we "assert that although there is little empirical research, what is there … is diverse in method, topic, and population" (177).

This text contributes to the discussion of appropriate uses for YAL in academic contexts, specifically the composition classroom. Furthermore, the issues and themes addressed in the YAL texts referenced in this collection provide ample opportunity for classroom discussion and academic exploration. YAL and the composition classroom fit together nicely as they can both be interdisciplinary explorations of words, culture, characters, and times. This text is designed for a variety of readers, including composition instructors (those that may use the "Practical Considerations for the Composition Classroom" sections in their own classrooms), composition and literature researchers including experienced scholars and graduate students, researchers interested in YAL and popular culture for educational purposes, and those interested in YAL and popular culture in a general sense.

In this collection's opening essay, Lacy Marschalk outlines the multiple ways in which Rainbow Rowell's contemporary YA novel *Fangirl* can be used in the composition classroom, and in particular in a themed class on identity she taught for honors composition students. While most YA novels involve characters who are still in high school, *Fangirl* is set during protagonist Cath Avery's first year at the University of Nebraska–Lincoln. First-year composition students will experience many college firsts right alongside Cath, and teaching this fictional but relatable text allows students to discuss difficult topics, including binge drinking, academic failure, and mental illness in a safe space.

Melissa Ames also discusses social responsibility in dystopian YAL. In capitalizing on student interests such as the popularity of YA dystopian novels and media, she and her students wrestled with ethical concerns regarding societal achievements, technological advancement, scientific discoveries, and so on. Likewise, Ames offers practical steps and models to make such connections between fictional texts and real-world problems.

Next, Mary McCulley shares the value of teaching the literacy narrative using *The Book Thief*, arguing, "literature can aid the larger goals of composition classes" in that "literature supports a democratic composition classroom because it helps foster empathy and identification with others while promoting critical reflection." The content of *The Book Thief* appropriately challenges students to consider literacy development and multiple perspectives of literacy as they read and explore their own journeys with writing and literacy.

Andrew Bourelle discusses *The Perks of Being a Wallflower*'s protagonist Charlie, and his unnamed "Friend" to whom he reveals the truth of his life. Bourelle's pedagogical approach to the text includes discussing its relevance, either in the classroom or through written assignments, as a persuasive piece that can be analyzed in first-year composition courses.

Further discussing the perceptions of young adult literature's place in academia, Mariam Kushkaki challenges the "No Vampires Policy" trend in first-year composition (FYC). In representing the overall aim of this text as a whole, Kushkaki criticizes faculty dismissal of young adult literature, linking the movement to the tension sparked by the *Twilight* series' popularity with teens. Kushkaki's essay explores how assignments incorporating YA literature in the composition classroom not only benefit students but also meet the WPA Outcomes Statement for FYC. Her work honors rigorous curriculum demands while also providing a framework for incorporating popular YA.

Mary-Lynn Chambers and Kathleen B. Gray then explore students' reactions to their own personal crises as a lens through which they read YAL. Specifically, the authors address the popularity of crisis-oriented YAL and the influence it has on college students in general and the composition classroom specifically. Chambers and Gray argue that by modeling the crisis-oriented writings established in the literature, the composition classroom can potentially help students establish that their pre-college experiences are not antithetical to their new college lives.

Tara Stillions Whitehead and Richard James Whitehead critically examine YAL and otherness, as well as using empathy as a rhetorical tool. Exploring diverse protagonists, the authors impress upon their students that "taking another's perspective does not mean surrendering to another's ideology." By encouraging openness to otherness and varying perspectives, students can improve critical thinking skills and become more intelligent writers.

Kelly F. Franklin goes on to argue that adolescents often develop opinions based on arguments represented in their social media feeds, and connects that idea to the nature of performance as it connects to student writers' online personas. Franklin presents the concept of imagined communities as relevant to Cory Doctorow's young adult dystopian novel *Little Brother*, providing first-year composition students the opportunity to explore "the notion that modern day is in fact a dystopia."

As many YAL protagonists struggled against the powerful forces in her social context, so too do young adults in general, argue Christi L. Cook and LeeAnn Olivier in their essay. "Like many of its protagonists, young adult literature is marginalized: it is an oft contested and sometimes suspect genre existing on the borderlands of the canon of adult literature," according to the authors. Yet, as is the case with most literature, several archetypes are prevalent in YAL. To help student writers identify archetypes and further incorporate them in their own compositions, the authors share a theoretical framework and pragmatic teaching strategies for including resonant mythological archetypes as a driving force when teaching *A Monster Calls* by Patrick Ness.

Padma Baliga and Namrata Harish follow, offering their perspective of dystopian fiction within the context of the Indian classroom. Since English is not their students' first language, the authors emphasize a pedagogy that focuses on reading and writing to "help students learn to use the language comfortably and profitably." Due to the courses being mandated, Baliga and Harish find that students are hesitant to read, but embracing a mix of graphic novels, film texts and YA novels lead to more eager responses from students. More specifically, the authors argue for the use of dystopian YAL in that "themes of family and peer pressure are juxtaposed with political ones; it is the most obvious bridge between fiction for children and that for adults."

Jenny Ferguson's essay next tackles the challenges of composition as a general education requirement through discussion of her creative writing as a composition course. Ferguson discusses her use of YAL social justice texts to foster student engagement in the reading and discussions. Her essay also describes assignments of narrative, modeling, mapping, and reader response.

Jenny L. Howe examines gender politics in Stephenie Meyer's worldwide bestseller, *Twilight,* with the goal of demonstrating the role gender studies and YAL can play in the development of college-level writing. Howe's essay considers how gender theory can inspire discussions of YAL and increase critical thinking (in general and in response to texts) with her students. This essay also discusses the position of YAL and popular culture versus the use of the classics as reading materials in a composition classroom.

Michele D. Castleman also uses classics; specifically, she discusses using myth to inspire composition students to pen their own myths. Castlemen discusses the use of Scott Westerfeld's *Afterworlds* to better understand the genre of writing and, further, to challenge students to consider the authorial experience of writing myths. She provides assignments to teach students about literary archetypes and reflect upon the use of archetypes in both classic and popular literature.

Kelly F. Franklin applies the notion of epic theater and theater for social change to Katniss Everdeen, protagonist of *The Hunger Games*, to argue that the futuristic post-apocalyptic heroine does more than entertain readers—she serves as an icon of social change, both within her own story and in real life. As a result, then, student writers in the composition classroom might debate concepts of icons of social change in discussions and essays.

Matthew D. Fazio follows and examines death tropes in YAL. By surveying the plots of numerous young adult novels, Fazio determines that, while not a popular way to start most genres of writing, many young adult novels begin with a death. He asserts that reliance on a death trope is to establish a level of comfort and familiarity with the audience. By understanding the death of YA characters, Fazio is able to offer a rhetorical inquiry project appropriate for use in the composition classroom.

Danielle Brownsberger studies representations of autism in YAL. Brownsberger's essay examines the depiction of autism in *The Curious Incident of the Dog in the Night-Time* in order to expose the unconscious ideologies that surround neurology in YAL. She provides discussion questions about *The Curious Incident of the Dog in the Night-Time* to foster student engagement and participation in the subject area and to provoke thought about social responsibility in the college composition classroom.

Tiffany M.B. Anderson writes about Gene Luen Yang's *American Born Chinese* and argues that "while Chinese mythology, legends, and folklore preserve Chinese culture, American popular culture disseminates stereotypes of minorities to Americans while simultaneously pulling minorities into mainstream American culture." Anderson's essay also considers how *American Born Chinese* expands the traditional understanding of text to include graphic images and allows students a new element of rhetorical analysis.

Overall, the diversity of theoretical frameworks, texts, and arguments presented in this collection further demonstrates the diversity within YAL itself. As a whole, this book presents a cogent argument for the use of YAL in the composition classroom, but each part serves that greater whole by furthering the argument in unique ways and also providing faculty and students practical examples for application. While we hope readers find this text beneficial for the reasons we intend, we look forward to a growing academic discussion of YAL in the composition classroom in the future.

WORKS CITED

Bartholomae, David. "Inventing the University." *When a Writer Can't Write: Research on Writer's Block and Other Writing Problems*, edited by Mike Rose. New York: Guilford, 1986, 134–166.

Baumbach, Abagail. "Changing Times: An Analysis of Diversity in Young Adult Literature." 2016. *Digital Commons @ Brockport.* digitalcommons.brockport.edu/cgi/viewcontent. cgi?article=1133&context=honors. Accessed 12 January 2017.

Cole, Pam. *Young Adult Literature in the 21st Century.* New York: McGraw-Hill, 2008.

Elliott, Joan B., and Mary Dupuis. *Young Adult Literature in the Classroom: Reading It, Loving It, Teaching It.* Newark, DE: International Reading Association, 2002.

Fernsten, Linda A., and Mary Reda. "Helping Students Meet the Challenges of Academic Writing." *Teaching in Higher Education,* vol. 16, no. 2, 2011, 171–182.

Graff, Gerald, and Cathy Birkenstein. *They Say, I Say: The Moves That Matter in Academic Writing.* 3d ed. New York: W.W. Norton, 2014.

Hayn, Judith A., Jeffrey S. Kaplan, and Amanda L. Nolen. "Young Adult Literature Research in the 21st Century." *Theory Into Practice,* vol. 50, 2011, 176–181.

Heath, Shirley Bryce. *Ways with Words: Language, Life, and Work in Communities and Classrooms.* Cambridge: Cambridge University Press, 1983.

LSU College of Human Sciences & Education hosts authors for Young Adult Literature Conference. 2016. https://sites01.lsu.edu/wp/lovepurple/2014/06/13/young-adult-literature-conference/. Accessed 5 February 2017.

Milliot, Jim. "Children's Books: A Shifting Market." *Publisher's Weekly.* www.publishersweekly.com/pw/by-topic/childrens/childrens-industry-news/article/61167-children-s-books-a-shifting-market.html. Accessed 5 January 2017.

Monseau, Virginia R., and Gary M. Salvner. *Reading Their World: The Young Adult Novel in the Classroom.* 2d ed. Portsmouth, NH: Heinemann, 2000.

Perl, Sondra. "The Composing Process of Unskilled College Writers." *Research in the Teaching of English,* vol. 13, no. 4, 1979, 317–36.

Rybakova, Katie, and Rikki Roccanti. "Connecting the Canon to Current Young Adult Literature." *American Secondary Education,* vol. 44, no. 2, 2016, 31–45.

Sarner, Lauren. "The Problem with New Adult Books." *The Huffington Post.* 14 October 2013. www.huffingtonpost.com/lauren-sarner/the-problem-with-new-adul_b_3755165.html. Accessed 13 January 2017.

Wallace, David L., and Helen Rothschild Ewald. *Mutuality in the Rhetoric and Composition Classroom.* Carbondale: Southern Illinois University Press, 2000.

"It's like swimming upstream"

Using Rainbow Rowell's Fangirl
to Alleviate Anxieties and Grow Writers

Lacy Marschalk

Increasingly in my composition classes, students ask for models. They do not merely want to be told—or, to discover—how to write a rhetorical analysis, a research proposal, or an argument of definition, but, quite reasonably, they wish to see well-crafted examples of these modes of writing. Peter Elbow has warned us of the dangers of treating texts "as sacred" or infallible, of "*serving* them" rather than "*using* them" ("Being a Writer" 74), but when used effectively, models can help emerging writers gain a better understanding of genre conventions, audience expectations, and organizational patterns and structures. Using models in this way is common in composition courses, as is modeling the writing process. Writing instructors often dedicate significant time to demonstrating prewriting techniques, discussing the various approaches to drafting (perhaps even creating a collaborative "live draft" in class), and providing checklists of what to focus on when revising and editing, all while giving students ample time to practice these stages for themselves.

These ways of modeling speak to our students intellectually; they allow students to feel more knowledgeable of rhetorical modes and better equipped to break apart and perform academic writing tasks. However, while most students can identify how, why, or even whether a model text works, and required portfolios might prove they are all capable of prewriting, producing multiple drafts, and following a checklist, these abilities alone rarely produce strong writing. Student writers (and really writers of all levels) need to spend time thinking about writing, feeling frustrated by writing, pushing through those frustrations, writing words and deleting those words, over and over again. They need to develop the fortitude to face the blank page head on, to detach themselves from their writing, to accept and even welcome feedback. They need to understand that writing is often mentally taxing and even confidence shattering, but it can also be a source of real joy and pleasure.

These aspects of the practice are far more difficult to model. For years I have been letting the masters do this work for me. I assign excerpts from Stephen King's *On Writing* and Anne Lamott's *Bird by Bird* at various points during the semester, and we draw inspiration from their words. From King we learn that it is okay to "approach the act of writing with nervousness, excitement, hopefulness, or even despair—the sense that you can never completely put on the page what's in your mind and heart" (106); and from Lamott we discover that "[v]ery few writers really know what they are doing until they've done it.... We all often feel like we are pulling teeth, even those writers whose prose ends up being the most natural and fluid" (22). There is a measure of comfort in knowing that even well-known, professional writers still struggle with their writing, but the lives these writers live are so far removed from the experiences of the typical eighteen-year-old sitting in a university classroom that it can be difficult for my students to see King and Lamott as models of the writing lifestyle. What they need is someone closer to their own age.

Enter Cath Avery, the protagonist of Rainbow Rowell's young adult (YA) novel *Fangirl* (2013). Cath is a freshman at the University of Nebraska—Lincoln, and she's an aspiring writer, which makes her rather unique in the realm of contemporary young adult fiction. While most YA novels involve characters who are still in high school—or who don't attend school at all because they are off fighting oppressive governments—*Fangirl* follows Cath from the very beginning to the very end of her first year of college. The novel is divided into two parts ("Fall 2011" and "Spring 2012"), and the story opens with Cath moving into her new dorm room and ends with "her last Friday night in Pound Hall" (430). Because my first-year writing students read *Fangirl* during the fall, they are experiencing many firsts right alongside Cath. First time sharing a room with a stranger. First time eating such questionable combinations as "[c]ottage cheese with peaches, canned pears with shredded cheddar ... [and] cold kidney and green bean salad" in the dining hall (29). First time performing poorly in a favorite subject. They can speak to the veracity of the "detergenty twang" of the dorm room air (14), the way in which time moves differently in college. "'Months are different in college,'" Cath's love interest, Levi, observes, "'especially freshman year. Too much happens. Every freshman month equals six regular months'" (174). *Yes*, my students agree enthusiastically. Rowell has captured this moment in their lives, the struggle to make new friends, to maintain long-distance relationships, to renegotiate family roles. And because Cath eventually finds her place, her people, and ends the year in a more hopeful place, she also gives them a glimpse into their more settled futures.

However, *Fangirl* is not just the story of Cath's journey from anxious, socially isolated incoming freshman to fully acculturated college student; it is also the story of her journey as a writer. Contemporary YA novels are replete with creative protagonists who profess their aspirations to become fashion designers, musicians, or future Picassos, but less common are portrayals of teen writers, and rarer still are accurate representations of the struggles teen creators face when confronting the blank page (or screen), when trying to balance the competing demands of life and art, or when receiving negative feedback. *Fangirl* is the rare YA novel that puts these struggles center-stage while also confronting a number of issues relevant to first-year college students, including anxiety and mental illness, binge drinking, learning disabilities, and academic failure. Rowell has a rare gift for grappling with such meaty, thought-provoking material without becoming melodramatic or maudlin, and assigning *Fangirl* creates an opportunity to address these important issues as well as a host of topics relevant to the composition classroom, including the writing process, originality and plagiarism, and rhetorical genre. In this essay, I will demonstrate the ways in which this "*Küntslerroman*, or artist's novel," as Jocelyn Van Tuyl has described it (199), can be taught as a model for first-year students struggling to form their own identities as writers.

"Writing is hard," and Other Lessons Cath Avery Teaches Us

Early in the semester, I confront the elephant in the room. I invite my composition students to complete the following sentence: "Writing is _____." The activity is anonymous, and the responses range from the jaded ("Writing is not useful to my major") to the clichéd ("Writing is how I express myself"). Most commonly, however, students say, "Writing is hard." I am expecting this response. I am prepared for it. "At what point do you think writing gets easier?" I ask. "When you finish this course? When you graduate college? When you've spent hours and hours practicing and perfecting your writing?"

They shrug noncommittally.

"Never," I say. "It never gets easier. It is always you against a blank page, you struggling to find the perfect words, to find the perfect way to arrange those words, and realizing you will never achieve perfection no matter how hard you try. You will get better at understanding when and how to use certain modes, how to research and outline and organize, but writing will always be hard. Writing is hard for me; it's hard for every publishing writer."

I quote Thomas Mann to them: "A writer is someone for whom writing is more difficult than it is for other people" (qtd. in Moore 13). I tell them, as

Nathanial Hawthorne supposedly said, that "[e]asy reading is damned hard writing" (qtd. in Barrett and Mingo 135). I show them tweets in which popular authors profess their struggles with the novels they are writing.

This speech might seem like the opposite of a pep talk, but inevitably many students perk up at the revelation that they are not alone. *Their professor, their favorite authors, also struggle with writing.* "Wow. That makes me feel better," a student in a recent class confessed. Writing can be a lonely business, and I want my students to know that it is okay to vent their frustrations, to acknowledge when the writing is not going their way.

"But why is writing hard?" I ask.

They know, but they cannot quite put a finger on it. The closest they come is *writing is work*.

In a previous position, as an academic coach, I helped struggling college students develop their study skills. At the center of these sessions was the concept of metacognition. I wanted students to learn to reflect on their thinking—to take a moment to contemplate how they were thinking, why they were thinking that way, and how they *should* be thinking. At a conference I had met Leonard Geddes, a former associate dean at Lenoir-Rhyne University and the creator of the LearnWell Projects, an organization that trains students and faculty to use a metacognitive approach to education so that deeper, more enduring learning takes place. This approach relies heavily on Bloom's Taxonomy, which I would teach to the students I coached so that they could identify not only the level of thinking they were performing but also the level of thinking expected by their professors.

Because I learned these strategies as an academic coach, I have applied them in my own teaching. In response to my own question—"Why is writing hard?"—I briefly explain the concept of Bloom's Taxonomy to my composition students. I draw the revised Bloom's pyramid on the board and label the six tiers, remembering through creating, and I ask them where writing falls. They quickly recognize that writing is creating, the highest order of thinking, while the majority of the studying they prefer to do—or that their previous educations prepared them to do—falls in the lower half of the pyramid—remembering, understanding, and applying. While these three levels are foundational to all forms of knowledge, college-level writing courses privilege the higher-order thinking skills—analyzing, evaluating, and creating. Explaining these concepts helps the students to understand why they lean so heavily on summary when writing their rhetorical analyses, why they overuse quotations in their research essays, or why they prefer to cite dictionary definitions instead of forming their own definitions of terms.

My goal in sharing Bloom with my composition students is to acknowledge what they have known all along—writing is hard work. More importantly, it should be hard; they are creating something new, stating something in a way that it has never been stated before. This lesson speaks to them intellectually, but I know it is also easy for them to slip back into previous habits, to start procrastinating on their writing assignments because they dread the mental work these projects demand. For this reason, I assign Rowell's *Fangirl* after the first paper has been submitted and returned, after the Bloom's lesson has become a distant memory.

On the surface, Cath Avery may not seem like the kind of student to whom most composition students will relate. An English major, Cath places out of the traditional composition sequence and receives special permission to take a junior-level creative writing class as a freshman. She is a prolific and popular fanfiction writer with dozens of short stories to her credit and thousands of readers who await her every word. Her stories are set in the universe of Simon Snow, a Harry Potter surrogate created by the fictional Gemma T. Leslie, the "most successful author of the modern age" (Rowell 262), and when *Fangirl* opens, Cath—or "Magicath," as she is known online—is in the middle of writing her magnum opus,[1] the slash novel *Carry On, Simon*. Cath is "only two-thirds of the way through" with the novel, and it is "already longer than any of Gemma T. Leslie's books" (50–51). Her new chapters regularly draw tens of thousands of hits (42), and fans have started making *Carry On, Simon* t-shirts and telling Cath "that they couldn't look at canon the same way after reading her stuff" (51). Cath is clearly a skilled and even influential writer, one with an audience and fan-base far larger than most students ever dream of having.

Despite her talent for fanfiction, however, Cath struggles in her fiction-writing class. She receives an F on her unreliable-narrator assignment because she writes her scene from the point of view of a Simon Snow character, which her instructor, Professor Piper, considers to be a form of plagiarism. To Cath, the work is original because the words and story are all her own—she only borrowed the characters and world—but to Professor Piper, "'The characters and the world *make* the story'" (107). As a fanfiction writer, Cath has never had anyone call into question the ethics of her work because, as she says, "'it's not illegal…. I'm not trying to sell [the stories]'" (107–108); she doesn't see a grade as a form of currency or understand the definition of plagiarism as her professor has defined it.

This scene with Professor Piper is short, only a couple of pages long, but it opens the door for an important conversation about what academic plagiarism is and isn't. When we read this section of the novel, students almost always side with Cath at first. Their own definitions of plagiarism are often framed by the size of the offense and the intent of the offender. By their estimation, Cath did the work herself; she did not copy someone else's writing into a document and submit it as her own. More importantly, Cath didn't think what she was doing was wrong; writing fanfiction is legal, after all. My students themselves have perhaps been guilty of doing something similar—using an idea from another source without giving credit, paraphrasing without including citations. Slowly, they come to realize that using an idea from another source is like borrowing someone else's characters or world—the idea *makes* the essay in the same way that the characters *make* the story. Cath's failure becomes their own, something that could easily happen to them, to any well-intentioned students, if they aren't careful.

Like many students who fail an assignment, Cath does not respond well. The thought of writing an original story paralyzes her, and she continually puts off starting her final project. With just days left in the semester, Professor Piper gives the class a familiar speech:

> "I know what it's like to be distracted. To seek out distractions. To exhaust yourself doing every other little thing rather than face a blank page.... A blank screen...
>
> "So if you haven't finished—or if you haven't started—I understand, I do. But I implore you ... *start now*. Lock yourself away from the world. Turn off the internet, barricade the door. Write as if your life depended on it.
>
> Write as if your *future* depended on it" [204].

Despite this warning, Cath continues to procrastinate. She sets writing goals for herself and then fails to meet them. She tries freewriting. She starts multiple stories and then deletes them. Then the unthinkable—or the very thing we frequently warn students about—happens: she is called home by a family emergency. She doesn't write the story, and she assumes she has failed the class. For various reasons, both academic and personal, she contemplates dropping out of college and moving home, but her father convinces her to finish out the year.

When Cath returns to UNL that spring, she is surprised to find that she has received an incomplete, not an F, in fiction writing. She has not heard anything from Professor Piper, and she can barely stomach the idea of going to her office. Twice she enters the building only to walk right back out. She considers changing her major. Then, on the third attempt, before she can make it back outside, Professor Piper spots her and asks her why she didn't submit the final project. Cath acknowledges that her father was hospitalized, but she also admits that she had already decided not to write the story. Based on her earlier failure, on Professor Piper's opinion of fanfiction, she has decided that creative writing is not for her. She does not feel that she can write original fiction, where the rules and characters have not already been established for her. "'When I'm writing my own stuff,'" Cath confesses, "'it's like swimming upstream. Or ... falling down a cliff and grabbing at the branches, trying to invent the branches as I fall'" (Rowell 262). Professor Piper mimes this gesture, grabbing at an invisible branch. "'*Yes*,'" she says. "'That's how it's supposed to feel'" (262).

Cath's writing analogies should resonate with anyone who has spent time at the pinnacle of Bloom's Taxonomy, practicing the highest order of thinking skills—i.e., anyone who has ever tried to create anything. Even Cath, the fanfiction writer with thousands of fans, struggles to create her own work. She doesn't entirely trust her own voice, her own stories. She would rather "pour" herself into an existing "world … than try to make something up out of nothing" (261). When writing is easy for us, as it is for Cath when she is writing Simon Snow stories, it is usually because what we are saying is not really our own creation. We are repeating other people's ideas, using clichéd language, overusing quotations. When it is hard, it is because we are on the brink of original thought, of new ways of describing the world in which we live, and that is a challenge for even professional writers. It is also why first-year students often struggle to see themselves as writers; to be a writer is to own and understand this process and to keep pushing forward anyway, in the hopes of eventually capturing that elusive original idea down on paper.

Professor Piper understands exactly how Cath feels, but in this moment, Cath cannot find comfort in this shared experience. She, like many emerging writers, is struck by a crisis of identity and a crisis of character. Cath's inability to see past her failures as a writer stems in part from what Carol Dweck has defined as a "fixed mindset." Cath is used to being the smartest writer in the room, so when Professor Piper challenges her, she not only loses confidence, but she becomes "practically fiction-phobic" (392). She does not know how to accept and utilize feedback to grow as a writer. She only wants affirmation that she is doing well.

Like many students, Cath has conflated failure to write with some innate inadequacy on her part. Because original writing is hard for her, she believes she is better off doing something else; clearly, if she were meant to be a writer, writing would come naturally to her. In her research on mindsets, Dweck discovered that when her subjects perceived their intellectual and creative abilities to be fixed (genetically predisposed, unable to change), failure "transformed from an action (I failed) to an identity (I am a failure)" (Dweck 33). Students who have not struggled to do well in the past are particularly susceptible to this kind of identity crisis when they are inevitably given a task that is more challenging. The novel emphasizes that Cath has always been a good student. She made a thirty-two on her ACT and is on scholarship at UNL. Until she receives the F on her unreliable-narrator assignment, the closest she has ever come to feeling like an intellectual failure is when her estranged boyfriend, Abel, breaks up with her for a girl who scored a thirty-four on the ACT. "'You're breaking up with me because I'm not smart enough?'" Cath asks Abel, ignoring the fact that they go to different colleges and have not spoken on the phone in weeks (Rowell 75). Even in this moment, when Cath questions whether she is smart enough for a coder like Abel, her identity as a writer is affirmed. Abel promises, "'We can still be friends. I'll still read your fic—Katie [the new girlfriend] reads it, too. I mean, she always has. Isn't that a coincidence?'" (76). Because Cath the person has become synonymous with her fiction—even in the eyes of her former long-term boyfriend—she cannot recognize the failure of a piece of a writing as anything other than a failure of the self. She cannot see that the same gifts for language, plot twist, and character development that made her famous in fandom can be cultivated and used to make her an excellent original fiction writer.

The students with whom I work, many of whom are honors students, have much in common with Cath. While they may not be famous fanfiction writers—at least not to my knowledge—few of them have truly struggled academically. To them, a B is unacceptable, and a C is incomprehensible. Getting their first essays back can be an eye-opening experience as they realize that writing formulaic five-paragraph essays at the eleventh hour—something I have warned them against since the first week—is not going to earn them the A's they are accustomed to making. They do not see a C as a chance to learn and grow but as a failure that reflects on them personally. Some of them receive that first C and do what Cath does initially—they shut down. They give up; they stop participating with the same kind of enthusiasm, and a few might even withdraw from the class. Writing is hard, and they still do not fully understand that writing is a skill that can be—that must be—developed through time and hard work.

For this reason, Cath's story is far more relatable after they have received that first essay grade, after they too have had a chance to experience disappointment. Some of them have received A's on their first papers, of course, but even those students now know that there are aspects of their writing that need work, that improvements can always be made. As we read Cath's story, we discuss the dangers of succumbing to a fixed mindset and of believing that our abilities are immutable; we discuss the need to cultivate a growth mindset and to view feedback as an opportunity to learn and become better. This lesson is richer because not only have they seen someone else—even if that someone else is fictional—have similar struggles, but because, in the end, that person is able to overcome her struggles and find success.

After all her starting, stopping, and agonizing over Professor Piper's assignment, Cath is finally able to complete the project by moving away from Gemma T. Leslie's world and solidly into her own. She writes a story based on her own life, based on the moment that changed her life forever—when her mother abandoned the family ten years earlier. On the last page of the novel, we are treated to an excerpt from this story, "Left," and we begin to understand that all of Cath's struggles and hard work have been worth it; not only has she finished her incomplete coursework, but "Left" has been awarded *Prairie Schooner*'s prestigious Underclassmen Prize (435). Cath does not give up fanfiction entirely, but she realizes that she is more than just Magicath—

she is also Cather Avery, a promising writer with her own stories to tell. Rowell's message here is clear; for those writers who persist in the face of obstacles and who are willing to write with truth, honesty, and originality, growth, success, and even joy are possible.

Practical Considerations for the Composition Classroom

Cath's journey as a writer provides an excellent model for composition students struggling with writer's block and procrastination, as well as those who are afraid of plagiarizing or of receiving poor grades and negative feedback, but the narrative structure of *Fangirl* lends itself to other discussions critical to the composition classroom as well. Although Rowell's primary narrative is linear, Cath's story is interpolated with excerpts from Gemma T. Leslie's books, Cath's fiction, and two fictional articles. While I use the primary narrative to confront the anxieties growing writers face, I use the interpolations to discuss rhetorical genre and voice, which can be difficult to teach. In their writing, my students often refer to memoirs as novels, books as articles, and poetry as "stories," and whether the misapplication of these terms is out of thoughtlessness or a lack of understanding is not always clear, but such an issue must be addressed. By reading fiction in the composition classroom, and especially by reading an interpolated novel like *Fangirl*, which weaves genres together, the distinctions between these genres can be taught as well as the importance of recognizing the conventions of different genres and of understanding how to use them in our own writing.

While the novel concludes with an excerpt from Cath's original story "Left," it opens with a piece that theoretically anyone could have written: the "Encyclowikia" page for "The Simon Snow Series" (Rowell 3), which readers will instantly recognize as mimicking the form and tone of a Wikipedia entry. Rowell uses this fake encyclopedia entry to introduce her readers to the Simon Snow series and to establish its importance to her story even before readers have been introduced to Cath or the primary narrative. The entry is only a page long and could easily be forgotten as one becomes immersed in Cath's narrative, but I use the Encyclowikia page as an opportunity to discuss the conventions of encyclopedia entries and to introduce the final course project: a collaborative Wiki page that a group of three to four students must write and edit together. When we get to this assignment, we look at example Wikipedia pages online, but we also examine Rowell's Encyclowikia page, and we identify and discuss the conventions Rowell employs to make her encyclopedia entry feel as if it were lifted from Wikipedia. Because her entry is brief, we also imagine what we might add to the entry based on the excerpts of the Snow novels that we have read throughout *Fangirl*. I challenge each group to draft a detailed outline of a revised Simon Snow entry that contains the kind of information readers want and expect from a Wikipedia entry. Then we look at and compare these revisions as a class. This exercise allows us to discuss what we and other readers most look for in a Wikipedia entry, including detailed, organized content; credible sources that are clearly and frequently cited; and a single, authoritative voice.

The other "non-fiction" passage embedded in *Fangirl* is an excerpt from a fake *Newsweek* profile about Simon Snow's online fan community (141). The passage is brief—only four paragraphs long—but it is substantive enough to start a discussion about the tonal and structural differences between popular and scholarly sources, as well as between fictional and non-fictional texts. I have the students perform a close reading of the passage, noting how this mode of writing differs from the others found throughout the novel, and then they find magazine and newspaper articles with the kind of language and structure Rowell, a former journalist, is mimicking. This exercise prepares them for their only creative assignment of the semester: to invent or appropriate an urban legend or folk tale and then write it as if it were being reported by a local newspaper or magazine.

The other interpolated pieces, which follow every chapter and are sometimes even embedded within chapters, are almost entirely made up of excerpts from Cath's and Leslie's fiction. Focusing on these interpolations can lead to productive discussions on voice, as well as on writerly growth. Scattered throughout the novel are dated excerpts from all seven of Leslie's Simon Snow novels (2001–2010), as well as excerpts from *Carry On, Simon* and eight of Cath's short stories. Those stories that were written by "Magicath" between 2006 and 2009 were co-written with her twin sister Wren (or Wrenegade, as she is known online), and those stories dated 2010 and after were written by Magicath alone. The dates—and names—are significant here because they mark the moment when Cath begins to come into her own voice; from 2010 on she no longer has to negotiate with her sister on plotlines or character development choices, and because there have been no new Simon Snow novels, she also does not have to compete with Leslie for ownership of the story. In fact, the reason Cath is writing so furiously on *Carry On, Simon* is because she wants her novel to be finished before the final installment of Leslie's series, which is scheduled to be released in May 2012. Rowell's primary purpose for embedding these excerpts is to juxtapose instances in Cath's life with those in Simon's, such as placing the chapter when Cath moves into her dorm room alongside the moment when Simon moves into his,[2] but when analyzed apart from the rest of the text, these excerpts also tell another story—the story of how Magicath, popular fanfiction writer, becomes Cather Avery, award-winning literary fiction writer. Over time, we see Cath becoming more experimental (she uses second person in "Left") and more willing to draw from moments in her own life in order to enrich the development of her characters (which are by now very different from those Leslie originally created). Voice can be a difficult topic to discuss with students, but by comparing Leslie's fiction with Magicath and Wrenegade's, and Magicath and Wrenegade's fiction with Magicath the solo writer's, and Magicath the solo writer's fiction with Cath Avery's, students can begin to note stylistic and tonal differences between these writings, as well as differences between these texts and the primary narrative. In the primary narrative, we are given access to Cath's struggles as a writer, but in the interpolations, we are able to see that, in the end, all that struggling produced a strong, original voice.

For decades, the debate over how and when and whether to use imaginative literature in the composition classroom has raged on, and one can imagine that the staunchest advocates for keeping literary and composition studies separate might find the use of a popular young adult novel in a composition class especially noisome. In her influential essay "Freshman Composition: No Place for Literature," Erika Lindemann says that the most important question composition instructors should ask is "what the purpose of a first-year writing course is" (312), and if the purpose is to teach academic discourse, then composition "neither requires nor finds particularly relevant a significant role for literature" (313). However, Peter Elbow has also argued that "[i]maginative language touches people most deeply; sometimes it's the only language use that gets through" ("The Cultures of Literature and Composition" 537). Intellectual lessons on mindset, metacognition, and Bloom's Taxonomy speak to my students' minds; Cath Avery's struggles with writing speak to their hearts. And if, as Lindemann asserts, the purpose of composition is to "provide opportunities to master the genres, styles, audiences, and purposes of college writing" (312), *Fangirl* can help with that, too. Rhetoric is the foundation upon which most composition courses are built, and it can be difficult for writing instructors to find a balance between teaching writing—the primary purpose of the course—and discussing readings, especially when the readings are fictional and not models that the students are expected to follow. *Fangirl*, however, presents a different kind of model: a model for how to survive the first year of college, for how to overcome academic adversity, and, most importantly, for how to embrace the challenges of writing and find joy in the process.

NOTES

1. Cath's sister Wren describes the novel, which Cath has been working on for two years, as Cath's "life's work" (400).

2. For more on these "metaleptic crossings," see Jocelyn Van Tuyl, "'Somebody Else's Universe': Female *Kunstler* Narratives in Alcott's *Little Women* and Rowell's *Fangirl*," *Children's Literature Association Quarterly*, vol. 41, no. 2, 2016, pp. 204–206. In particular, Van Tuyl

examines Rowell's use of *mise en abyme* as reflective of "the ways in which fanfiction 'operat[es],' as Tisha Turk puts it, in the 'metaleptic mode'" (204).

WORKS CITED

Barrett, Erin, and Jack Mingo. *It Takes a Certain Type to Be a Writer: And Hundreds of Other Facts from the World of Writing*. Newburyport, MA: Conari, 2003.

Dweck, Carol. *Mindset: The New Psychology of Success*. New York: Ballantine Books, 2007.

Elbow, Peter. "Being a Writer vs. Being an Academic: A Conflict in Goals." *College Composition and Communication*, vol. 46, no. 1, 1995, pp. 72–83.

_____. "The Cultures of Literature and Composition: What Could Each Learn from the Other?" *College English*, vol. 64, no. 5, 2002, pp. 533–546.

King, Stephen. *On Writing: A Memoir of the Craft*. New York: Scribner's, 2000.

Lamott, Anne. *Bird by Bird: Some Instructions on Writing and Life*. New York: Anchor Books, 1994.

Lindemann, Erika. "Freshman Composition: No Place for Literature." *College English*, vol. 55, no. 3, March 1993, pp. 311–316.

Moore, Dinty W. *The Mindful Writer: Noble Truths of the Writing Life*. Somerville, MA: Wisdom Publications, 2012.

Rowell, Rainbow. *Fangirl*. New York: St. Martin's Griffin, 2013.

Van Tuyl, Jocelyn. "'Somebody Else's Universe': Female *Kunstler* Narratives in Alcott's *Little Women* and Rowell's *Fangirl*." *Children's Literature Association Quarterly*, vol. 41, no. 2, 2016, pp. 199–215.

Using Dystopian Texts to Promote Social Responsibility in the Composition Classroom

MELISSA AMES

Since the Colonial period, educational institutions in the United States have been tasked with developing character as well as academic skill. While in earlier epochs such character education would have been explicitly tied to morality as defined within Christian contexts, today's character education takes on a more secular form, focusing on developing skills related to social responsibility. By definition, social responsibility is "a personal investment in the well-being of people and the planet" (Berman 15). Despite the fact that many feel that public schools and universities are ideal sites for this type of training, research has found that instructors are often reluctant to discuss controversial issues within their classrooms because of the potential negative ramifications. A recent study found that only "11% of students reported spending time in their classes on 'problems facing the country today'" (Wolk 667). Further research has found that such issues "receive little attention in schools because in the culture of schooling, and the culture of society, many controversial topics and issues are taboo" (Evans, Avery, and Pederson 295). Ultimately, these cultural taboos "impose severe disabilities on teaching and thinking," impacting the decisions instructors make concerning course content and classroom management (Evans, Avery, and Pederson 295). Resistance—perceived or real—from students, parents, or administrators result in curricula that are divorced from contemporary events pertaining to social inequality. As a result of this self-censorship, students exit the educational sphere ill prepared to be active citizens of the world.

When instructors do go against the societal grain and merge such subject matter into their courses, some common issues surface. Brian K. Payne and Randy R. Gainey describe two likely scenarios that instructors will be faced with when controversial topics are at the center of classroom discussion: "(a) a small number of students may want to voice their opinions at the expense of excluding other students, or (b) all of the students may simply avoid eye contact and hope the professor will not make them talk about their ideas" (55). To further complicate the situation, other factors can also impact how likely a class is to engage in critical thinking practices surrounding social topics. Payne and Gainey explain that various "gender and demographic differences" may "affect an individual's beliefs and attitudes toward many controversial issues," as well as their willingness to openly discuss their views (55).

Despite these difficulties, studies have found that there are numerous benefits to crafting a course that forces students to engage in such critical inquiry. Research finds that the study of controversial topics, if discussed within an open and supportive classroom environment, promotes "increased political interest and civic tolerance and decreased dogmatism" (Evans, Avery, and Pederson 297). In "Teaching Supercharged Subjects," David Pace, an Associate Professor in the History Department at Indiana University, discussed a challenging course he taught on "The Dawn of the Atomic Age." Throughout many of his first attempts at teaching this course, he found that students quickly "began to assume uncharacteristically extreme positions, and conflicts within the class threatened to poison interactions for the remainder of the course" (Pace 42). Pace was further troubled by the way the students' unwavering views affected him as a teacher. He writes, "the extreme nature of many students' comments pushed my 'buttons,' and the emotional and intellectual chaos of the argument made me less effective as an agent of critical thinking" (Pace 42). Ultimately he was able to restructure the class so that it produced more favorable results, and he highlights ten strategies that ultimately worked to produce a more productive classroom atmosphere. Some of these strategies include: providing students with the necessary skills to engage with the debate (e.g., analyzing a question from multiple perspectives, supporting an argument with research); setting the foundation for the controversial issue and controlling the instructional pace (e.g., exposing students to a controversial topic slowly and incrementally); and managing the classroom dynamic and conversation (e.g., ensuring the conversation stems from the students but intervening as necessary and making sure that logic rather than emotion motivates arguments) (Pace 43–45).

Other best practices for tackling tricky topics within classroom study include creating an inquiry unit where the teacher begins with a question, or set of questions, that connect the various topics of discussion and textual analysis (Wolk 666). Such an approach allows the overarching thematic focus of the class, more so than the individual topics of conflict, to be the foundation to build upon. This umbrella places various debates in dialogue with one another and broadens the conversation, while also helping to prevent students from disengaging if one specific topic is not appealing to them. Another crucial component to crafting a successful course that encourages social responsibility is text selection. Payne and Gainey encourage instructors to select texts that engage students in critical thinking about social issues because they provide a specific context in which to explore a larger social critique (57). This is where fictional narratives—particularly young adult literature (YAL) following in the utopian and dystopian tradition—can be extremely useful.

Discussing novels in particular, Carrie Hintz and Elaine Ostry argue that dystopian "literature encourages people to view their society with a critical eye, sensitizing or predisposing them to political action" (7). They suggest that "exposure to these types of texts can lead young readers to see inequality in their own communities and countries" (Hintz and Ostry 8). Scholars such as Jacqueline N. Glasglow encourage utilizing dystopian novels in social justice units. She argues that "social justice education has the potential to prepare citizens who are sophisticated in their understanding of diversity and group interaction, able to critically evaluate social institutions, and committed to working democratically with diverse others" (54). Similarly, Steven Wolk believes that reading dystopian novels allows "students to question the world we have and envision a better world we could have" because these texts "offer unique opportunities to teach these habits of mind" (668). Although these stories are often set in the future, usually in post-apocalyptic settings, Wolk argues that "thematically they are really about the present" (668).

This essay discusses the successes and challenges of teaching a particular cross-curricular composition course that focused on controversial issues appearing in scientific research and dystopian literature. The course capitalized on student interests (e.g., the popularity of YA dystopian novels and media) and studied narratives that wrestle with ethical concerns surrounding the idea of progress (societal achievements, technological advancement, scientific discoveries, and so forth). Contemporary debates and specific issues addressed throughout this course included cloning, stem cell research, black market organ transplants, human trafficking, surveillance technology, euthanasia, and capital punishment. In alignment with research concerning best practices in teaching social responsibility topics, this course was centered on a set of inquiry questions that stretched across all units, texts, discussions, and writing assignments. It utilized narratives as the site of inquiry—as the safe space in which to wrestle with these controversial issues. In this class students analyzed various fictional dystopian texts (novels, film, and television) that critique the above-mentioned issues, and class discussion revolved around the following questions: what do we do when human survival and societal progress come at extreme costs, and how might such advancements question our faith in humanity? The theme of indebted bodies—bodies created by technology, dependent on technology, governed by technology, or punished by technology—was present in all of the literary and media texts students covered (see Figure 1). The young adult novels, in particular, often served as gateway or anchor texts, priming the analysis of canonical literature (read in entirety or in excerpts), media, and nonfiction texts.

An Interdisciplinary Composition Course: Studying Science, Law, Medicine and Literature

This course was designed as a general education composition course for undergraduate students. The normal composition of such a class is 18–21 students, primarily non–English majors of freshman to junior status. The course objectives were designed so that by the end of the semester students would be able to demonstrate the following skills:

1. Develop skills in critical reading, viewing, and listening for understanding and evaluating culturally diverse course materials and for becoming more discerning reader/viewer/listener.

2. Engage in reading and writing experiences about literature in order to demonstrate an increased understanding or an appreciation for social, cultural, intellectual, and aesthetic ideas and their discovery.

3. Understand the relationship that narratives have to one another (despite differences in media or genre) and to the cultural/social/historical milieu in which they are created, produced, and consumed.

4. Showcase skills and best practices for analyzing various genres and composing arguments about their purpose, value, and functionality.

5. Recognize multiple perspectives and be able to logically integrate, expand on, and/or counter them when formulating one's own argument.

6. Develop research skills, including effective use of source materials and the principles of MLA documentation, as well as the abilities to annotate, paraphrase, summarize, quote, and synthesize written material accurately and ethically.

7. Apply research from outside disciplines (e.g., science, law, ethics) to the study of literature, film, television, and other artifacts from popular culture.

8. Demonstrate mastery of the writing/design process by creating multiple products that arrive at their final state through the stages of pre-writing/pre-planning, drafting, revising, editing, and proofreading.

9. Revise documents by participating in peer review workshops and writing conferences.

10. Work collaboratively in order to explore ideas, formulate arguments, and present findings in a scholarly fashion.

While these were the objectives articulated on the syllabus, the course also aimed to teach social responsibility—an outcome not as easily measured as those listed above.

This course was divided into three thematic units: (1) Exploring the Consequences of Technological Progress; (2) Critiquing the Changing Justice System; and (3) Ethical Debates within Science and Medicine. Each unit was further divided into sub-units focused on specific technological advances or instances of human progress. These sub-units contained textual sets where students analyzed the topic of focus within a literary work, film, and various non-fiction texts from contemporary discourse (see Figure 1).

Figure 1. Course Themes & Texts

Themes	*Print Texts*	*Media Texts*
UNIT I. EXPLORING THE CONSEQUENCES OF TECHNOLOGICAL PROGRESS		
Human Dependence on Information Technology	M.T. Anderson's *Feed*; Mark Baurelien's "The Dumbest Generation"; Nicholas Carr's "Is Google Making Us Stupid?"	
The Evolution of Robotics	Isaac Asimov's *I, Robot*; Brian Aldiss's "Super Toys"	Steven Spielberg's *A.I. Artificial Intelligence*
Technology and the Human Body	Scott Westerfeld's *Uglies*; Aldous Huxley's *Brave New World*	
UNIT II. CRITIQUING THE CHANGING JUSTICE SYSTEM		
Human Surveillance	Cory Doctorow's *Little Brother*; Philip K. Dick's "The Minority Report"	Steven Spielberg's *The Minority Report*
Capital Punishment		Alan Parker's *The Life of David Gale*
UNIT III. ETHICAL DEBATES WITHIN SCIENCE AND MEDICINE		
Cloning and Stem Cell Research	Kazuo Ishiguro's *Never Let Me Go*	Michael Bay's *The Island*
Human Trafficking	Margaret Atwood's *The Handmaid's Tale*	Miquel Sapochnik's *Repo Men*

Making and Resisting Connections Between the Fictional Texts and Real World Problems

One theme that students studied pertained to the consequences of advanced technology. In their early readings, they were forced to entertain the arguments of academics who specifically critique their generation's dependency on technology:

> We have entered the Information Age, traveled down the Information Superhighway, spawned a Knowledge Economy, undergone the Digital Revolution, converted manual workers into knowledge workers. [...] And yet, while teens and young adults have absorbed digital tools into their daily lives [...] taken more classes, built their own Web sites, enjoyed more libraries, bookstores, and museums [...] young Americans today are no more learned or skillful than their predecessors, no more knowledgeable, fluent, up-to-date, or inquisitive, except in the materials of youth culture [Baurelein 8–9].

Baurelein laments the current societal conditions: "instead of opening young American minds to the stores of civilization and science and politics, technology has contracted their horizon to themselves, to the social scene around them" (10).

Baurelein's criticisms align well with the social commentary provided in *Feed*. After only hours of being disconnected from the feed, a constant stream of information that automatically flows through people's minds, the main character, Titus, begins complaining about its disappearance through an interior monologue that showcases just how crucial he and his peers feel this technological apparatus is to their daily existence:

> I missed the feed. I don't know when they first had feeds. Like maybe, fifty or a hundred years ago. Before that, they had to use their hands and their eyes. Computers were all outside the body. They carried them around outside of them, in their hands, like if you carried your lungs in a briefcase and opened it to breathe [Anderson 47].

In this course students were trained to study not only the content of the narratives but their form as well—although they were not equally skilled at both tasks.

Despite being able to easily grasp the social commentary present within these narratives, students struggled when it came to analyzing how the authors' stylistics underscored those. Both Anderson's *Feed* and Westerfeld's *Uglies* perform their social commentary about the negative effects of technology through various formal techniques. For example, both authors draw upon informal diction (the use of slang and improper syntax) to highlight the ignorance of the characters within their novels. While students understood that the authors were mocking their main characters or, at least, depicting their lack of critical thinking and formal education, they resisted reading these characters as analogous to themselves. They did not want to see themselves in these young adult protagonists—which is abnormal for a genre that is known for its relatability—indicating that the students were hesitant to grapple with the critique about their own dependence on technology and the detrimental effects that it may produce.

Less student resistance was seen when the critiques concerning technology did not implicate them directly. Another thematic thread surfacing throughout many of the narratives studied in this course were the effects that technological advancements have on the environment. Although many narratives touch on this theme briefly, the novel that most explicitly does so is *Feed*. Throughout the novel the declining state of Earth is shown through depictions of suburbs existing under protective domes; dead seas that can only be visited when wearing protective suits; and discussions of national parks being eliminated in order to build air factories (Anderson 88, 129, 179). Anderson is clearly critiquing human waste at various points in his novel in sometimes comical and sometimes serious ways. One ridiculous scene finds the main character's mother and brother crinkling up "the disposable table" so that it can be thrown away after just one use (Anderson 129). And in a more emotional scene toward the end of the novel, the father of a dying girl makes this enraged speech about the wasteful practices of American citizens: "We Americans are interested only in the consumption of our products. We have no interest in how they were produced, or what happens to them once we discard them, once we throw them away" (Anderson 290).

This theme of waste surfaces in Aldiss's short story about artificial intelligence, "Super Toys." Consider this excerpt from a speech made by the CEO of a company who invented the first robotic child:

> Though three-quarters of the overcrowded world are starving, we are lucky here to have more than enough, thanks to population control. Obesity's our problem, not malnutrition. I guess there's nobody round this table who doesn't have a [technology implant] working for him in the small intestine, a perfectly safe tape-worm that enables its host to eat up to fifty per cent more food and still keep his or her figure [195].

The various films viewed throughout the term show the consequences of human waste as only a visual display can. The most striking of these are the closing scenes of Speilberg's *A.I.*, which depicts a destroyed vision of New York City, first in ruins and later under water. The film ends with a scene two thousand years in the future—long past the end of humanity during a time in which aliens reside on Earth and humans cease to exist. In class discussion and writing activities, students easily connected the environmental critiques made in these texts to contemporary problems such as global warming, dependence on fossil fuel, water pollution, and animal extinction.

Another theme that students connected well with was the societal critique concerning the effects of the media and celebrity culture on society. Westerfeld's YA series grounds its commentary on the current surge in cosmetic surgery and offers "an impetus for an important dialogue about beauty standards and our culture's" captivation with them (Scott and Dragoo 11). In one scene, the main character of *Uglies*, Tally, is flipping through old celebrity magazines from the "Rusty Era" (a period meant to refer to our contemporary times). Her interior monologue demonstrates how drastically she and her contemporaries have been brainwashed into believing that physical differences amount to only imperfections:

> She'd never seen so many wildly different faces before. Mouths and eyes and noses of every imaginable shape, all combined insanely on people of every age. And the bodies. Some were grotesquely fat, or weirdly over muscled, or uncomfortably thin, and almost all of them had wrong, ugly proportions. But instead of being ashamed of their deformi-ties, the people were laughing and kissing and posing, as if all the pictures had been taken at some huge party [Westerfeld 198].

This topic is broached in *Feed* also. In this novel Anderson depicts the characters as being mindless trend followers, quickly running off to change their hairstyles or self-mutilate their bodies if the current fashion trend demands it. In an interview with James Blasingame, Anderson notes that, in addition to serving as a cautionary tale about the misuse of technology, his novel was intended to scrutinize the current culture of instant gratification, aspects of herd psychology, and individuals' refusal to tackle serious societal problems (4). Although resistant to aligning themselves with the authors' commentary about their generation's dependence on technology, students were quick to apply the critiques about societal beauty standards to their own lives. Perhaps because as young adults they are heavily influenced celebrity culture and media messages concerning body image, this topic was the most selected when students had the opportunity to focus their own research on one of the course themes.

Practical Considerations for the Composition Classroom

The assessments in this class strived to show mastery of textual connections through written products involving textual analysis and interdisciplinary research. Writing instruction and tasks were scaffolded so that students developed and practiced a range of writing skills and produced a range of compositions that increased in length, difficulty, and genre variation as the course progressed. Students completed four formal writing assignments and two impromptu writing pieces throughout this 15-week course. The first two assignments are the most traditional, while the other two highlight an attention to genre and interdisciplinary boundary blurring not always found in a composition class.

Response Journal

Students completed this ongoing project throughout the semester in order to document their careful reading and literary analysis, as well as their attentive viewing of in-class films (see Figure 2). The goal of this collection of essays was to practice writing skills and assist them in completing other course work. Therefore, students were asked to craft a 1–2 page entry for each literary work we read and each film we viewed in class. They were encouraged to use these entries during our class discussion when called upon to participate in the analysis of the narrative and to consider these documents as a form of pre-writing for larger writing projects.

Figure 2. Response Journal Criteria

Format for Responses: For each entry devoted to a print text you should include the following components:

- *Bibliographic Citation* (formatted according to MLA—see OWL Purdue's website for assistance)
- 1–2 paragraph *Summary* of the text (a brief synopsis of the story in your own words)
- 1–2 paragraph *Analysis* section (a discussion of the text's importance, overall message, and the social critique implicit within the narrative)
- *Explication* of a key passage/scene or set of related quotes/scenes (you should type out a substantial section of the text—an important paragraph or bit of dialogue—or a few linked quotations and then discuss its/their importance in relation to the text as a whole; for media texts you could also attend to filmic devices (editing, lighting, sound, setting, camera angles), discussing their effects
- *Discussion Questions* (a list of at least 10 questions/issues that you would like to discuss in class or explore in future projects—these can be general questions but more useful might be questions that point to specific moments in the text that were interesting/confusing; it is suggested that you include potential page numbers to turn to during discussion)

Although these response journals were collected periodically throughout the semester for informal feedback on comprehension and writing development, they were ultimately assessed as a whole when they were formally submitted for a grade. Students were then assessed based on the four major skill areas described above (summary, analysis, explication, and questioning) and in three more procedure-orientated categories (language/mechanics; bibliographical citation; and completeness).

Literary Analysis Essay

The second, rather standard, assignment given to this class was a traditional literary analysis essay. Students were asked to craft a research paper integrating outside source material to formulate an argument concerning how a controversial issue is addressed through various narratives. They were to study how these fictional texts provided a social commentary and/or critique about this issue. They were further directed to tackle the overarching questions posed by the class: (1) what ethical concerns surround the area of progress explored in their chosen narratives and (2) what these narratives suggest we do when human survival and societal progress come at extreme costs. This essay was assigned at midterm in order to ensure that students were mastering the material and key skills.

Multi-Genre Research Project

While the literary analysis essay asked students to pair texts, the final individual assessment of the course, the multi-genre research project, allowed students to focus their study on one text alone. Also, while all of the other formal assignments found students writing in traditional academic genres, this assignment allowed them to create a multimodal composition demonstrating advanced research skills through various writing items and creative pieces. In order to showcase a comprehensive understanding of one selected work/pairing, students created projects that creatively captured the literary work's overall narrative, theme, and social commentary. While a traditional essay could have met the same goals, this allowed students more freedom and flexibility when relaying their understanding of the text. This assignment encouraged students to apply their knowledge from the primary text to a variety of genres, thus creating a meta-narrative about the work. It also allowed them to showcase their understanding of how various genres (some which we studied in class) function.

From this description it might appear that students had an endless choice when it came to the construction of their final projects; however, this was not actually the case. Students were directed to choose one genre from various categories—categories specifically selected to demonstrate different skills and levels of comprehension (see Figure 3). In the end, they crafted seven unique pieces for inclusion in their projects.

Figure 3. Artifact Options for
Multi-Genre Research Project

A. *Newspaper Component*: Compose an item that would appear in a fictional newspaper published in the hometown/area of the narrative text. This item should conform with the genre in question in terms of content, length, tone, and layout.

CHOOSE ONE OPTION FROM BELOW:

Obituary: a brief (½ or 1 page) blurb about the death of a character from the narrative. This could take place during the narrative or in some perceived (fictional/extended) future. Relevant details from his/her life should be present.

Letter to the Editor: a 1–2 page (double-spaced) letter taking a stand on an issue that occurred within the text. (Note: this cannot be the same issue explored in the research section below).

Advice Column: a 2-part advice column (from the character seeking advice and the fictional expert responding to it). The content of the entry posed by the narrative's character should pull from the storyline and should fit his/her personality.

Front Page Feature Story: a 2-page (double-spaced) article highlighting a key event that took place in the narrative—something that would be "front page" news. This should be fashioned after a real newspaper and should start with an attention grabbing title, important information up front, and it should address all the important W's (who, what, when, where, and why).

Personal Advertisement: a brief personal (dating) advertisement for one of the characters in the text. This should conform to genre standards/length and should fit the character's disposition.

B. *Artistic Analysis Piece*: Select a literary/cultural artifact that (a) is intended to capture the essence of the narrative text (i.e., a book jacket cover) or (b) that they feel represents/captures the essence of the narrative text (i.e., an unrelated text that they feel aligns well with text of study). This item can be found (but then should be cited properly) or originally crafted. Accompanying this piece should be a 1 paragraph justification of why this artifact does (or does not) fit the narrative of study.

CHOOSE ONE OPTION FROM BELOW:

Poetry (found or original)

Music Lyrics (found or original)

Product/Company Advertisement (found or original)

Book Cover/Jacket (original design or written analysis/comparison of two different versions in print)

Movie Poster (original design or analysis of published poster's design)

C. *Visual Artistic Application Piece*: Select a piece of visual art that they feel represents/captures the essence of the narrative text. This item can be found (but then should be cited properly) or originally crafted. Accompanying this piece should be a 1 paragraph justification of why this visual fits the narrative of study.

CHOOSE *ONE* OPTION FROM BELOW:
   Photograph (found or original)
   Sketch/Drawing (found or original)
   Political Cartoon (found or original)

D. *Character Insight Piece*: Craft an item that provides insight into one of the characters from the text. This item will require close reading and a review of the narrative in order to select specific characteristics, behaviors, descriptions, etc. Using direct quotes/paraphrases is suggested.

CHOOSE *ONE* OPTION FROM BELOW:
   Journal/Diary Entry: a 1–2 page (single-spaced) entry (or set of entries) from a character's perspective detailing a moment from the narrative from his/her vantage point.
   Facebook Page: a mock Facebook page for a character including relevant biographical details, likes, friends, and posts. Some of this material should stem directly from the text but others can be inferred based on his/her personality.
   Vanity License Plate: a realistically designed vanity license plate (use proper layout) that would represent the character's personality. Attached to this artistic piece should be a 1 paragraph justification of why this vanity plate fits his/her persona as showcased in the narrative.
   Text Message/IM exchange: a 1–2 page (single-spaced) transcript for a text message or IM exchange between two characters. The contents of this narrative must be loosely based on the narrative but embellishments are allowed as long as they fit the characters participating in the conversation.

E. *Informational Essay*: Write in an established genre relevant to book production/review. Proper organization, tone, mechanics, and proofreading are expected.

CHOOSE *ONE* OPTION FROM BELOW:
   Book Review: a 1–2 page (double-spaced) evaluation essay written in the form of a book review that might be published in a newspaper, magazine, or website. Although some summary will be present, this should be balanced against critique and commentary. Be careful not to be "spoiler" heavy for the audience's sake.

Back of Book Synopsis: a 1–2 page (double-spaced) summary of the book as would be found on the rear side of a published text. This summary should serve to entice readers, encouraging them to buy/read the text, but should not spoil key plot points (such as the ending).

Compare/Contrast: a 2–3 page (double-spaced, MLA formatted) compare & contrast essay discussing the print narrative against its film counterpart. (For texts other than "Minority Report," this requires an outside film viewing of the adaptations of the works).

F. *Research Component I. (Traditional Essay)*: Demonstrate synthesis writing and documentation skills through a traditional essay formatted according to MLA standards.

CHOOSE *ONE* OPTION FROM BELOW:

Author Biography: a 2–3 page essay about the author (using proper MLA citation & at least 3 scholarly sources)

Book's Reception: a 2–3 page essay discussing the book's reception/popularity/reviews (using proper MLA citation & at least 3 sources—source types will vary)

Literary Analysis: a 2–3 page essay integrating scholarly research (journal articles), analyzing a key aspect of the text (MLA citation required)

G. *Research Component II. (Applied Research Item)*: Demonstrate the ability to research a controversial issue (one highlighted in the text) in order to provide a social commentary (similar or opposite as to that found in the text). Regardless of the option selected below, include a works cited page for this section that lists all of the sources you consulted when crafting this piece.

CHOOSE *ONE* OPTION FROM BELOW:

Public Service Announcement (as would be used by one side of issue in narrative): a public service announcement (print advertisement, faux billboard, commercial, video) advocating for one side of the controversial issue researched (must use material from research).

Poster/Flier/Brochure Advocating One Side of Issue: a print item meant for display/distribution that one side of the issue (supporter or opposition) would utilize to publicize his/her stance on the issue (must include material from research).

PowerPoint Presentation about Debate: a traditional PowerPoint presentation one might use if instructing a class on this controversial issue (must use material from research).

Students were assessed by scores earned in each of the seven categories listed above as well as two additional categories based on assembly and design (which included elements related to organization/design, as well as mechanics/writing).

Group Research Presentation

While most of the assessments throughout the course were based on individual accomplishments, one assignment took on a group format. This collaborative group project allowed students to study a contemporary controversy occurring in the fields of science, law, and/or ethics—one that has infiltrated mainstream media and popular culture. This cooperative learning activity required out of class meetings, research compilation, and a formal group presentation.

Students were able to select from ten different options (see Figure 4) and they were placed into two or three person groups based on their interests. These presentations were staggered throughout the semester, aligning with the texts and topics being covered, allowing the students to become co-instructors at various moments throughout the semester.

Figure 4. Group Research Topics

The Effects of Social Networking (On Human Relationships/ Communication)
Artificial Intelligence (Progress and Potential Outcomes)
Plastic Surgery (Effects of Media/Beauty Standards)
Global Warming (Human Progress and Environmental Consequences)
The Death Penalty (The Debates Concerning Legislation)
The Patriot Act (Surveillance and National Security Issues)
Assisted Suicide/Euthanasia (Ethical Debates and Mainstream Examples)
Stem Cell Research (Scientific and Political Debates)
Cloning (Scientific Accomplishments and Ethical Debates)
Human Sex Trafficking (Global Instances and Ethical Debates)

After groups were assembled, students researched their assigned topic and crafted a 15–20 minute presentation on the debates surrounding it. Students were required to use five scholarly sources, craft a visual to aid in their presentation, and complete an essay that documented their individual and group research processes. As some of these are controversial issues, students were cautioned to be objective when presenting the material. The purpose of this presentation was not that of a persuasive speech where they would take a stance on the issue but an informative one where they would objectively relay the main points of both sides of the debate without reflecting bias toward one side or the other.

Conclusions: The Successes and Challenges of Teaching an Interdisciplinary Course

Overall, the course succeeded with the desire to teach social responsibility as students did begin to show concern about the well-being of various subgroups and the planet as a whole. As research predicted, the fictional narratives were a productive space to engage with controversial topics and by the end of the term students were able to easily locate the social commentary present within narratives and apply those critiques to the world around them. The young adult novels, in particular, proved to be ideal anchor texts in subunits that explored a range of texts and issues. However, the promise within many scholars' claims that such study would predispose students "to political action" and increase their "political interest and civic tolerance" was not always seen (Hintz and Ostry 8; Evans, Avery, and Pederson 297). While the course may ultimately impact students' political consciousness, there was no way to determine with any accuracy if this will in fact occur. Class discussion and individual writing pieces indicate that students were able to objectively critique the society of which they are a part, but these critiques did not often extend into discussions of how to resolve such cultural problems. For example, while students were quick to agree with scholars who claim that their generation is overly dependent on technology—and students even shared their worries that such dependency could decrease their intellectual capabilities—they never suggested abandoning their favorite technological gadgets, social networking sites, and so forth. However, the fact that these students were able to "evaluate social institutions" and honestly discuss "problems and injustices" is a solid starting place for continued growth (Glasglow 54; Wolk 667).

The only surprising outcome of the course was the lack of group debate it inspired. As a course grounded in supposedly controversial issues, there was an overwhelming consensus on most of the topics. The students almost always agreed with the social commentaries provided by the authors and directors of the various texts and offered very little in terms of counter arguments. Having only taught this particular course once, I am unable to determine if this was the result of the classroom dynamic, the individual personalities within the class, or if the issues or texts themselves did not cater to divergent viewpoints.

And finally, in terms of the course's cross-curricular focus: I was pleased that students were able to apply the motifs present within the fictional narratives to work being completed in other disciplines. Along the same lines, students were also able to study how these controversial topics were being discussed in other discourses and understand how that conversation—and the research being carried out in diverse fields—was being co-opted by the creators of fictional texts in productive ways.

WORKS CITED

A.I. Artificial Intelligence. Directed by Steven Spielberg. Warner Brothers, 2001.

Aldiss, Brian W. "Super-Toys Last All Summer Long." *Man in His Time: The Best Science Fiction Stories of Brian W. Aldiss,* edited by Brian W. Aldiss. New York: Atheneum, 1989. 194–201.

Anderson, M.T. *Feed.* Somerville, MA: Candlewick Press, 2002.

Asimov, Isaac. *I, Robot.* New York: Ballantine Books, 1977.

Atwood, Margaret. *The Handmaid's Tale.* New York: Anchor, 1998.

Bauerlein, Mark. *The Dumbest Generation: How the Digital Age Stupefies Young Americans and Jeopardizes Our Future, Or, Don't Trust Anyone Under 30.* New York: Penguin, 2009.

Berman, Sheldon. *Children's Social Consciousness and the Development of Social Responsibility.* New York: State University of New York Press, 1997.

Blasingame, James. "An Interview with M.T. (Tobin) Anderson." *Journal of Adolescent and Adult Literacy,* vol. 47, 2003, pp. 98–99.

Carr, Nicholas. "Is Google Making Us Stupid?: What the Internet is Doing to Our Brains." *The Atlantic.* www.theatlantic.com/magazine/archive/2008/07/is-google-making-us-stupid/306868/. Accessed 18 August 2012.

Doctorow, Cory. *Little Brother.* London: Tor Teen, 2010.

Evans, Ronald W., Patricia G. Avery, and Patricia Velde Pederson. "Taboo Topics: Cultural Restraint on Teaching Social Issues." *The Clearing House,* vol. 73, no. 5, 2000, pp. 295–302.

Glasglow, Jaqueline N. "Teaching Social Justice Through Young Adult Literature." *The English Journal,* vol. 90, no. 6, 2001, pp. 54–61.

Hintz, Carrie, and Elaine Ostry. "Introduction." *Utopian and Dystopian Writing for Children and Young Adults,* edited by Carrie Hintz and Elaine Ostry. Abingdon-on-Thames: Routledge, 2003, pp. 1–20.

Huxley, Aldous. *Brave New World.* New York: Harper, 2010.

I, Robot. Directed by Alex Proyas. Twentieth Century Fox, 2004.

Ishiguro, Kazuo. *Never Let Me Go.* New York: Vintage, 2010.

The Island. Directed by Michael Bay. Dream Works, 2005.

The Life of David Gale. Directed by Alan Parker. Universal Pictures, 2003.

Minority Report. Directed by Steven Spielberg. Twentieth Century Fox, 2002.

Pace, David. "Controlled Fission: Teaching Supercharged Subjects." *College Teaching,* vol. 51, no. 2, 2003, pp. 42–45.

Payne, Brian K., and Randy R. Gainey. "Understanding and Developing Controversial Issues in College Courses." *College Teaching,* vol. 51, no. 2, 2003, pp. 52–58.

Repo Men. Directed by Miguel Sapochnik. Universal Pictures, 2010.

Scott, Kristi N., and M. Heather Dragoo. "The Baroque Body: A Social Commentary on the Role of Body Modification in Scott Westerfeld's *Uglies* Trilogy." *Academia.edu.* Accessed 25 July 2011.

Westerfeld, Scott. *Uglies.* Simon Pulse, 2011.

Wolk, Steven. "Reading for a Better World: Teaching for Social Responsibility with Young Adult Literature." *Journal of Adolescent & Adult Literacy,* vol. 52, no. 8, 2009, pp. 664–673.

Of Myths and Thieves

Teaching the Literacy Narrative with The Book Thief

Mary McCulley

On the first day of class, first-year composition students appear either confused or excited as they scan the required reading and spot Markus Zusak's *The Book Thief* on the list. In one end-of-the-year reflection, a student openly expressed his initial incredulity, saying, "I thought this was going to be an ordinary composition class until I saw there was READING involved!" Such a reaction would have been less common only a couple of decades ago when first-year composition courses were often taught with anthologies of literature. However, the famous Lindemann-Tate debate raised the question of whether literature had a place in the composition classroom at all. Now, many students entering composition programs have already internalized the divide they perceive between writing and literature.

The question of literary integration continues to beset English faculty, inviting scholars to develop defenses and compromises in collections of essays such as *Teaching Composition/Teaching Literature* (2003) and NCTE's *Composition and/or Literature: The End(s) of Education* (2006). While the debates admirably seek to rectify the marginalization of composition studies and re-evaluate literature's appropriate use for addressing composition program goals, teachers like myself may feel more pressure to defend their choice of literature, especially Young Adult Literature (YAL), in a course designed primarily to teach the writing process for academic and public audiences. My conviction that teaching YAL benefits the composition course echoes Edith M. Baker's conclusion that literature can aid the larger goals of composition classes. She explains that an effective approach to literature in a composition class will "teach students the thinking skills necessary to critique dominant power structures, as well as the disciplines within the university," "move students from self-centered positions and to an understanding of other narratives," and allow students to "gain knowledge of multiple approaches to a single topic" while reflecting on personal understandings of moral and ethical issues (172–173). In other words, literature supports a democratic composition classroom because it helps foster empathy and identification with others while promoting critical reflection.

I propose that *The Book Thief* offers an excellent resource for approaching these composition goals. The novel invites students to critically examine beliefs about literacy and literacy development, understand multiple perspectives about literacy, and develop empathy for others through literary imagination. Through a unit structured around a literacy narrative assignment, students use this YA text and their own experiences to challenge assumptions and evaluate what Harvey J. Graff theorized in his 1979 tome as "the literacy myth," or the belief that traditional literacy equates to both personal success and increased social morality. As students construct more complex understandings of literacy, they use class discussion and small group conferencing as spaces to write and revise their own ideas about literacy in personal narratives. Zusak's intentional use of literary tools such as figurative speech provides a model for students to imitate effective rhetorical strategies that help convey memorable messages to audiences.

As I relate how the literacy conversations transpire in the course, I first define literacy, the literacy narrative assignment, and the literacy myth, all ideas central to the five-week unit. Then, after a brief synopsis of *The Book Thief,* I explain how the class explores the following ideas in literacy studies: literacy events, literacy sponsors, authentic writing, and multiple literacies. Following these explorations in literacy studies, I deliver an extended analysis of the text, showing how its complexity challenges students to confront ambivalent perspectives regarding literacy and to take responsibility for their own agency in performing various literacies for social good. At the end of this essay, I offer my assignment prompt with a brief explanation regarding exercises leading up to the final essay and the evaluative process. The assignment asks students to write a story that details memories of their own literacy development and to think critically about how their literacy has shaped their identity and beliefs.

According to the NCTE website, "Literacy has always been a collection of cultural and communicative practices shared among members of particular groups" ("Definition of 21st Century Literacies"). While these "cultural and communicative practices" include reading, writing, and speaking, literacy scholars such as Brian Street extend the definition beyond an "acquisition of skills" relating to traditional literacies to recognize a range of competencies or "multiple literacies" (77). Street argues that "new" literacy studies looks beyond the specific skills and foregrounds questions about "dominant," "marginalized," and "resistant" uses of language (77). The literacy narrative, now a staple in composition courses, asks students to reflect upon these larger questions concerning literacy development, practices, and beliefs. Mary Soliday explains that the assignment not only "tells what happens when we acquire language, either spoken or written," but also focuses "upon those moments when the self is on the threshold of possible intellectual, social, and emotional development" (511). In other words, the literacy narrative allows students a space to transcribe who they are becoming as they critically examine their defining "cultural and communicative" experiences in various social situations.

As students begin their literacy narratives, they tend to recite two limited grand narratives that scholars call into question. The first part of "the literacy myth" as theorized by Graff, articulates the "belief ... that the acquisition of literacy is a necessary precursor to and invariably results in economic development, democratic practice, cognitive enhancement, and upward social mobility" (qtd. in *Literacy Myths, Legacies, & Lessons* 35). Students re-tell this myth uncritically when they repeat assumptions that the acquisition of literacy will automatically improve society. Graff clarifies in his article that looks back on thirty years of scholarly work surrounding the "literacy myth" that he never intended to say that literacy was unimportant as some critics accused ("Literacy Myth at Thirty" 637). However, he challenges critical thinkers to discard the assumption that literacy, as an agent in and of itself, *necessarily* results in economic, social, or moral advancement. He prompts his readers to confront the myth and strategically use it to "serve more equitable, progressive humane goals" (652). In other words, it is important that humans possess the agency, often through the tool of literacy, to enact change, but we cannot expect literacy development to default in an advanced society. The second part of the "the literacy myth," as "encouraged by an assessment-focused education system," encourages students to rank their literacy level according to standardized testing scores, grades, or informal declarations of their literacy performances (DeRosa 1). Susan DeRosa identifies the proclivity for re-telling this aspect of "the literacy myth" as one of the key inhibitors to successful narratives because these labels often stunt students from recognizing their potential as effective communicators (1).

Before I ask students to reconsider these myths in their own literacy narratives, they quickly recognize them as problems when they identify with the protagonist in *The Book Thief*, Liesel Meminger. Students often find the story so compelling that they become more willing to discuss seemingly abstract theories of literacy that take on life and meaning through the characters and plot. YAL provides an invaluable resource for engaging students in these discussions about literacy because, according to Crag Hill, it "immerses readers in the experiences ... of young adults" while encouraging readers to identify with and develop empathy for the characters and their struggles (8). In recent YA scholarship, such as Sarah K. Herz and Donald R. Gallo's *From Hinton to Hamlet: Building Bridges between Young Adult Literature and the Classics,* more scholars are noting the benefits of using YAL as a bridge to classic books or texts that may not be immediately or apparently accessible to some adolescents. In the same way, I believe that YAL offers a bridge to academic theories, such as those relating to literacy that may not initially interest students. Through narrative, students can see the concept of literacy development move from an abstract concept to a real event. They more easily discuss the impact of literacy sponsors through a discussion of characters who become personal to them. They learn to identify multiple literacies as we look at Liesel's reading and writing, Hans's music, and Max's drawing. Almost always, students take on the role of detective and discover less obvious literacies such as Rudy and Liesel's thievery. These discussion of the YAL text allow their imaginations to make sense of abstract concepts. Because Liesel's story becomes important to these students, they begin to see the importance of their own literacy narratives.

Zusak's novel employs the unique semi-omniscient narrator Death, a structural device that never ceases to intrigue students. Death tells Liesel's story through his own memories of collecting bodies in Germany during the destruction of World War II and through his rendering of the protagonist's memoir, which he salvages in the aftermath of the bombing of Himmel Street where she lives. Liesel's story recounts her pre-adolescent through adolescent years in which she is adopted by a German couple, Hans and Rosa Hubermann because, as she discovers later, her parents are in trouble with the government for being communists. At first, the young girl comprehends very little regarding the political events or the personal happenings in her life; however, as her insatiable desire to acquire reading literacy is met through her loving foster father's patient teaching and her own book thievery, she grows up into a perceptive young woman responding to the atrocities of the world around her by promoting human dignity through the power of words. Alongside her narrative, readers get a glimpse into the life of Max Vandenburg, the Jewish man who hides in the Hubermann's basement. His friendship with Liesel prompts him to turn his violent anger and aggression toward Hitler into drawings and stories that express the travesty of Nazi power while offering hope to those who dare to see the world differently and resist the tyranny of evil.

Literacy Events and Sponsors

The belief that literacy presumes social interaction plays out as a prominent theme in *The Book Thief.* Yetta Goodman calls the moments in which a child learns literacy, "literacy events" and explains, "it is important to remember that children's development of literacy grows out of their experiences and the views and attitudes toward literacy they encounter as they interact with social groups" (317). The association a child makes between specific social interactions and literacy matters far more than the actual texts consumed or produced. Death traces Liesel's early literacy events from the moment she steals her first book (*The Grave Digger's Handbook*) at the site of her brother's funeral, through her humiliating struggle to read in front of her class, to her intimate nighttime basement reading and writing sessions with "Papa" Hans. Most likely students don't relate to Liesel's thievery, but many can relate to the various struggles that accompany her literacy development.

At the beginning of the story, Liesel is not a "strong" reader by educational standards. Her early difficulties in reading are relatable to reluctant readers, who do not possess her appetite for books. Amanda Sladek notes that the literacy narrative assignment is often not appealing to these students because "not every student enters the academy with a deep connection to reading and writing" (64). Sladek admits that her own interests caused her to "[assume] that literacy would be a driving force in [her] students' lives" (63). However, many students have struggled with the various pressures in their schools or home that have played a role in their own identify construction as "bad" readers and writers. Students relate to the difficulties of performing literacy in the one-size-fits-all classroom, which is often focused on progress testing rather than natural development. During the "progress tests" at Liesel's school, "[e]very child was made to stand at the front of the room and read from a passage the teacher gave them" (75). Liesel is unable to accomplish the task because she has not yet progressed in her reading as far as the other students in her age group. My students readily express sympathy with Liesel, remembering moments when they, too, felt like they were reading something "written in another tongue" (77). The incident invites students to form their own critique of literacy testing as they share anecdotes about what practices encouraged or discouraged their progress in reading or writing in their educational experiences.

Interestingly, as students evaluate the ubiquitous problem of standardized testing, they, like Liesel, draw attention to moments in which their worth as individuals felt closely attached to their literacy development. Liesel equates her performance to her own worth because her teacher Sister Maria employs corporeal punishment in response to what she sees as Liesel's impertinent behavior. Sister Maria is an example a "literacy sponsor," what Deborah Brandt defines as an authority figure who plays a role in determining how a student accesses or values literacy. The title includes "older relatives, teachers, priests, supervisors." or anyone who serves as a "reminder that literacy learning ... has always required permission, sanction, assistance" and often "coercion" (556–557). In effect, students learn from their sponsors that there is a certain type of literacy and an appropriate display of literacy that earns one favor or garners punishment and disapproval. In prompting students to critique and evaluate how they have experienced "literacy sponsors" in both beneficial and damaging ways, I attempt to be honest as we recognize the constraints of the composition classroom, with both the institution and me as their professor acting as "literacy sponsors." I acknowledge that even in this assignment I am articulating in some form or another acceptable literacy "discourses," or "ways of being in the world" that "integrate words, acts, values, beliefs, attitudes, and social identities" (Gee 526).

Many students choose to write about positive examples of literacy sponsorship as modeled by Hans Hubermann. Liesel's literacy lessons begin when she starts wetting the bed during a nightmare. Instead of punishing her, Hans uses these moments to assure her that he will protect and cherish her regardless of the circumstances. He provides this assurance to her through reading lessons. Liesel realizes that when reading with Hans "books and words started to mean not just something but everything" (30). Only as she builds relationships through her reading does she learn that words hold a power to help and heal, or hurt and kill. Hans's reading level is not much more advanced than Liesel's as Rosa reveals he dropped out of school in fourth grade. Still, every night, he faithfully carries out a ritual reading with his adopted daughter, teaching her to write the alphabet with his "thick painter's pencil and a stack of sandpaper" (67). He requires Liesel to paint the words she doesn't know on the wall until she learns their meanings. In his unconventional style, he adds a bit of humor to the alphabet lessons by assigning Rosa's famous epithet "SAUMENSCH!" (German for pig) to the letter "s." Hans thoughtfully adds these personal touches—from using his work supplies to incorporating family jokes—to create moments in the first half of the book which betray an overarching argument about the importance of socialization in literacy development in contrast to speed, skill, and standardization. In Liesel's own words reflecting on these days, she writes, "*but it was not so much the school who helped me to read. It was Papa*" (64, emphasis in original).

Because Liesel's story is so unique, the students attempt to craft their stories as series of one-of-a-kind literacy events while still imitating some of the descriptive strategies Zusak uses to create memorable scenes. One student Madison,[1] for instance, had internalized a certain propriety associated with literacy as embodied by her older sister, who had been labeled a "good" reader at school. Madison's narrative employs a fairy-tale like description of her older sister, who, crowned with perfect brown hair, would sit regally in a chair while reading. By observing her sister and observing school procedures that required students to read quietly at one's desk, Madison appropriated the idea that literacy was equivalent to solitude, quietness, and what she saw as "perfection." In her narrative, she represents herself as the antithesis of the respectable learner by using descriptions of herself as the "wild" and "hyper-active" child with "untamable" curls who could not sit still to read a book in the "appropriate" way.

Madison's mother, her heroic literacy sponsor, rescues Madison from these stifling literacy beliefs. To convey the essence of her mother, Madison imitates the thoughtful description chosen for Hans in *The Book Thief*. Zusak stirs together a sense of crudeness and comfort exuded in Han's smell—"a mixture of dead cigarettes, decades of paint, and human skin" (37). In Madison's narrative, she needed the hero to embody a sophisticated, regality she associated with literacy. Madison describes listening to her mother's voice fluctuate perfectly as the "smell of Clinique-lotion" wafted through the room. Yet, Madison's mother encouraged her to read aloud while standing up at the kitchen table, an act that sanctioned what Madison saw as a more "uncon-ventional" literacy practice. In her narrative, Madison attributes the devel-opment of her confidence in speech and interpersonal relationships to her mother's literacy sponsorship.

Another one of my first-year composition students, Caleb, approached the critique of literacy sponsors through a risky, yet ultimately rewarding strategy. At the beginning of his narrative, he cheekily critiques the language I use in the assignment prompt as he says, "Honestly, literacy has not 'shaped my life' in any significant way, but I can probably stretch some stuff from my life's experience, take some other stuff out of context, put it all together, and punch out around 800–1200 words." Had he stopped there, I could have read his story simply as a mockery of the assignment; yet I know from talking with Caleb in small group conferences that he genuinely wanted to write in a way that entertained his audience, including me. When I first encouraged him to use the humor I recognized in his early journal writing, he was reluc-tant because he thought it wouldn't be serious enough, and he was genuinely concerned about alienating his readers. I realized that Caleb had internalized the idea that appropriate literacy was serious as opposed to playful.

His essay helped explain, too, that his aversion to reading stemmed from his feelings of insecurity within his family who all enjoyed serious reading. In his essay, he relates how his dad "a pastor … reads books with massively obnoxious titles like *The Ancient Church's Theology on Predestination, Hermeneutics, and Another Really Big Word vol. 17* just for the fun of it" while his "mom is into those Francine River-love-flower-sappy-type books." Even his two youngest brothers "are at the beginner-to-amateur reading stage where they [read] *Lord of the Rings*-type books." Each member of his family was reading something socially sanctioned, but Caleb humorously expresses his fear that his own lack of pleasure in "serious" reading positioned him as an outsider and possibly a disappointment to his literacy sponsors—his parents and teachers. Caleb expressly acknowledges his own hesitation in revealing this part of himself to the audience as he writes, "I know very well that this paper is a *literacy* paper and will ultimately end up in the hands of my composition professor, so I would like to warn you that what I am about to write will most likely make you think that I am a horrible person—*I am not a big reader*" (emphasis in original).

Throughout his narrative, though, Caleb still positions his parents as positive literacy sponsors. He remembers his mom reading the very traditional children's book *I'll Love You Forever,* but he admits that he primarily recalls the amusing "picture of the toddler on the front cover pulling all of the toilet paper off of the rack" which he thought was "really cool." His narrative creatively grapples with his literacy development struggles through witty critique of an ideal that is subconsciously propagated by his otherwise caring literacy sponsors—that literacy should be a serious, moral endeavor (whether the literacy sponsors truly believe this or not). Toward the end of his essay, Caleb admits that while he still does not enjoy reading, his reading experiences and observations of his family's reading were important to him in understanding them and connecting with each one. His essay also revealed to him that he enjoys writing humor and hopes to try his hand at it again somewhere down the road.

Authentic Writing and Multiple Literacies

Another problem students quickly identify in educational settings is the lack of authentic writing opportunities. Liesel sees very little value in her writing at school because she seeks authentic writing experiences. For Liesel, authenticity is not directly related to the type of text or type of assignment, but rather it marks any purposeful use of literacy within social relationships. After giving an assignment to write a letter to a classmate, Sister Maria heavily sanitizes the meaningful banter in the letters between Liesel and her best friend Rudy. Liesel reflects that this literacy event, this "letter writing" assignment "meant nothing" because it provided no positive means for Liesel to use words to connect personally with someone else (94–95). Grant Wiggins explains that authentic writing is that which "ensure[s] that students have to write for real audiences and purposes, not just the teacher in response to generic prompts" (30). He argues that authentic writing also requires the student to feel that there is a "real *difference* to be caused" by their writing (30). Liesel intuitively recognizes this, so while her teachers see her as underperforming academically, she is searching for more meaningful ways to use the literacy she is learning.

The literacy narrative assignment may feel "inauthentic" to students because it does not translate into a form of writing students would find themselves engaged in outside of the college composition classroom. Even Wiggins downplays genres of college writing that are less than pragmatic. Still, his criteria for authentic writing simply identifies those endeavors that students perceive make a difference for a specific audience. I encourage students to consider their literacy narratives a social activity, choosing a specific audience other than me, who would benefit from or simply enjoy the narrative they tell. The most successful narratives are often inspired by an intimate idea of audience. One student Tammy, for instance, a self-proclaimed "mediocre writer," chose to write about her experiences as a bilingual in America. She admitted that she and her sister had once described to each other the sensation of not being able to find the correct words as having bubbles in their mouths. She writes about how the Portuguese and English laughter would "foam" from their lips as her sister would sing her "Portlish" in "frothy giggles." Tammy was unsure if anyone else would understand the image, but she was confident her sister would; she only knew exactly what she wanted to say once she decided to direct the narrative for her sister. This choice helped Tammy illustrate her experiences in a richer, more memorable way that not only enabled the reader experience a bilingual's dilemma, but would more importantly (for Tammy) make her sister chuckle with understanding. Tammy's experience also illustrates what DeRosa strives to accomplish through the literacy narrative. She argues that "literacy narratives encourage writers to develop an awareness of the flexibility of their roles; as writers, they are not defined by the static 'labels' that may have been previously assigned to them" (7). Tammy is able to move beyond the label she embraced of "mediocre" writer and gain control of her own persona as a writer, giving credence to the bilingual literacies that shape her as an individual.

To promote more authentic literacy narratives, I encourage students to write about any type of literacy that they personally value. I ask that however they interpret literacy they simply indicate in their narrative that they are showcasing a *competency* that requires *communication* or *social engagement.* Like Sladek, I believe that allowing students to write about "alternative literacies" makes the assignment more valuable and relevant to their lives outside the English classroom" (64).

Some students are reluctant to make the creative move because they feel unsure whether they can justify a certain hobby or experience as a "literacy event." *The Book Thief*, though, allows us as a class to discuss how one can write about the communicative and social aspects of different literacies such as drawing, playing the accordion, house-painting, and even (as one of my students pointed out) thievery. I ask the students to perform a close analysis of Max's drawings in his books "The Standover Man" and "The Word Shaker."

As a class, we also perform a close reading of a small passage in the book in which Liesel develops a greater sense of admiration for Papa's multiple literacies. Death describes the scene:

> As far as the painting itself was concerned, probably the most interesting aspect for Liesel was the mixing. Like most people, she assumed her papa simply took his cart to the paint shop or hardware store and asked for the right color and away he went. She didn't realize that most of the paint was in lumps, in the shape of a brick. It was then rolled out with an empty champagne bottle…. Once that was completed, there was the addition of water, whiting, and glue, not to mention the complexities of matching the right color. The science of Papa's trade brought him an even greater level of respect…. Competence was attractive [356].

This glimpse into the thoughtfulness and skill Papa put into mixing paints is made even more significant by the realization that he set aside a portion of his meticulous labor each evening he and Liesel painted the alphabet or unfamiliar words on the wall together. Papa also garnered an unflattering name for himself in the community for being the only painter who didn't refuse jobs in the Jews' corner. Liesel eventually recognizes the incredible selflessness of her Papa as she sees precious skill, time, and labor invested in mixing the paints that provided the wordless acts of protest within an anti–Semitic community.

The various examples of characters developing their skills, unveiling the processes behind their competency, and using these literacies in some form to connect with others opens a wide range of possibilities for students to choose their own literacy narratives. So far, I have read narratives on audiobooks, comic books, musical instruments, DIY (do-it-yourself) projects, piloting, screenwriting, drawing, woodworking, sports, health, cooking, computer coding, intercultural sensitivity, and even the use of a prosthetic limb. As students write about what is meaningful to them and learn to challenge their assumptions and beliefs, they are also enlarging understandings of literacy for their peer readers and me.

Ambiguities and Agency

While students identify with Liesel as a protagonist, struggling through her literacy development and searching for meaningful relationships, they often feel disconnected from Liesel's world and the atrocities of the Holocaust. Jenni Adams notes that the "novel is unusual for a Holocaust text" because Zusak uses what she calls "doubleness" in Death's first-person narration. She claims that he is an ironically compassionate narrator, who is used "to simultaneously … confront the adolescent reader with the fact of death (in both an abstract and a historically located sense) and to offer protection from the most unsettling implications of this fact" (223). In short, Death is a menacing friend. In the end, Zusak manages multiple audience expectations. For children, the sad events culminate in a happy ending as Liesel lives and her book is eventually shared. For older readers, though, the ending is unsettling as they realize Liesel's entire world and her innocence is crushed in the very moments she produces her book.

Similarly, Zusak offers a "doubleness" in his representation of literacy. In many ways, the novel offers an optimistic hope that the words and stories of those like Max and Liesel who value all human life can indeed foster democratic change as well as personal cognitive and social advancement. Readers witness how Liesel's literacy development accompanies her development of cognitive and moral sensibilities. Before she can read or write effectively, she comprehends little of the world around her and innocently salutes her "Heil Hitler"s as a participant of the BDM (League of German Girls), a part of the Nazi Party youth movement. In one of her most defining moments, the Nazi book burning in Mulching, Liesel salvages a book from the "corpse of collected books" a literacy event that reorients her perspective against the Nazi party (114). She begins to see people's writing as the personification of those individuals. Death gives voice to Liesel's recognition as he details the carnage of books just as he would detail the life of a human character. The book Liesel steals from the book burning—*The Shoulder Shrug*—introduces Liesel to a Jewish protagonist, opening her mind to challenge an oppressive regime that hatefully censored ideas and dehumanized real people. This important moment in her literacy development specifically prepares her to embrace Max once the Hubermanns agreed to hide the Jew in their basement.

Max's story "The Word Shaker" advances the theme that literacy promotes good as well. Max repurposes his copy of Hitler's *Mein Kampf* by painting over the anti–Semitic words and creating an outlet to express his fears and burdens that plague his violent daydreams and night terrors. His story, written for Liesel, illustrates the power of words through the image of a seed growing into large tree that overshadows the evil trees planted by the Führer. His visual metaphor assures readers and Liesel that good will triumph over evil through the power of words.

This seminal idea of literacy as the key to moral victory, though, is not wholly optimistic. It carries the weight of "doubleness" that Adams describes in the book. She argues that in examining Max's book, the "visual style of the narrative ... evokes its ambivalent situation" (225). She observes how "Hitler's words are still visible in places through the paint, with the effect that the anti–Semitic tract is both hidden by the fable and exposed within it, the story both confronting and protecting its young reader, Liesel, from the ugly truth about Germany" (225). The words creeping up underneath the paint on the pages of Max's story remind readers, too, that literacy is a double-edged sword, useful for good and evil. Students are quick to point out that one of the most successful, literate characters in the story is Hitler himself, whose oratory and writing influenced an entire nation to turn against the Jews. In addition, literacy does not "save" everyone at the end of *The Book Thief.* Again, the doubleness of interpretation arises in one of the most heartbreaking moments of the story. As Liesel stays up late in the basement to write her book, she unknowingly protects herself while she can do nothing as Himmel Street is bombed and her beloved family and neighbors are killed in their sleep. While literacy "saves" her life in one sense, it also isolates her from all the relationships she has worked throughout the story to establish.

Despite the ambiguities readers must wrestle with at the end of the story, most students believe that Liesel ultimately finds agency or power through her words in the construction of her own narrative. By recognizing this, students begin to see the value in writing their own stories. DeRosa argues persuasively that the literacy narrative assignment is a space in which students "become active participants in the construction of their literacy development" and help students "develop a sense of critical agency about their literacy practices" (2). By reflecting on their literacy practices, students may, DeRosa posits, "identify and reflect on their roles and responsibilities as writers" and "develop awareness of their 'literacy in action'—the ways that their writing can effect change in their communities" (2).

Practice Considerations for the Composition Classroom

The literacy narrative is a staple genre in many first-year composition courses. I design an entire literacy narrative unit in which we use *The Book Thief* as our core text both for discussing definitions and issues regarding literacy and also as an example of engaging narrative writing. Below, I have included the prompt for the essay assignment I use in my class, including an introductory definition of literacy as written by the National Council of Teachers of English, which I have excerpted by bolding the key words that indicate for students what ideas should feature prominently within their narrative.

The definition of "literacy," according to the NCTE (National Council of Teachers of English), is "a collection of **cultural and communicative practices** shared among members of particular **groups** ... a wide range of **abilities and competencies**." We don't often take time to reflect on how our own personal stories and life experiences have shaped our identities and beliefs. A literacy narrative asks you to think about how your own experiences, in reading, writing, or some other form of literacy, have shaped your identity and beliefs as an individual. Sharing literacy narratives also helps you communicate what you believe to a specific audience to challenge or to inspire them. We can understand through our own stories why we believe what we do about the power, struggles, pleasures, benefits, or necessity of various literacies. Your job is to narrate a memory or a series of memories related to your literacy development and explain why this story is significant to you now. 800–1000 words.

Preliminary Exercise

Before students write complete drafts, I spend one 50-minute class period on descriptive writing. I ask students to collect their favorite descriptive passages from the book, and we perform a close reading of several sections as a class to determine what makes the passage work. In the last 10–15 minutes of class, students select a couple of strategies (imagery, figures of speech, sentence structure, sentence rhythm, etc.) and imitate them creating a scene for their literacy narratives. These passages usually end up in their final drafts and are often some of the strongest passages in their narratives.

End Goals/Rubric

Along with the assignment prompt, I provide students with a rubric. This is a condensed list of the features I expect to see in class. I usually devote a class day (or an online lesson) to each:

1. Show meaningful reflection and discovery[2]
2. Express a clear understanding of "literacy" per the key words in the definition provided
3. Employ story-telling devices (plot, characters, action, setting)
4. Rhetorically use vivid description and avoid cliché
5. Avoid overt persuasive/moralizing tone
6. Provide a memorable, focused main idea (take-away) for a specific audience
7. Use strong sentence structure and active verbs
8. Demonstrate purposeful revision and editing

The literacy narrative unit spans about five weeks with the bulk of the reading finished in the first two weeks. I find most students will manage the three to four hours outside of class reading per week because we do a lot of the writing such as the reflections, exercises, and some drafting in class. In addition to *The Book Thief,* I assign one professional non-fiction essay (like Amy Tan's "Mother Tongue") and one sample student essay for students to use as models. During the first two weeks, I conduct the class in small breakout groups and whole class discussion on the novel and begin every class day with an eight-minute free-write to get students brainstorming for their essays. In the final two weeks, I meet with each three-to-four-person writing group to discuss the essays in progress. I flip the classroom[3] by having students read revision and editing strategies online, apply them to their essays, and then come to their writing group meeting to discuss their ideas and revision process.

The literacy narrative is often the piece students find the most satisfaction in writing, according to their responses in author's notes and journal reflections. I, too, find their insights on their literacy processes some of the most engaging and thought-provoking essays I read all semester, especially when they truly take the time to examine their own assumptions or societal norms in relation to literacy. The more students feel an attachment to the material they are writing about the more then invest in the writing process, too. Their audiences become more real because their work is meaningful and personal.

The most challenging aspect of this assignment is pushing students to move past cliché or uninspired narratives about "the big (sports) game," or that philanthropy trip they took last summer. I hesitate to downplay any important experiences in these students' lives, so, as much as I can, I encourage students to question what they know and perhaps discover a fresh way of understanding these important events as processes of social communication. I tell them that their essays should not simply leave readers with a good feeling; rather, they should leave readers re-thinking how they understand and value certain literacy practices. While not all students produce amazingly thought-provoking essays, the most successful essays often employ critical thought that emerges from our discussions about literacy myths and societal assumptions. These papers engage in a growing body of social knowledge that can transform how we understand and value multiple literacies.

Conclusion

As I have claimed throughout this essay, using YAL in the composition course to accompany a literacy narrative unit encourages students to explore ideas about literacy (literacy myths, sponsors, events, etc.) and to practice rhetorical story telling. I take pleasure in reading students' final reflections on the novel. Many say they will share the book with others or read it again. Others express various visceral and cathartic reactions they have in their reading experiences—crying, laughing, or sighing in pain and relief. In the most recent semester of teaching *The Book Thief*, one student expressed the general tenor I find within the end-of-book reflections: "Where do I begin? I just finished *The Book Thief*, and the images of the last fifty pages still swirl in my head. The story of Liesel was so captivating. It enriched my view of WW2 and caused me to think about my own life deeply."

My hope is that along with the reading experiences, the process of writing a literacy narrative becomes a significant and positive literacy event in the lives of these students. I want students to leave with a more critical understanding of literacy and be inspired as active agents who use their literacies and their stories for the well being of others. After all, it is the act of storytelling that is part of what makes us human, makes us feel, and makes ideas matter. Rick Altman sums up saying that narrative is the "essential strategy of human expression and thus a basic aspect of human life ... [it] commands our attention. If we would understand the ways in which humans interact, we must take up the challenge of narrative" (1).

NOTES

1. All students are referred to with pseudonyms.
2. Kara Poe Alexander's article, "From Story to Analysis: Reflection and Uptake in the Literacy Narrative Assignment," analyzes how teachers perceive successful reflection and provides concrete strategies for articulating "reflection" requirements to students.
3. See McCallum, et al. for research on flipping the classroom in higher education.

WORKS CITED

Adams, Jenni. "'Into Eternity's Certain Breadth': Ambivalent Escapes in Markus Zusak's *The Book Thief*." *Children's Literature in Education*, vol. 41, no. 3, 2010, pp. 222–33.

Alexander, Kara Poe. "From Story to Analysis: Reflection and Uptake in the Literacy Narrative Assignment." *Composition Studies*, vol. 43, no. 2, Fall 2015, pp. 43–71.

Altman, Rick. *A Theory of Narrative*. New York: Columbia University Press, 2008.

Baker, Edith M. "Composing English 102: Reframing Students' Lives through Literature." *Composition and/or Literature: The End(s) of Education*, edited by Linda S. Bergmann and Edith M. Baker. Urbana: National Council of Teachers of English, 2006.

Bergmann, Linda S., and Edith M. Baker. *Composition and/or Literature: The End(s) of Education*. Urbana: National Council of Teachers of English, 2006.

Brandt, Deborah. "Sponsors of Literacy." *College Composition and Communication*, vol. 49, no. 2, 1998, pp. 165–85.

DeRosa, Susan. "Literacy Narratives as Genres of Possibility: Students' Voices, Reflective Writing, and Rhetorical Awareness." *Ethos*, vol. 15, 2008, pp. 1–14.

Goodman, Yetta. "The Development of Initial Literacy." *Awakening to Literacy*, 1984, pp. 102–9. Rpt. in *Literacy: A Critical Sourcebook*, edited by Ellen Cushman, et al. New York: Bedford/St. Martin's, 2001, pp. 316–24.

Graff, Harvey J. "The Literacy Myth at Thirty." *Journal of Social History*, vol. 43, no. 3, 2010, pp. 635–61.

_____. *Literacy Myths, Legacies, and Lessons: New Studies on Literacy*. Piscataway: Transaction Publishers, 2011.

_____. *The Literacy Myth: Literacy and Social Structure in the Nineteenth-Century City*. Cambridge, MA: Academic Press, 1979.

Herz, Sarah K., and Donald R. Gallo. *From Hinton to Hamlet: Building Bridges Between Young Adult Literature and the Classics*. Santa Barbara: Greenwood Press, 2005.

Hill, Crag. "Introduction." *The Critical Merits of Young Adult Literature: Coming of Age*. Abingdon-on-Thames: Routledge, 2014, pp. 1–24.

Lindemann, Erika. "Freshman Composition: No Place for Literature." *College English*, vol. 55, no. 3, 1993, pp. 311–16.

McCallum, Shelly, Janel Schultz, Kristen Sellke, and Jason Spartz. "An Examination of the

Flipped Classroom Approach on College Student Academic Involvement." *International Journal of Teaching and Learning in Higher Education,* vol. 27, no. 1, 2015, pp. 42–55.

"NCTE Definition of 21st Century Literacies." NCTE Executive Committee, February 2008. http://www.ncte.org/positions/statements/21stcentdefinition.

Poe Alexander, Kara. "From Story to Analysis: Reflection and Uptake in the Literacy Narrative Assignment." *Composition Studies,* vol. 43, no. 2, 2015, pp. 43–71.

Sladek, Amanda. "The New Literacies Narrative." *Writing on the Edge,* vol. 26, no. 1, 2015, pp. 65–72.

Soliday, Mary. "Translating Self and Difference through Literacy Narratives." *College English,* vol. 56, no. 5, 1994, pp. 511–26.

Street, Brian. "What's 'New' in New Literacy Studies? Critical Approaches to Literacy in Theory and Practice." *Current Issues in Comparative Education,* vol. 5, no. 2, 2003, pp. 77–91.

Tan, Amy. "Mother Tongue." *The McGraw-Hill Reader: Issues Across the Disciplines.* Ed. Gilbert H. Muller. 11th ed. New York: McGraw-Hill, 2011. 76–81.

Tate, Gary. "A Place for Literature in Freshman Composition." *College English,* vol. 55, no. 3, 1993, pp. 317–21.

Tokarczyk, Michelle M., and Irene Papoulis. *Teaching Composition/Teaching Literature: Crossing Great Divides.* Bern, Switzerland: Peter Lang, 2003.

Wiggins, Grant. "EJ in Focus: Real-World Writing: Making Purpose and Audience Matter." *The English Journal,* vol. 98, no. 5, 2009, pp. 29–37.

Zusak, Markus. *The Book Thief.* New York: Knopf, 2006.

Love Always

The Perks of Being a Wallflower
as a Rhetorical Text

ANDREW BOURELLE

In Stephen Chbosky's epistolary novel *The Perks of Being a Wallflower*, the protagonist, Charlie, writes to an unnamed "friend" whom he feels he can confide in. In each letter, he narrates what has happened recently in his life and concludes with the closing "Love always,/Charlie." Because of this format, *The Perks of Being a Wallflower* can be interpreted as a letter to whomever is reading the novel, and, as a result, the novel can be seen as more than just a coming-of-age story—it can also be read as an argument. Charlie's message is one of empathy, open-mindedness, support, friendship, and finally love. With each concluding, "Love always," Chbosky makes an argument to readers that they should "love always."

Because *The Perks of Being a Wallflower* can be read as a narrative and a rhetorical text, it is an ideal book to use in a first-year composition course. Students can read the book in its entirety, or in excerpts; additionally, they can either discuss the rhetoric of the novel in class or in written assignments. In this essay, I will provide example rhetorical analyses of two excerpts of *The Perks of Being a Wallflower* as well as advice about how instructors can use the book in their classes. I hope this essay is merely the beginning of a larger discussion of the possibilities of using *The Perks of Being a Wallflower* in composition courses. I would like to see instructors take the suggestions made here, adjust them to fit their own curricula, and build upon the ways in which *The Perks of Being a Wallflower* can be used in college writing classes.

The Perks of Using Perks

First, it seems important to explain why *The Perks of Being a Wallflower* is an appropriate and interesting text for first-year composition students to read, analyze, and write about. Set in the early 1990s, the novel follows the character of Charlie during his first year of high school. Charlie begins the year as a shy introvert who has difficulty fitting in among the more sociable and socially adjusted teenagers around him. During the course of the year, Charlie makes friends, finds a mentor in his English teacher, falls in love, experiments with drugs, and, in short, grows up. The book never shies away from sensitive topics, such as abortion, bigotry, bullying, child molestation, domestic violence, drug abuse, homosexuality, and suicide. The book does not address these topics in contrived, didactic ways; *The Perks of Being a Wallflower* is not written as a stereotypical after-school special. Rather, the novel tackles tough-to-discuss issues with honesty and verisimilitude.

While the book is categorized as young adult literature (YAL), it handles "adult" material deftly and maturely—making it appropriate for college-age students. Much of Charlie's perspective is relatable for students in their freshman year of college. Charlie is venturing into unexplored territory—a fish out of water, if you will—as he enters high school. Likewise, many students taking composition courses experience similar feelings of insecurity and loneliness when first attending college. Moreover, even though Charlie is a freshman in high school, his sister and several of the friends he ends up making are seniors; therefore, the book emphasizes going off to college, leaving home, growing up and moving on—all themes that most first-year composition students can relate to. Even though the characters in the book are predominantly high school students, most college students, having recently graduated from high school, can appreciate and understand the experiences described in the text. And because the book tackles universal coming-of-age issues, even nontraditional students will likely connect with the material. The book was written and published in the 1990s—in an era before smart phones, text-messaging, and social-media dominated the lives of teenagers—but the story is one that anyone who has experienced high school, whether recently or in earlier generations, will be able to relate to in some capacity.

While the book is fiction, the prose very much resembles memoir-type genres that are often employed in composition classes and can be found in numerous composition textbooks, such as Richard Johnson-Sheehan's *Writing Today* (described as memoir), Duane Roen, Greg Glau, and Barry Maid's *The McGraw-Hill Guide* (as writing to share experiences), and John J. Ruszkiewicz and Jay Dolmage's *How to Write Anything* (as narrative). Even though *The Perks of Being a Wallflower* is a novel, not a memoir, I would argue that it is a relevant text to use because it showcases examples of narrative/memoir writing in form. As M. Thomas Gammarino suggests, fiction and nonfiction "have more in common than not, and […] the delineation is more elusive than it may at first seem" (20–21). The difference, Gammarino states, is "more a distinction in subject matter than in technique" (21). Moreover, narrative—whether fiction or nonfiction—can and often does have rhetorical purposes. *The Perks of Being a Wallflower*, then, is an excellent text for first-year composition because it is a narrative *and* because it is rhetorical.

Narratives—whether fiction or nonfiction—can make powerful rhetorical statements, even if they are not as commonly studied for their rhetorical elements as commentaries, evaluations, or proposals. As Elizabeth A. Stolarek and Larry R. Juchartz state, "Not all narrative arguments […] are made explicitly. In an *implicit* narrative argument, the 'moral of the story' isn't stated; it's the job of the reader to determine the point or points the author seems to be making" [emphasis in the original] (337). Not all narratives necessarily make arguments, or they can be interpreted with ambiguity. "But," Stolarek and Juchartz state, "carefully examining the rhetorical elements of a text can help a reader decide to what extent the author is attempting to persuade an audience through narrative argument" (337). *The Perks of Being a Wallflower*, therefore, demonstrates the rhetorical potential of narrative, both in fiction and of the memoir-type writing it emulates. The book provides students with an opportunity to carefully examine its rhetorical elements, looking for the implicit arguments throughout and ultimately providing a model that could be used for their own narrative arguments.

The *Perks of Being a Wallflower* is written as a series of letters, and, for that reason, the book could be used in its entirety or in excerpts. Many of the letters function as stand-alone stories, and, with a little contextualization from the instructor, students could read one or a few, rather than the entire book. For the purposes of providing examples, I will focus on the first two sections of the book, providing thorough rhetorical analyses that could be used as a model for how to discuss the text with students. I have chosen the first two letters because, together, they show the range of possibilities available in the novel. The first section sets the stage for the rest of the novel and makes arguments about some of the novel's thematic elements. The second letter is shorter, and it serves to demonstrate how even brief sections of the novel have strong rhetorical messages.

Rhetorical Analysis: First Letter

The opening section of the novel is a letter Charlie writes to his mysterious "friend" on the eve of his first day of high school. In the five-page section, Charlie reveals some background about his family life: details about his parents and two siblings, an explanation about his friend's suicide, and an introduction to his Aunt Helen, who is dead, but remains an important part of Charlie's life and of the novel.

The narrator begins the first letter saying he is "writing to you because she said you listen and understand and didn't try to sleep with that person at that party even though you could have" (2). Charlie has never met the "friend" he is writing to and requests that this person—i.e., the reader—not try to figure out who he is. Charlie states that he "just need[s] to know that someone out there listens" (2). From the start, then, the novel is set up to create the perception that Charlie could actually be writing to whomever is reading the book. From the first page, the reader is being told directly that "other people look to you for strength and friendship" (2). This has the effect of asking—or arguing—for readers to engage with the narrative from a sympathetic perspective. Charlie is telling the reader directly that he or she should be the type of person who will understand his story and will sympathize, or at least empathize, with what he has to say.

Charlie then proceeds to state, "I am both happy and sad and I'm still trying to figure out how that could be" (2). Charlie tells the story of his friend Michael's suicide the previous school year. He heard the announcement over the loudspeaker at school, stating that Michael had died. Afterward, he and a few other people "who actually liked Michael" (3) sat with guidance counselors to discuss how they were coping with Michael's death. Crying, Charlie doesn't understand why Michael did it, and one of the counselors replies that Michael probably "didn't feel like he had anyone to talk to" (4). "Then," Charlie explains in the letter,

> I started screaming at the guidance counselor that Michael could have talked to me. And I started crying even harder. He tried to calm me down by saying that he meant an adult like a teacher or a guidance counselor. But it didn't work and eventually my brother came by the middle school in his Camaro to pick me up [4].

Here is a powerful rhetorical move made by the author. By showing Charlie's reaction and emphasizing that Michael did have someone he could have talked to about his problems, Chbosky deftly makes an implicit argument that anyone feeling depressed should look for someone to talk to. The character of Michael could have potentially found catharsis in speaking to Charlie. And the reaction of Charlie, the friend left feeling guilty and confused because he couldn't help, shows the damaging effects on others that suicide causes. The passage can speak to readers in different ways. To someone considering suicide, the passage can be rhetorically persuasive about seeking help. To others, the passage can speak to the importance of being open and ready to help a depressed friend or loved one—even, perhaps, if the person has not asked for help.

Because the counselors say that Michael had "problems at home" (4), Charlie continues his narrative by describing his own home life and contemplating whether he, too, has problems at home. He has an older brother, who is a football player in college, and a sister, who is a senior in high school and gets straight A's. His dad "works a lot and is an honest man"; his "mom cries a lot during TV programs" (5). The narrator establishes his family as ordinary, believable, and somewhat dysfunctional. He recounts a story when his Aunt Helen lived with the family, and Charlie, at seven years old, kept asking her about a bad thing that happened. She cried because of his pestering, and, consequently, Charlie's father slapped him for "hurting [his] aunt's feelings!" (6). (Charlie points out later in the book that this is the only time his father ever harmed him.) After his mom has a few glasses of wine, she reveals to Charlie what happened to his Aunt, and while he doesn't tell his "friend" what the bad thing is, he concludes, "Some people really do have it a lot worse than I do. They really do" (6).

While this part of the narrative doesn't contain a rhetorical message quite as obvious as the suicide discussion earlier in the section, there is still a rhetorical message here. By establishing some details about Charlie's household, the narrator does more than introduce the other family members as characters. He establishes that he has an imperfect yet realistic family—one that, with its imperfections, might seem relatable to readers. The rhetorical effect of establishing the nature of the family—as well as the trauma that his aunt apparently endured—can work to put readers in Charlie's shoes, thus making an argument: while you may have "problems at home" or problems in life, you are not the only one.

Moreover, throughout the first section of the novel, the text shows Charlie to be a sensitive, sad, socially uncomfortable individual who is attempting to make sense of the world around him. Aristotle states that there is persuasion "through character whenever the speech is spoken in such a way as to make the speaker worthy of credence; for we believe fair-minded people to a greater extent and more quickly [than we do others], on all subjects in general and completely so in cases where there is not exact knowledge" [brackets in original] (1.2.4). While Aristotle's comments were originally applied to oratory, his discussion is applicable here. Charlie's ethos as the narrator—and therefore Chbosky's ethos as the author—is quickly established; he is fair-minded and knowledgeable about a certain coming-of-age perspective. We know from the beginning that Charlie is someone who, simply put, does not fit in. The text therefore makes the argument to those reading, especially those that feel a similar sense of loneliness, confusion, and despondency, that they are not alone either. Most readers can probably relate to Charlie's situation in some way, even those readers who don't have much in common with Charlie. In fact, for those readers who are nothing like Charlie (those who "fit in," if you will), I think the text makes a different argument—one for empathy. Readers who may not be the same type of "wallflower" as Charlie are given a glimpse into a world they are unfamiliar with, and, therefore, the book argues for them not to judge that world negatively. Charlie establishes the ethos to be his readers' fair-minded guide into the world of a high-school student who does not fit in. Readers will trust Charlie, as Aristotle says, "in general" and "completely so" regarding Charlie's world that they might not be familiar with.

Rhetorical Analysis: Second Letter

The second letter in the book is shorter, barely covering two pages, and focuses primarily on one particular coming-of-age problem: bullying. Most of the section is devoted to a situation in which, as Charlie describes it, "only one kid named Sean really seemed to notice me" (7). In a detached, distant tone, Charlie describes how Sean waited for Charlie after gym class and said "really immature things" and told Charlie he was going to give him a "swirlie" (7) "He seemed pretty unhappy as well, and I told him so," Charlie explains, adding, "Then, he got mad and started hitting me" (7). Charlie's brother had previously taught him how to fight—"Go for the knees, throat, and eyes" (7)—and so Charlie ends up hurting the boy. "And then I started crying," Charlie explains (7). He adds later, "Some kids look at me strange in the hall-ways because I don't decorate my locker, and I'm the one who beat up Sean and couldn't stop crying after he did it. I guess I'm pretty emotional" (8). Charlie was briefly afraid that he would get into trouble for fighting, but another kid, a witness, stands up for Charlie and explains that he fought in self-defense. In the end of the section, Charlie explains that he hasn't met any friends yet. "I was hoping that the kid who told the truth could become a friend of mine, but I think he was just being a good guy by telling the truth" (8).

Thus, the section ends on a lonely note. Charlie was able to defend him-self, but not without becoming very upset, and he longs for a friend. The same messages of empathy can be seen in this passage, but this time through the lens of bullying. One could interpret that the section makes an argument for fighting back against bullies—Charlie hurts his attacker, after all. However, this seems like a reductive interpretation. Charlie might come through the event physically unscathed, but emotionally he is a mess. This shows how everyone loses when it comes to bullying. Even when a victim successfully defends himself, the "winner" is emotionally distraught. So while there is likely an argument to fight back, the clearer argument is to bullies themselves: such acts lead to emotional and physical pain. Dunking someone's head in the toilet is not a harmless prank. Readers, one would hope, would be less likely to bully in any form after reading the section.

Finally, the presence of the witness in the story also makes a rhetorical statement. This person is not Charlie's friend, yet he tells the truth about the attack. Readers can likely assume that this witness fits in at school at least a little better than Charlie does. Still, he reports the truth about the incident, standing up for Charlie, which encourages readers who witness wrongdoing to ultimately do the right thing. Whether it's a college campus or the workplace, bullying is present in settings besides high schools, and so readers can take this message to heart even if they haven't been in high school for quite some time.

The second section of the book also includes a few paragraphs about Charlie's interactions with Michael's old girlfriend, Susan. By Charlie's description, we can tell that she used to be one of the students who, like Charlie and Michael, did not fit in. "But," Charlie explains, "over the summer she had her braces taken off, and she got a little taller and prettier and grew breasts" (6). As a result, Susan "acts a lot dumber in the hallways, especially when boys are around" (6–7). She won't say hi to Charlie anymore. "I think it's sad because Susan doesn't look as happy," he says (7).

In these few paragraphs, we get a description of a secondary character who is trying to fit into the world around her. She is doing so with more success than Charlie, at least on the surface; however, it appears that she is no longer happy. From this, readers can deduce another of Chbosky's arguments: people such as Charlie, who feel alienated or socially uncomfortable, should strive for happiness, not popularity. Susan apparently is becoming more popular, but she is not coming any closer to finding herself or finding happiness. This is a journey that Charlie is trying to make, a journey of understanding, not one of pretext where he is pretending to be something he is not.

As you can see, this section of the book, the second letter to the unnamed "friend," is short yet full of significant rhetorical implication. I wanted to describe it because it shows how even brief excerpts from the book can be used for in-depth analytical discussions. This section, as with all the others, concludes with the words "Love always," showing that Charlie, who has no friends and who is bullied, is still capable of unconditional love.

The themes—or arguments—established in the first sections of the book are addressed throughout the novel, but Charlie's letters continue to address even more coming-of-age issues and controversial topics. As Charlie narrates his experiences and reflects upon the world around him, Chbosky makes implicit rhetorical statements about child molestation, bigotry against homosexuals, domestic violence, drug use, and more—all with a rhetorical undercurrent arguing for empathy. More than that, each section concludes with the statement "Love always," thus making an argument for unconditional love.

Thomas Newkirk states that "[t]he personal essay dramatizes thought by showing the writer as someone open to the potentially transforming effects of a life sensitively encountered" (13). While the letters in *The Perks of Being a Wallflower* are not personal nonfiction essays, they function in a similar way. While they have the verisimilitude of fiction rather than veracity of nonfiction, the effect is the same: they show a realistically portrayed world sensitively encountered by a trustworthy narrator. As Newkirk adds, "Even confessions of inadequacy, insensitivity, and cruelty are redeemed by those reflexive turns that show the writer has—often, it seems, through the act of writing—achieved a measure of self-understanding and moral growth" (13). Through Charlie writing these letters to his "friend"—i.e., the reader of the novel—*The Perks of Being a Wallflower* demonstrates the self-understanding and moral growth possible through writing. I believe the book, and its sections, also argues for such self-exploration from its readers.

Practical Considerations for the Composition Classroom

There are a variety of ways to actually use the text within a composition classroom. As I said before, the book could be read in its entirety or in parts. However, I recommend asking students to discuss a limited section, with the instructor facilitating the rhetorical analysis. Analyzing the implicit narrative arguments that the book makes can be a more challenging task than simply asking students to identify ethos, pathos, and logos in a magazine advertisement or a TV commercial; therefore, students will likely need some help to do a thorough, deep reading of the book. My review of the first two sections of *The Perks of Being a Wallflower* can serve as a model for what instructors might discuss; however, there are ample sections of the book rich with interpretive rhetorical potential if an instructor wants to choose another.

Once students have seen how they can rhetorically analyze the text, they could be asked to write analyses of other sections, or of the book as a whole. These could be short writing assignments or major assignments. Students could do this work individually or in groups. Because the novel tackles a variety of topics—bigotry, abortion, drug use, etc.—different students or different groups of students could be tasked with rhetorically analyzing certain themes within the book. What is the novel's argument about homosexuality? About bullying? About suicide? Because the book is rich with discussion topics, students need not be asked to consider every rhetorical aspect of the book. Focusing on just one topic—such as teenage sexual activity or teenage suicide—would be more than enough for a student, or a group, to write about or present on.

In addition, analysis of the book could be used as a launching pad for an assignment that asks students to write *Perks*-type personal memoirs—or even letters to "friends"—reminiscent of the implicitly rhetorical stories in the book. Students could write, as the character Charlie does, about stories from their own lives that influenced or changed them, that led to their personal growth, and that have a rhetorical power as well. According to Newkirk, autobiographical essays that show the author's "turn" toward a new realization consequently "dramatize learning, they illustrate the possibility of personal growth, and they celebrate, indirectly, the heuristic power of writing itself. *Writing is the hero of the writing*" (emphasis in original) (14).

Such an assignment takes the often-used memoir genre and emphasizes the rhetorical aspect of the writing as well as the commonly used narrative and storytelling components of the writing activity. As Candace Spigelman states,

> Chief among objections to teaching personal forms of writing to first-year students is concern that it fosters in developing writers a naïve investment in some kind of "pure" and unmediated disclosure. For this reason, it is important that students and teachers appreciate the ways in which experience is rhetorically assembled [66].

Even though it's a novel, *The Perks of Being a Wallflower* can demonstrate this rhetorically assembled personal form of writing—a personal narrative that makes arguments in addition to reflecting upon experience. Students need not tackle topics such as rape or domestic violence; however, any narrative that calls for empathy, shows personal growth and maturity, and prompts readers to pause long enough to think about their own lives in relation to the text will be a rhetorically successful communicative act. *The Perks of Being a Wallflower* perfectly demonstrates the rhetorical potential of narrative, making it a perfect text to use in conjunction with lessons about writing personal, rhetorical narratives.

Conclusion

In summary, I argue that *The Perks of Being a Wallflower* could be used for students' rhetorical analyses, as well as a model for writing their own memoir essays wherein they do more than render experience—they add a rhetorical component as well. *The Perks of Being a Wallflower* could be included in a multi-week lesson that emphasizes rhetorical narratives—or it could be concluded in a single class, if students are merely asked to read and discuss one section of the book. Whether students are rhetorically analyzing *The Perks of Being a Wallflower* or writing arguments in the form of rhetorical memoirs that are mimetic of the storytelling techniques of the novel, the book offers ample opportunity for analysis and discussion.

While I have provided an analysis of the first two sections of the book and offered some suggestions for implementing the book into composition classes, I encourage instructors to take my suggestions, change them to fit their individual needs, and build upon them in order to continue exploring the ways in which the novel can be used in first-year composition. As a book that provides the perspective of a teenager and tackles sensitive subject matter, *The Perks of Being a Wallflower* is a novel that is both appropriate for first-year composition—and one that most students will find engaging, entertaining, and thought-provoking.

Works Cited

Aristotle. *On Rhetoric*. 2nd ed., translated by George A. Kennedy. Oxford: Oxford University Press, 2007.

Chbosky, Stephen. *The Perks of Being a Wallflower*. New York: MTV Books/Gallery Books, 2012.

Gammarino, M. Thomas. "Class Barriers: Creative Writing in Freshman Composition." *Currents in Teaching and Learning*, vol. 1, no. 2, 2009, pp. 19–27.

Johnson-Sheehan, Richard, and Charles Paine. *Writing Today*. 2nd ed. Boston: Pearson, 2013.

Newkirk, Thomas. *The Performance of Self in Student Writing*. Portsmouth, NH: Heinemann, 1997.

Roen, Duane, Gregory R. Glau, and Barry M. Maid. *The McGraw-Hill Guide: Writing for College, Writing for Life*. 2nd ed., New York: McGraw-Hill, 2010.

Ruszkiewicz, John J., and Jay Dolmage. *How to Write Anything: A Guide and Reference*. New York: Bedford/St. Martin's, 2010.

Spigelman, Candace. *Personally Speaking: Experience as Evidence in Academic Discourse*. Carbondale: Southern Illinois University Press, 2004.

Stolarek, Elizabeth A., and Larry R. Juchartz. *Classical Techniques and Contemporary Arguments*. London: Pearson, 2007.

"They should not … engage students in writing about vampires"

Reconciling First-Year Composition with Young Adult Literature

Mariam Kushkaki

There is no question that young adult literature (YAL) already occupies, in some capacity, a place in the high-school English classroom. Many of us have read the canonical coming-of-age stories in school—*The Catcher in the Rye* or *The Outsiders*, perhaps—and learned of literary and social themes in a much more accessible and relevant fashion than, say, something written by Shakespeare. There's also no question that YAL has, in a greater capacity, a tight hold on readers outside of the classroom. We need not look far to see just how extensive YAL's influence is in popular culture. A good number of movies today and from the past several years are adaptations of YA books with multiple films per series: the *Harry Potter* stories, *The Chronicles of Narnia, The Hunger Games, Twilight, Divergent*, and *Maze Runner,* to name a few. And it isn't just the fantastical or dystopian stories getting screen time; we also have the more everyday stories like *The Perks of Being a Wallflower* and *The Fault in Our Stars* rounding out our options. A notable number of these movies invariably lead to merchandising endeavors that include everything from clothing and fashion accessories to figurines and posters. I've seen my fair share of Mockingjay pins attached to backpacks and Elder Wand bumper stickers affixed to cars, to say the least.

The massive surge in YA-books-turned-movies is indicative of a larger trend: YAL is (and has been) on the rise—and not just with young adults.

Publishers Weekly in 2012 cited a study from Bowker Market Research, indicating, "55% of buyers of works that publishers designate for kids aged 12 to 17—known as YA books—are 18 or older, with the largest segment aged 30 to 44." Since then, YA book sales have continued to soar, with the Association of American Publishers stating that YAL "saw sales increase 22.4 percent from January to September 2014."

Yet even with such success, YAL has not quite permeated the college-level mainstream curriculum. While students might see the occasional YA book in a course curriculum or two, YAL is certainly not the default genre in higher education. This is not to suggest YA stories don't have academic value, however. Indeed, their value goes beyond the English class that focuses on character development, symbolism, plot, and other topics of literary analysis. *The Hunger Games*, for example, has been used throughout the nation to teach math (specifically probability), with an official lesson plan even developed by the National Council of Teachers of Mathematics. Coleen T. Sheehy and Karina R. Clemmons also examine how YAL can function in not just math, but music, science education, and world languages in "Beyond the Language Arts Classroom: The Dynamic Intersection of Young Adult Literature and Technological, Pedagogical, and Content Knowledge." But there is certainly still a great deal of resistance to YAL's place in the college classroom, with one of the arenas of tension appearing in first–year composition (FYC). Interestingly, FYC occupies a unique position not unlike YAL. Both tiptoe the line between legitimacy and illegitimacy in the academic setting, and FYC and YAL have an overlapping audience of teenagers at the end of high school and just entering the college level. It would seem, therefore, that these two subjects could be reconciled (or perhaps should be reconciled by now), especially since both often function under the larger "English" umbrella.

This essay seeks to explore this tension to determine how YAL can be integrated into the composition classroom while meeting the outcomes for FYC. I begin with a brief examination of YAL's contentious place in the classroom, followed by a discussion of how and why the field of composition resists YAL. I then present an outline for reconciling composition with YAL in an FYC curriculum and provide a sample composition assignment that draws on older YA texts—namely, the *Wonder Woman* and *Batman* comics from World War II—for students to rhetorically and contextually analyze. Using these texts simultaneously enables students to explore long-standing arguments surrounding YAL while linking those texts to modern-day interpretations via the superhero genre boom in television and films. Ultimately, it is my hope that this essay offers writing instructors a framework for integrating YAL into their classes while honoring the demands of a rigorous composition curriculum.

The Benefits and Perceived Shortcomings of YAL

The topic of YAL's value in the classroom has been discussed for decades, but it's often regulated to middle school and high school classrooms, with one of the most salient points that is consistently brought up being YAL's ability to connect with students. Jeffrey S. Kaplan describes the change in YA stories that strengthen their appeal for younger readers:

> Instead, nowadays, contemporary young adult realistic fiction covers every conceivable concern that teenagers face in their lives (Sturm & Michel, 2009; Veit & Osada, 2010). From the trauma of rape and incest to the agony of recognizing one's sexual identity, books for young adults are a haven and respite for adolescents to read about what is real and self-evident in their lives [21].

To clarify, it is not just the purely "realistic" YA stories that incorporate such elements. Even the more fantastical tales have what would be considered the "serious" topics of young adulthood, and students in middle and high schools can refer to YAL to help navigate their own lives. The personal connection to YAL has the added benefit of otherwise disinterested students engaging with reading—and, if linked to canonical texts, a means of bridging the gap between student interest and the literary classics.

Despite its mature themes—themes that draw both a younger and an adult crowd—there is still a stigma attached to YAL, one that is grounded in the assumption that stories geared toward young adults are "too simple." Ruth Graham of *Slate* outright declares to adults, "Read whatever you want. But you should feel embarrassed when what you're reading was written for children." Her biggest critique of adults reading YAL is that "these books consistently indulge in the kinds of endings that teenagers want to see, but which adult readers ought to reject as far too simple." While adult readers of YAL in the general population might strongly disagree with Graham's sentiment, many scholars and instructors in higher education have indicated similar thoughts, thus shaping perspectives on YAL. Sean P. Connors relates his experiences leading a prerequisite YAL course for preservice teachers, where he was met with hesitance from the instructors-in-training: "As one student recently put it, 'I can see the logic in using YAL … but I wonder whether we're cheating high school students when we ask them to read books that are less challenging than the literature they'll be expected to read in college'" (70). Connor's experiences are complemented in "Furthering the Cause: The Study and Teaching of Young Adult Literature," in which Lynne Alvine and Marshall A. George recount a personal communication with Joan Kaywell, who states, "Not only is young adult literature no longer required by the Department of Education in Florida in teacher preparation programs, but the teaching of literature is being replaced in the public schools by the skill and drill of test-preparation booklets" (82).

The explicit removal or avoidance of YAL in the classroom is evident at the postsecondary level as well, particularly with FYC courses. Writing scholars like Linda Adler-Kassner have expressed great concern about the teaching of core concepts of writing (contextual awareness, textual analysis, organizational skills, and so on) and how to transfer those concepts to new contexts. In her article "The Companies We Keep *or* The Companies We Would Like to Try to Keep: Strategies and Tactics in Challenging Times," Adler-Kassner tells of the "No Vampires Policy" she has instituted in her own classes:

> Writing classes, especially first year classes, must absolutely and always be grounded in Writing Studies, must always be about the study of writing. They should not, as I heard recently and anecdotally, engage students in writing about vampires—nor about political issues, nor about recent controversies, nor about other things that are not about *writing* [132].

A dismissal of popular culture as a whole, including YAL—of the vampires Adler-Kassner mentions, which I wager can be traced back to YAL and the *Twilight* series—indicates the tension between the demands of FYC and the literary interests of our younger students, resulting in many composition programs banning fiction altogether from their curricula. As the next section shows, the field of composition's resistance to YAL stems from a deeper rift with literature as a whole.

Composition's Push Against Young Adult Literature

The field of composition has and continues to push for not only a disciplinary identity, but for academic capital as well. Composition, being often listed under the "English" heading, is not unaccustomed to being cast under literature's shadow as the lesser of the two. The strain between literature and composition has a long history, but the objections to composition's legitimacy are succinctly addressed by Sherry Burgus Little and Shirley K. Rose in their article "A Home of Our Own: Establishing a Department of Rhetoric and Writing Studies at San Diego State University." In recounting their proposal for a writing department separate from the English department, Little and Rose dispute several assertions that composition would be better off housed in English. For instance, previous studies have indicated that "the teaching of composition holds an inferior position in the hierarchy of English departments" with the "teaching of composition ... regarded as an 'academic sweatshop'" (22). This disdain for the teaching of writing can be traced back to the assumption that the study of writing cannot be removed from the reading of literature, which Little and Rose are quick to attack: "this argument equates reading with reading only the *belles lettres*, assuming that the study of literature alone guarantees full literacy or a humanistic education. This assumption is false and, we suggest, arrogant" (20).

Since separating from what Little and Rose deem "the arrogance" of the English department by developing a separate Department of Rhetoric and Writing Studies at San Diego State University in the early 1990s, the overall field of composition still has not come to a consensus as to what the function of writing—specifically FYC—should be. The complexities of the student-teacher-field dynamic don't make things any easier, either. In "Writing at the Postsecondary Level," Russel K. Durst provides a historical overview of composition studies from 1984 to 2003, breaking up the areas of focus into three groups: the students, the teachers, and the contexts surrounding writing. In regards to students, research has been done on the writing process, academic discourse, and political, social, and economic factors that shape students and their writing. On the other hand, teachers are a topic of study when it comes to politics, collaboration, cultural studies, and critical pedagogy, while the contexts of writing as a whole are linked to issues of assessment, technology, and institutional factors. With all of these subsections of composition studies, it is clear that there are an incredible number of factors to consider when developing a writing curriculum.

To complicate the situation further, the end goals of FYC are also up for debate. For some scholars, a genre-based approach is ideal for FYC to create adaptable writers that can transfer their knowledge into new situations:

> These courses are underscored by the position that if and when learners adopt the position that the study of writing involves consistent analysis of relationships between contexts, purposes, audiences, genres, and conventions and learn to conduct that analysis, they are ... likely (so the theory goes) to be more adaptable writers [Adler-Kassner, Majewski, and Koshnick, "The Value of Troublesome Knowledge"].

However, scholars like Elizabeth Wardle wish to overhaul the current idea of FYC altogether and replace it with "Writing about Writing" courses. Wardle is particularly concerned with "mutt genres" plaguing FYC, which, she says, are "mimic genres that mediate activities in other activity systems, but within the FYC system their purposes and audiences are vague or even contradictory" (774). In other words, FYC courses teach students genres of writing, like a personal narrative, an observation, and an evaluation or review (to name a few), yet "their specific characteristics, their rhetorical situations, are quite different" than genres found outside of FYC (773). In a sense, then, these types of writings that Wardle identifies after a survey of twenty-two FYC courses are not enabling students to think of their writing in abstractions that could be applied elsewhere. Meanwhile, for James Berlin, social-epistemic rhetoric is the way to go, since it can transform the writing classroom into a liberatory site that challenges "unequal power relations in the authoritarian classroom, a place where the teacher holds all power and knowledge and the student is the receptacle into which information is poured" *á la* Freire's banking concept of education (491).

Because of the strained relationship between English (read: literature) and writing, the field of composition strives for recognition as a legitimate discipline. As a result, though, FYC is approached in multiple ways (as seen with Durst's history) and has multiple end-goals (as mentioned with Adler-Kassner, Wardle, and Berlin). Would it not be possible for YAL to still be integrated into a composition curriculum to meet some of these goals?

A Place for Young Adult Literature in First Year Composition

With dismissive views of both YAL and of FYC—and with FYC itself seemingly resistant to YAL—the question to ask is whether these two fields can function together in the same space. If we think back to all of the elements of composition studies Durst mentions, including gender, race, and cultural influences, it would seem like YAL would fit in FYC since its storylines and characters reflect on these topics as well, thereby giving students a chance to engage with such topics too. In turn, FYC students would also be engaging in the social-epistemic rhetoric promoted by Berlin.

Yet YAL's place need not be so political. According to Anne Beaufort, "There is no consensus on what is appropriate subject matter in academic writing courses, nor is there any overarching heuristic to guide writing teachers in their choice of subject matter or course themes." FYC has been a site for thematic content for quite some time now, and, as Kathleen Blake Yancey, Liane Robertson, and Kara Taczak explain, "Students in these FYC courses find themselves studying and writing about topics of interest to faculty, from medical narratives and video games to comic books and British history" (5). They also cite Michael Donnelly, who claims that "there is no 'must' content; the only thing(s) that really matters is what students are *doing*—i.e., reading, thinking, responding, writing … when these things are primary, and whatever other content remains secondary, we have a writing course" (5).

Beaufort and Donnelly are undoubtedly not alone in their open perspectives of what content can or should be in a writing course. In her response to Adler-Kassner's "No Vampires Policy," Sandie Friedman argues that theme-based courses that include topics like vampires grounded in YAL and popular culture has multiple benefits, and that that "especially in challenging times, when students are pressured to take a pragmatic, career-oriented approach to college, it's important for them to be able to choose content … it may be one of the few times … when students can explore something that interests them for its own sake" (79). To dismiss student choice—or, at least, to dismiss their interests—"is not only to exclude instructors not trained in writing studies, but also to limit students' choices—and thus, to reduce the possibility of engagement" (81).

Furthermore, we cannot ignore the fact that using YAL in FYC still offers students the chance to engage with and strengthen their own writing. Jerome Evans is particularly sensitive to the intersections of literature and writing in "From Sheryl Crow to Homer Simpson: Literature and Composition through Pop-culture." He explores specific lesson plans between popular culture and canonical literature, highlighting the impact of popular culture specifically on critical thinking and writing: "Students can readily practice critical-thinking skills—supporting assertions with specific evidence," and "students also successfully develop their writing skills through topics related to and models from popular culture," underscoring the need for more emphasis on composition through a pop culture lens (37).

Fortunately for instructors, there is some guidance in articulating what FYC hopes to accomplish. The WPA Outcomes Statement for First-Year Composition (3.0), adopted by the Council of Writing Program Administrators, acknowledges "that the process of learning to write in any medium is complex," and offers an explanation of writing as "both individual and social and demands continued practice and informed guidance." The outcomes themselves reflect this notion, with the Statement honing in on four main overarching concepts that shape FYC: (1) Rhetorical Knowledge, (2) Critical Thinking, Reading, and Composing, (3) Processes, and (4) Knowledge of Conventions. Combine these outcomes with the flexibility of the content choice for FYC in the vein of Beaufort, Donnelly, and Friedman, and we can work towards coupling YAL with FYC.

It is important to note that of the WPA's learning outcomes, the third on writing processes can be covered with most, if not all, writing assignments to begin with. The fourth on knowledge of conventions can still apply to multiple writing assignments as well (since each type of writing assignment typically has its own conventions, whether it be a research paper, a personal narrative, or anything else). The first and second learning outcomes (rhetorical knowledge and critical thinking, reading, and composing) can be much more focused on specific texts.

The sample assignment that follows therefore emphasizes the first two outcomes outlined by the WPA. Moreover, the assignment follows in the footsteps of Beaufort and Donnelly, running on the idea that thematic approaches are not inherently problematic as long as composition is the primary focus—and, to be sure, the assignment emphasizes attention to both argumentative and story composition in terms of audience, purpose, and context. I liken this to a middle ground between Adler-Kassner's "No Vampires Policy" and Friedman's "pro-vampire" stance—a project that acknowledges students' interests outside of academia while still respecting and dissecting the nuances of both textual and visual composition in an academic setting.

Practical Considerations for the Composition Classroom

One of the projects I often include in my own FYC courses is a contextual analysis of the comic book industry, something I consider to be writing both *with* and *about* YAL. No doubt that the current obsession with the superhero genre of movies will resonate with many students, but the purpose of this project is to dig deeper into the history of superheroes in comics so that students may better understand how arguments about a genre typically deemed "childish" have evolved.

First, some history behind this topic before delving into the assignment details. In his article "Why 100,000,000 Americans Read Comics" from *The American Scholar* in 1944, William Moulton Marston—a scholar, psychologist, and the creator of Wonder Woman—tells of how the comic book industry of the 1940s worked toward producing comics that could be entertaining *and* educational:

> We have inaugurated the policy of introducing into continuities a certain percentage of words which are above the average child-reader level, with the result that children soon determine the meanings and add these new words to their vocabularies. Excerpts from Superman have been used successfully in teaching English in the public schools, notably in a junior high school at Lynn, Massachusetts, where a special Superman workbook was compiled by a progressive young English teacher [42].

Marston's seminal scholarly essay from 1944 is one of the first of its kind, both celebrating and defending the then-recent boom of the comic book industry and explaining why such a boom had occurred. The comic book industry experienced incredible success during World War II, and Marston uses this correlation between industry success and the war to support his argument about the legitimacy of popular and mainstream texts as educational tools (both academically and personally), claiming that comics act as an antigen to the effects of the excessive violence children witnessed during wartime. For example, comics taught young readers to embrace righteousness, to love rather than kill enemies (as demonstrated by Superman and Wonder Woman repeatedly), and to aspire to a level of greatness reflected by the heroes themselves. What's more, in keeping with the feminist push during

World War II—the "We Can Do It!" mentality espoused by Rosie the Riveter—Marston proclaims that Wonder Woman specifically teaches young girls to be proud of their femininity and reveals to young boys that the oft-feminized qualities of love and compassion are, in truth, noble characteristics to possess (42).

Despite Marston's report of the effectiveness of comic books as educational tools, the inclusion of popular culture in the classroom was (and still is) met with resistance on multiple fronts. Marston himself acknowledges resistance to comic books from scholars who adamantly believe comics "are not literature—[they say] adventure strips lack artistic form, mental substance, and emotional appeal to any of the most moronic of minds" (36). A decade after Marston's article, psychiatrist Fredric Wertham wrote *Seduction of the Innocent*, building on the critique of popular culture—especially crime and horror comics—by declaring that such texts were corrupting the minds of the American youth and robbing children of "proper" academic education. With the rise of violence in America in the late 1940s and early 1950s, Wertham considered the comic book industry to be the source of the increased violence among juveniles. According to Wertham, stories and images found in comic books caused psychological damage to children, prompting them to become murderers, sexual deviants, and drug users. In this regard, Wertham counters all of the assertions made by Marston a decade prior: comic books were still educational, but not in the way Marston assumed. Instead, says Wertham, comic books teach children immoral behavior and, when incorporated into the classroom, present misinformation about history and the great literary texts usually taught. He cites, for instance, a *Superboy* comic in which Superboy is part of America's history, helping George Washington cross the Delaware River (17). Wertham also references a comic version of *Macbeth* in which he laments the genius of Shakespeare being overshadowed by gory illustrations (68). Thus, for Wertham, using these pop-culture texts as teaching material would severely hinder the development of young minds into scholars and functional adults.

For this FYC assignment, then, students look at both YAL itself, as well as the arguments *about* it. Specifically, students learn about superheroes—Wonder Woman and Batman—by looking at the arguments and contexts shaping the comic book industry. We begin by reading *Wonder Woman* and *Batman* comics from the 1940s and 1950s and explore how they are shaped by the social and political contexts of those times. For instance, Wonder Woman offers students an introductory overview of the social and political values of the 1940s. In one scene of "Wonder Woman Comes to America," both men and women are startled by the heroine's outfit as she walks through the city. An elderly lady calls Wonder Woman a "hussy," yet several men are captivated by Wonder Woman showing off more skin than the average woman

(14). Furthermore, the fact that Wonder Woman's outfit is very American-looking in terms of color (red, white, and blue) reflects the patriotic values of Americans who were, at the time, wrapped up in World War II. Thus, students can reference this scene for both the 1940s values about women and the sense of patriotism of the time that shaped Wonder Woman's appearance.

Once students grasp the contexts shaping the comics themselves, they can consider more scholarly works that make arguments *about* comics. I ask my students to read and analyze the aforementioned texts—Marston's "Why 100,000,000 Americans Read Comics" and Wertham's *Seduction of the Innocent*. We review the social and political contexts surrounding these two works as well, and connect the *Wonder Woman* and *Batman* comics to the arguments of these two men. Marston, for example, notes that comics can teach children to show compassion to others, and students can link this statement with scenes from Wonder Woman in which the heroine saves her enemies instead of killing them. Or, students can connect Wertham's criticism of the excessive violence in comics to Batman's use of lethal force to kill multiple criminals throughout the *Batman* comics from the 1940s.

Thus, through this unit, students begin to appreciate how texts are linked together and shaped by external forces, rather than seeing writing as being limited to the classroom or existing in a vacuum. Their rhetorical knowledge (the first learning outcome of the WPA Outcomes Statement) is strengthened, since they "learn and use key rhetorical concepts through analyzing … a variety of texts" (WPA Outcomes Statement). Their critical thinking, reading, and composition skills (the second learning outcome) are also honed, as they develop the "ability to analyze, synthesize, interpret, and evaluate ideas, information, situations, and texts," especially by considering the graphical elements of comics and the textual messages about comics in tandem—what the WPA deems "the interplay between verbal and nonverbal elements." Add to the project the fact that students work in a pre-drafting, drafting, and revising stages, as well as write within the conventions of an analytical essay, and the third and fourth outcomes listed by the WPA's statement can also be met.

A Hopeful Reconciliation

The purpose of my project here is not to assert that all writing classes should use YAL, nor is my purpose to suggest that other methods of teaching composition are not as valuable or effective. What I am asserting, though, is that instructors should consider both student interest and their own biases about what constitutes "real" literature or texts that deserve a place in the classroom. To be sure, I do understand the concerns held by instructors and scholars who oppose widening the curriculum to include not just literature, but young adult literature as well. If YAL is not used effectively in the classroom, the overall course goals may not be met, and we composition instructors would be doing a disservice to our students. However, the quick dismissal of YAL altogether is just as much of a disservice to the genre and to the students who may otherwise not find themselves interested or invested in the course material.

The solution, I believe, must come from both sides: we must approach YAL with a cautious optimism, balancing our and our students' interests with concrete learning outcomes for our writing classes. At times, we may need to look at the YAL stories, the characters, the plot, the settings, the themes, but we can also take this time to consider these elements rhetorically, asking how genre, audience, and purpose come into play. Above all else, we ask our students to *write*.

In writing of the cultures of literature and composition, it is only appropriate to close with Peter Elbow's eloquent reflection on the two:

> Here again I'm trying to escape either-or thinking—escape the tired habits in which the sophisticated look down on the naïve, while the naïve look back down just as haughtily. There's no need for higher or lower, better or worse, with these two ways of being. We can have sophistication without snobbery, elitism, or condescension.... And it is perfectly feasible for *both* cultures, literature and composition, to help both styles to flourish [544].

Doing otherwise would be a disservice for all.

WORKS CITED

Adler-Kassner, Linda. "The Companies We Keep *or* the Companies We Would Like to Try to Keep: Strategies and Tactics in Challenging Times." *Writing Program Administration,* vol. 36, no. 1, 2012, pp. 119–140.

Adler-Kassner, Linda, John Majewski, and Damian Koshnick. "The Value of Troublesome Knowledge: Transfer and Threshold Concepts in Writing and History." *Composition Forum,* vol. 26, 2012, pp. 1–17.

Alvine, Lynne, and Marshall A. George. "Conversations from the Commissions: Furthering the Cause: The Study and Teaching of Young Adult Literature." *English Education,* vol. 37, no. 1, 2004, pp. 80–84.

Beaufort, Anne. "College Writing and Beyond: Five Years Later." *Composition Forum,* vol. 26, 2012.

Berlin, James. "Rhetoric and Ideology in the Writing Class." *College English,* vol. 50, no. 5, 1998, pp. 477–494.

Bush, Sarah B., and Karen S. Karp. "Hunger Games: What Are the Chances?" *National Council of Teachers of Mathematics,* www.nctm.org/Publications/mathematics-teaching-in-middle-school/2012/Vol17/Issue7/Hunger-Games_-What-Are-the-Chances_/. Accessed 22 April 2012.

Connors, Sean P. "Challenging Perspectives on Young Adult Literature." *English Journal,* vol. 102, no. 5, 2013, pp. 69–73.

Dilworth, Dianna. "Book Sales Up 4.9% in First ¾ of 2014: AAP." *GalleyCat,* www.adweek.com/galleycat/book-sales-down-6-5-in-q1-aap/107000. Accessed 2 September 2015.

Durst, Russel K. "Writing at the Postsecondary Level." *Research on Composition: Multiple Perspectives on Two Decades of Change.* Ed. Peter Smagorinsky. New York: Teachers College, Columbia University, 2006. 78–100. Print.

Elbow, Peter. "The Cultures of Literature and Composition: What Could Each Learn from the Other?" *College English,* vol. 64, no. 5, 2002, pp. 533–546.

Evans, Jerome. "From Sheryl Crow to Homer Simpson: Literature and Composition Through Popular Culture." *The English Journal,* vol. 93, no. 3, 2004, pp. 32–38.

Friedman, Sandie. "This Way for Vampires: Teaching First-Year Composition in 'Challenging Times.'" *Currents in Teaching and Learning,* vol. 6, no. 1, 2013, pp. 77–84.

Graham, Ruth. "Against YA." *Slate,* www.slate.com/articles/arts/books/2014/06/against_ya_adults_should_be_embarrassed_to_read_children_s_books.html. Accessed 10 September 2015.

Kaplan, Jeffrey S. "The Changing Face of Young Adult Literature: What Teachers and Researchers Need to Know to Enhance Their Practice and Inquiry." *Teaching Young Adult Literature Today: Insights, Considerations, and Perspectives for the Classroom Teacher.* Eds. Judith A. Hayn and Jeffrey S. Kaplan. Lanham, MD: Rowman & Littlefield, 2014. 19–40. Print.

Little, Sherry B., and Shirley K. Rose. "A Home of Our Own: Establishing a Department of Rhetoric and Writing Studies at San Diego State University." *WPA,* vol. 18, no. 1/2, 1994, pp. 16–28.

Marston, William M. "Why 100,000,000 Americans Read Comics." *The American Scholar,* vol. 13, no. 1, 1943, pp. 35–44.

Moulton, Charlie. "Wonder Woman Comes to America." *Wonder Woman: The Greatest Stories Ever Told.* Eds. Dan DiDio and Anton Kawasaki. New York: DC Comics, 2007. 8–20. Print.

"New Study: 55% of YA Books Bought by Adults." *Publishers Weekly,* www.publishersweekly.com/pw/by-topic/childrens/childrens-industry-news/article/53937-new-study-55-of-ya-books-bought-by-adults.html. Accessed 11 May 2014.

Sheehy, Colleen T., and Karina R. Clemmons. "Beyond the Language Arts Classroom: The Dynamic Intersection of Young Adult Literature and Technological, Pedagogical, and Content Knowledge." *Teaching Young Adult Literature Today: Insights, Considerations, and Perspectives for the Classroom Teacher.* Eds. Judith A. Hayn and Jeffrey S. Kaplan. Lanham, MD: Rowman & Littlefield, 2014. 225–240. Print.

Wertham, Fredric. *Seduction of the Innocent.* New York: Rinehart & Company, 1954.

Yancey, Kathleen B., Liane Robertson, and Kara Taczak. *Writing Across Contexts: Transfer, Composition, and Sites of Writing.* Logan: Utah State University Press, 2014.

Dystopian Literature in the Multi-Cultural College Composition Classroom

A Catalyst for Self-Reflection

MARY-LYNN CHAMBERS *and*
KATHLEEN B. GRAY

Dystopia is a trendy, moneymaking genre for would-be novelists and moviemakers. Can it also be a platform from which students can engage in critical thinking and self-analyzed reflection and writing? This is a question that is promoting discussion amongst college composition professors who are willing to consider the inclusion of the current with the classical in their college composition classroom (Ames). The use of dystopian literature has had a rich past within academia. It is not just a 21st century trend or a novel idea bent on catching the attention of our technology-distracted students. Three dystopian novels considered classics of the genre are Aldous Huxley's *Brave New World* (1932), George Orwell's *1984* (1949), and Ray Bradbury's *Fahrenheit 451* (1953). These works paved the way for dystopian writing and the attraction it holds with American readers while addressing important political, economic, and cultural shifts. Since there is precedence regarding the validity and usage of dystopian literature for student engagement in a composition classroom setting, then it is valuable to consider the role of contemporary dystopian fiction for today's students.

Given its huge popularity, can dystopian young adult literature engage an increasingly more diverse college student population? Are traditionally underserved populations, like African American and first-generation students, likely to be drawn to this genre? Our research investigates the potential barriers to, and effective strategies for, using this literature in African American and multi-cultural college composition classrooms by assessing African American student interest in dystopian stories. We also discuss ways to use this literature to engage students who are struggling to find their place in systems of higher education and to make connections between course content and their own social and political standpoints.

What Is Dystopia?

The dystopian genre is based in a futuristic society that incorporates elements of present day life and provides an allegorical appeal through a fictional storyline. The first time the term was used was in 1868 in a speech given to the British Parliament. Eventually, the term was used to represent a genre that is antithetical to the representation of a utopian society (Kizilkan 1). *Utopia*, introduced by Thomas More in 1516, is an alternate world in an alternate setting that presents a positive yet imaginary environment where individuals are free to express themselves without the fear of judgment (Ryan 3). The term "utopia" evokes a world that is working toward a better alternative social order. Dystopia, on the other hand, examines the darker side of utopian ideals; it addresses the challenges of dealing with a repressive society that constricts freedom and individuality. Devin Ryan explains, "dystopia is a future world that extends and distorts modern day issues into an inexhaustible and dehumanized state in which controls have been forced upon society and its inhabitants through social and physical limitations that restrict many aspects of life" (4). These controls that are forced on the characters within the novel are relatable to the family and institutional controls that the students may believe are also managing their experiences.

In 1965, Frank E. Manuel, et al, popularized the term dystopia when they identified that the prefix *dys-* suggests a movement toward a less favorable state (Dimock, Kuyper, and Dimock 92). Therefore, the term dystopia "is the most appropriate term for literature that describes the progressive degeneration of the body politics" (Lederer 1135). Richard Lederer goes on to suggest that dystopia is not just a place that doesn't exist, but it is the fabric of the "never-never" land that is intrinsic to fantasy, a place that could never be, yet might be. It is the combination of a nightmare world with underpinnings of a possible place we may experience at some point in the future (1135).

Dystopian literature is generally known for its dangerous storyline and daunting landscape; however, there are four specific traits shared by dystopian novels that provide a helpful framework for discussion of this literature in the composition classroom. Dystopian literature includes

- a vivid and descriptive setting.
- individuals in charge with absolute power.
- a strong protagonist shaped by the current situation.
- a conclusion that has elements of unease and hope.

Within this literature, there is a fear amongst the "individuals in charge with absolute power" that diversity will breed conflict within the dystopian society. The result is a required uniformity, and it is this uniformity that is challenged by the protagonist, revealing the value of individuality as well as "elements of unease and hope" (Reeve 36). There are many different voices speaking into the definition and development of the dystopian genre; however, April Spisak effectively summarizes an element within the dystopian novel when she clarifies that the dystopian fictional collection includes stories of a "messed up society where freedoms are curtailed in order to protect its citizens from imagined future terrible events" (55).

Why Should Dystopian Literature Be Used in the Composition Classroom?

Composition classes that are literature-based expand student knowledge and transform student writing, and this occurs when the literature engages the students and provides a good writing model. Separately, literature classes are often viewed as product focused, and writing classes are often viewed as process focused, but when you have a literature based writing class, then the intertwining of product and process can serve as a catalyst for further student development (Elbow 534–5). Typically, the composition classroom gathers inspiration for writing prompts from varied venues including news events, blockbuster movies, poetry, interviews, and anthologies of classic writings, so it is no surprise that the dystopian genre has found its way into the college classroom.

Kenneth Carano, Robert Schueller, and Matthew Hettwer share their belief that dystopian literature incorporated into a college civics course can be an effective tool to promote student engagement. These authors suggest that when the topic is relatable, the students will develop a greater awareness regarding current issues (46). When you consider the personal and societal challenges faced by the protagonist in dystopian writing, it becomes obvious that this genre metaphorically represents the challenges faced by some YA readers who are experiencing peer pressure that forces uniformity (Reeve 36). When students can form a connection between fantasy and reality, dystopian literature can become a useful agent within the composition classroom. Melissa Ames, at Eastern Illinois University, highlights dystopian literature in her college course entitled "Studies in 20th Century American Literature & Culture: Remediating 9/11." According to Ames' course description, the examination of the dystopia genre provides a decade of proof that the cultural trends that evidence the gravitation toward dystopian literature are worth examination within academia. This course provides the opportunity for students to analyze how tragedy and fear are crafted within dystopian literature and how the various texts address the concerns of varied cultures (1).

Ames is not the only college professor who sees the value of dystopian literature as an inspiration for critical thinking. Gwen Tarabox, at Western Michigan University, teaches a course entitled "Dystopian Literature: A Survey of Modern Book Series" (Ryan 2). Other colleges that incorporate or highlight dystopian literature in their syllabi include Oxford, Berkeley, Willamette, Vanderbilt, the Mythgard Institute, and Amarillo College (Ryan 13). This testifies to the growing popularity of pedagogies that use dystopia in the college classroom and its value as a rhetorical tool that engages students on a personal level.

James Dimock, Chad Kuyper, and Peggy Dimock affirm the value of using dystopian literature as a means to engage college students with current issues that are part of the college students' experience. The sense of possibilities based in social or political trends provides a platform where a student may consider the implications of the world in which he or she is situated, while engaging the imagination (93). Within dystopian literature, issues like genetic engineering, freedom of choice, or government control are examined. Some of the other elements within this genre are the loss of civil liberties, intolerable living conditions, constant surveillance, violence, mind control, and uniformity (Kizilkan 2). These topics, along with others, establish dystopian fiction as a viable resource where the instructor is able to address current issues and allow the students to write to those current issues from their own perspective.

Because dystopian literature grapples with questions of power, struggle, and systematic oppression, it may be particularly relevant to the lives of traditionally underserved student populations. While all students may struggle with feelings of alienation or concerns with uniformity, first generation college students, students of color, and students from lower-income backgrounds may be particularly familiar with the themes associated with dystopia because these underserved populations are more likely to have experienced stressful life events prior to coming to college (Boyraz, et al). African American students, in particular, are typically identified as traditionally underserved population, which means they are more likely to experience crime in the immediate family (both as victims and as perpetrators), illness and disability, parental divorce or separation, and economic difficulties (Charles, Dinwiddie, and Massey 1359), than the typical college student. Also, this group is more likely to experience discrimination during their college experience (Huynh and Fuligni). Asked to overcome the barriers associated with poverty or racism, these students may be particularly drawn to the injustice at the heart of many dystopian stories despite the fact that they do not see their own racialized social location reflected in the demographics of the main characters.

The connection that can occur in the classroom is not only with the genre's choice of settings based in societal challenges, but with the characters and the individual challenges the characters face. A personal connection with the characters has the potential to fuel students' interest in the lesson. Ryan explains, "constant surveillance, oppressive ruling regimes, lack of freedom, and forced conformity are all aspects of adolescent life that teenagers deal with on a daily basis" (2). An oppressive atmosphere that originates with an authority figure can leave many young adults searching for ways to free themselves or distance themselves from their current, oppressive situation. In reaction to the perceived oppression, students often select a college that provides distance from parental supervision and their rules. As a result, the plight of the protagonist who struggles under the oppression of an authority figure often resonates within the student reader. Similarly, for African American students who have experienced discrimination before and during their college experience, literature detailing a protagonist's response to oppressive authority structures may be particularly compelling. Dicle Kizilkan, understanding the relatability of the student with protagonist, cites this genre as "a tool [that] sensitize[s] young people's perceptions by creating room for empathic responses to the protagonist's plight, [thus establishing] … a platform for critical thinking individuals" (4). It is the dystopian author's strategy to illicit an empathic response within the student reader based on the creation of a high-stakes scenario that provides conflict and adventure, but also spawns sympathy for the protagonist.

Another aspect that provides a connection between the protagonist and the YA reader is the ongoing process of identity formation. Kelly F. Franklin suggests that dystopian literature "inspires young adult readers to find their true identity by showcasing characters in the process of identity construction" (iii). Thus, a number of authors have indicated that the development of identity within the protagonist and the student audience is based in performance that involves a power struggle. Kelly Wissman promotes the use of YAL within the educational experience because it is an "efficacious practice for self-discovery and social understanding" (149). This author goes on to cite studies indicating student use of YAL to "seek meaning and inspiration in their surroundings; to resist ascribed identities, and to search for a sense of belonging in the sociopolitical landscape in which they are often marginalized due to their race, gender, youth, and/or language" (149). This may be particularly compelling project for traditionally underserved students whose struggle with race and class may otherwise be excluded from public discourse or ignored within classroom discussions of literature and composition.

In addition to their struggles with systems of oppression related to race and class, traditionally underserved students are likely to question their place in college and doubt their ability to meet cultural and academic expectations of higher education institutions. These students are more likely to doubt the authenticity of their emerging college student status and question their ability to transition into the role of a college educated adult (Cox 21). By inviting students to grapple with the protagonist's process of identity formation, dystopian literature may normalize a student's own process and demonstrate that making meaning of shifting identities is part of, not antithetical to, the academic experience. As students analyze the protagonist's efforts to find a place within large, often unyielding, social structures, students may feel less anxiety about their own ability to fit into the structures within the university setting.

Since there is such a great potential for student engagement when dystopian literature is used in the composition classroom, then it is important for the college composition professor to identify which stories would provide the best options for improved student engagement based on their student population.

What Are the Popular Dystopian Series Utilized Within Academia?

One of the earliest YA dystopian novels to emerge in recent years is Lois Lowry's *The Giver*. In this storyline, everything is controlled by the Elders and dictated to the citizens. The characters are required to follow the Elder's edicts concerning who they will marry, the children they will receive, and the job they will work. Jonas, the narrator and protagonist in the story, has specialized insight into history and reveals the flaws in his present society. His mission becomes the unveiling of knowledge to the enslaved citizens. This foundational novel, *The Giver* (1993), provided a backdrop for dystopian writing that grew in response to the September 11, 2001, terrorist attack on New York City's Twin Towers. This attack confirmed American fears regarding the possibility of a new world order based on a cataclysmic event. The 9/11 event also provided a catalyst for YA authors to develop storylines set in a post-apocalyptic world where unreasonable controls are set in place (Ryan 5; Ames 4).

Moving away from YA literature based on monsters, vampires, and werewolves, the new development of dystopian settings and themes allowed for a closer look at the relationship of the individual to the community (Spisak

55). At the end of the 20th century, the introduction of Harry Potter created a magical frenzy as the literature was devoured by YA readers. This fantasy fiction has many dystopian qualities that allows for the blurring of the genres. In 2012, Suzanne Collin's *Hunger Games* trilogy (2008–2010) surpassed the sales of the *Harry Potter* series becoming the best-selling book series on Amazon (Connors). Collin's *Hunger Games* trilogy was financially successful, providing a strong indicator of the relatability of the genre for YA readers (Ryan 6).

The *Hunger Games* trilogy is based in a futuristic society called Panem, which is divided into twelve districts. Each year, a boy and a girl from each district are selected to fight to the death while the rest of the districts watch. This futuristic society is in an economic crisis with an opulent capitol oppressively controlling the citizens. The female protagonist, Katniss Everdeen, emerges as a beacon of hope as she defies the power figures and their rules. Phillip Reeve suggests that the influence of Collin's trilogy has created a desire within teens to start picking up more YA dystopian texts and find connections and solutions within their own lives, since the literature provides a social commentary on current issues while providing a sense of hope (35). This YA series is the most commonly referenced dystopian literature in academic writing that addresses 21st century dystopian literature, and, as such, provides many discussion points for the composition classroom.

The next dystopian series to emerge was James Dashner's *The Maze Runner* (2009–2011), which is set in a post-apocalyptic world that resulted from solar flares and widespread disease. The protagonist, Thomas, is dropped into a new world called the Glade. This all male society fights monsters, known as Grievers, while trying to engineer their escape through the maze. The entrance of a female, Teresa, initiates the beginning of change and remembering. The dominant masculine theme and the mystery behind the authority figures that hold all the power, can be very useful when discussing gender issues and identity confusion in the composition classroom.

Then there is Veronica Roth's *Divergent* trilogy (2011–2013) that is set in a futuristic Chicago that is split into five factions: Abnegation (selflessness); Amity (peace); Candor (honesty); Dauntless (bravery); Erudite (intellect). Once a citizen in the society has determined and selected a faction, transition to another faction is not allowed. Yet, within this society of order, there is a segment of the population who are divergent—those who are able to operate effectively in multiple factions—and these divergent members of society are feared because of the potential for nonconformity and rebellion. Certainly, this series touches on issues of conformity and character development in a society that pre-determines what is perfect, and these elements can spawn discussion and writing within the composition classroom.

When the college classroom services underrepresented populations like the African American community, it is valuable to include African American dystopian writers who incorporate race and culture into the dystopian storyline. In Octavia Butler's Parable series, the *Parable of the Talents* (1998) continues the developing story of a new religion, new community, and a new, female, black leader, Olamina. It is her daughter, Lauren, who narrates the story that emerges out of the Apocalypse, referenced as "the Pox" within the storyline. This disruptive crisis lasted 15 years and was caused by society's refusal to address the critical areas that needed to change. Religion and race are dominant themes in this dystopian novel that offers a presidential candidate whose slogan is "Make America Great Again." Two decades after the publication of this novel, college students are hearing this slogan being used by President Trump who succeeded Obama. The political, historical, and cultural conversations that can emerge from the reading of *Parable of the Talents* makes it a worthy dystopian writing that will engage the imagination of composition writers.

Is Dystopian Literature Useful with Underserved Students?

Dystopian literature, with its strategic and context-specific claims, is an important part of social criticism. It provides a platform for comparative dialogue that can offer the students insight into the discourse of identity formation within a political setting. Also, within a dystopian society, there is a systematic "otherness" framed within an alternative society, which may make this literature particularly compelling for traditionally underserved students feeling out of place in higher education institutions. Potentially, dystopian literature could be a useful tool for helping students connect with the composition course curriculum and find their place in their new college setting. This is especially true if students are already reading and engaging with dystopian literature, or if they are drawn to the literature when it is presented in a composition course. The research already presented establishes the validity of dystopian literature in promoting the rhetorical process in an academic setting. Our research helps contribute to our understanding of underserved, African American student populations and their receptivity to dystopian literature by measuring levels of student exposure and interest and suggesting ways to incorporate this literature into the composition course given the stated preferences of the students surveyed.

Method

The purpose of this research was to determine African American undergraduate students' receptivity to reading and relating to dystopian YAL in composition classes. As stated above, dystopian YAL is increasingly popular and many dystopian books have been turned into movies, widening their cultural influence. Due to this popularity and the compelling topics covered by this genre, dystopian literature has the potential to engage and inspire students in general. Yet, it remains unclear the extent to which traditionally underserved students are exposed to and are relating to these stories. In order to determine the appeal and applicability of dystopian YAL for African American students, we administered a survey that asked students the extent to which they (1) read or watch dystopian stories, (2) relate to the characters in dystopian stories, and (3) show interest in seeing these stories included in composition classroom assignments.

The Sample

We collected 59 anonymous surveys from African American students (28 men and 31 women) taking a Composition and Vocabulary course as part of their General Education curriculum. These students attend a small, liberal arts, Historically Black University in North Carolina. Although two respondents were ages 31+, 96.6 percent of our respondents reported being between the ages of 18–23. Of the 57 respondents who answered our questions related to family member college attendance, 49.1 percent reported that their parents and grandparents had not attended college. These respondents would be considered first-generation college students. As noted in an earlier section, first generation African American college students, as an underserved segment of the college population, may feel uncertain about their place in higher education. Understanding the extent to which course material resonates with this population is an important way to help ensure their engagement in class as new material is introduced.

The Survey

The survey contained questions related to student exposure to the storylines and characters in dystopian literature. We listed the most popular dystopian titles and asked students if they had read these titles or seen the movies based on them. We then asked open and closed ended questions about the features of dystopian stories that drew them to the genre and what discouraged them from reading or watching dystopian stories. We asked students if they would like to see dystopian literature used in their composition courses and gave them a chance to suggest writing prompts. Finally, to determine whether the race of the protagonist influenced student interest in dystopian YA literature, we asked if they were comfortable with the current racial status of characters or would prefer more African American characters in these stories.

Findings

Due to the tremendous publishing success, blockbuster movie sales, and overall popularity of dystopian YA titles, we expected that a large percentage of our sample would have either read a dystopian YA book or seen a film based on a book. We offered six suggestions regarding YAL titles: *The Giver; The Maze Runner; Divergent; The Hunger Games; The Chaos Walking; Legend Trilogy*. However, only 32 respondents (54.2 percent) saw or read at least one of the dystopian YA stories that were listed. The titles respondents had read or seen included *The Giver* by Louis Lowery and any title in *The Hunger Games* series by Suzanne Collins, *The Maze Runner* series by James Dashner, and the *Divergent* series by Veronica Roth. No respondents reported reading *The Chaos Walking* series by Patrick Ness or the *Legend Trilogy* by Marie Lu. Gender had very little impact on rates of exposure as only 53.6 percent of all men and 54.8 percent of all women reported having seen or read at least one title. For each gender group and among students overall, a little less than half of our respondents (45.8 percent) reported no familiarity with any title.

We had hypothesized that the appeal of dystopian YAL among African Americans would be somewhat mitigated by the fact that most of the characters in these stories are white. To test this hypothesis, we asked respondents if they were "okay with 'white' main characters" or if they "prefer more African Americans" to be highlighted in the literature. Twenty respondents (33.9 percent) either circled that they "prefer more African Americans," or wrote in a response that explained they want both white and African American characters featured equally in these stories, which would require more African American characters be added to dystopian literature. Only six respondents (10.2 percent) reported being "okay with 'white' main characters." This suggests that there is some interest in more racially inclusive literature. However, of the 20 students who reported wanting more African American characters, 75 percent had read or watched a dystopian story. This is higher than the percentage of the overall sample that had exposure to these titles (54.2 percent) and implies that a preference for more African American characters does not necessarily deter African American students from choosing the dystopian genre.

Overall, our data suggests that African American students hold a range of opinions about racial representation in literature and film. Fifteen respondents (25.4 percent) provided a written indication that they did not really care about the race of the main character. Eighteen respondents (30.5 percent), including seven who had read or seen a dystopian book or movie, chose not to answer the questions related to race. This non-response rate could reflect some discomfort with the question, but it could also suggest that students are ambivalent about the role of racial representation in literature.

While instructors cannot change the extent to which students of color are represented in dystopian young adult literature, they can acknowledge the lack of consensus about racial representation and the potential for students' ambivalence when discussing issues of inclusion and diversity in class. This may facilitate classroom conversations about race in literature and make composition assignments based on dystopian literature more accessible to students of color and to all students in mixed-race classrooms.

Our research suggests that even students who have not yet read or watched a dystopian storyline may be willing to engage with this literature in a composition class. Of the 34 respondents who reported being drawn to dystopian literature or movies, 10 had not read or seen any dystopian YA titles on our list. This suggests that levels of potential interest in this type of literature may be greater levels of current exposure to this genre. Although only 54.2 percent of our sample had been exposed to the themes of dystopian YAL through books or movies, respondents still expressed interest in seeing these themes explored in composition classes. Twenty-five respondents (78.1 percent of the 32 respondents who were familiar with dystopian titles) reported wanting to see these titles used in composition class. And 44.4 percent of those who had not read or seen these titles (12 respondents) also wanted these titles used in class. Taken together, 62.7 percent of our sample would welcome the use of dystopian YAL in a college composition assignment.

Reasons for Interest

Reasons for enjoying dystopian literature varied. Of those who read or watched a dystopian title, 59.4 percent reported that the story "feeds the imagination" and 75 percent reported that "it is fun to read/watch." This suggests that students do see value in the literature. Some respondents even felt that dystopian themes could be inspiring—40.6 percent reported that these stories "show triumph against the odds," 37.5 percent reported that these stories give "perspective on overcoming obstacles," and 31.3 percent reported that they "provide inspiration regarding doing what's right." Table 1 summarizes these findings.

Table 1: Reasons for Enjoying Dystopian YAL

Response on the survey	% of respondents
Feeds the imagination	59.4%
Fun	75%
Show triumph over the odds	40.6%
Provides a perspective on overcoming obstacles	37.5%
Provides inspiration regarding doing what's right	31.3%

Not all respondents found dystopian themes to be as relatable as we had expected. We had hypothesized that respondents would relate to themes of an underdog fighting against the system in a world structured by oppression. Yet, only 15.6 percent of respondents who had read or seen these stories reported that they "like to see youth going against the system." However 43.8 percent of respondents reported that they "relate to one of the characters" and 31.3 percent "relate to living in a broken world." This limited research suggests the possibility that there is a potential pedagogical connection between dystopian YAL and traditionally underserved populations. This small sample size indicates that African American and first generation college students may see themselves or their lives reflected in these stories. Further research is needed to see the extent of this correlation and the extent to which these findings apply to other minority groups within the college student body. Also, the lack of diversity among the characters in dystopian literature may explain why only 54.2 percent of respondents had chosen to read books or watch movies in this genre. However, this study did not specifically investigate the connection between lack of racial representation within the genre and the lack of interest in reading the genre. Furthermore, the lack of racial representation within the genre may be particularly alienating for students of color in predominantly white institutions, and we recommend further research be done at a predominately white institution (PWI) where minority students might have a different response to the racial representation within dystopian literature.

Summary of Findings

Research demonstrates that the inclusion of dystopian YAL in a college composition classroom can be an effective strategy for encouraging student engagement. The research conducted for this essay has provided further insight into the role dystopian literature can play for students who are traditionally underserved in the college setting.

College composition instructors can't assume students will have familiarity with dystopian themes or with specific books or movies. Traditionally underserved populations, such as African Americans and first-generation college students, may not be reading or watching dystopian young adult literature despite its overall popularity. Still, many students are and so some interest/familiarity can be assumed. It is important for instructors to be aware that a lack of racial representation within the dystopian literature may decrease the overall appeal of this genre amongst students of color, and the use of this literature may be alienating for some students of color in predominantly white institutions. Our research suggests that some students prefer more racial inclusivity in their literature and movies while others may have ambivalent feelings about racial representation. However, many respondents indicated that they don't care about the race of the characters, which suggests instructors should not automatically exclude literature with predominantly white characters. Instead, instructors can work to engage all students by explicitly grappling with questions of representation and race.

Since dystopian literature is a viable resource for all college composition courses, and since it can also serve as a tool for engagement for underserved college student populations, then it would be helpful to consider ways in which the literature might be incorporated into writing assignments and classroom discussion.

Practical Considerations for the Composition Classroom

Since there appears to be a potential pedagogical benefit to incorporating YAL into the composition classroom where underserved students are a part of the class roster, then it would be helpful to consider some strategies or ideas that would make that incorporation possible.

Prompts for Composition Writing

THE GIVER:

1. In *The Giver*, Jonas was forced into a job that was designed to serve his community, but this job resulted in personal sacrifice. As you embrace an education that will lead to an occupation, how has societal pressure influenced or dictated your career path? Do you feel that individuals from your social status are equally welcome in all careers?

2. In response to the 9/11 attack, how has the American government become more like the ruling powers in *The Giver*? Has the American government's reaction to the threat of attack helped to create hope or fear in the hearts of the American people?

3. Authority figures, whether parental, occupational, institutional, or governmental, can have an impact on personal relationships. The governing authority in *The Giver*, tried to place relational controls on Jonas. Do you see the same type of control in your own life, and how do you respond to that?

THE HUNGER GAMES:

1. In *The Hunger Games*, the tributes had to fight to the death in order to appease the controlling forces in their society. Do you, in your

own life, experience a form of "death" in order to appease an authority figure? If so, then how do you manage that tension and determine what is worth fighting for?

2. Every society has their "haves and have nots." In *The Hunger Games*, Katniss leads a revolt designed to level the economic and social playing field. How are your academic aspirations going to level the playing field for your future?

3. How does the storyline within *The Hunger Games* provide a commentary on current social issues within your own society? Katniss and Peeta provide hope to the people of the districts who are grappling with difficult issues, so how are you offering hope to your community?

THE MAZE RUNNER:

1. As in *The Maze Runner*, there are times in life when we feel like we are trying to escape from a maze created by someone else. Share a time in your life when you were navigating such a maze, and detail how you triumphed over the maze while engineering your "escape."

2. There are events in our life that are more easily forgotten then remembered; however, remembering is the first step in dealing with the issues at hand. Remembering is a strong theme in *The Maze Runner*. How has remembering in your life played a key role in discovery and freedom?

3. The Glade, in *The Maze Runner*, was a male dominated society. The introduction of a female brought change. Reflect on a time in your own life where the dominance of one group and the infiltration of another provided important change.

DIVERGENT:

1. Reflect on the five factions in *Divergent* [Abnegation (selflessness); Amity (peace); Candor (honesty); Dauntless (bravery); Erudite (intellect)] and how those five factions represent the division of groups in your own society.

2. In the *Divergent* series, the inability to conform created fear. Do you see that same pattern emerging in today's society? Also, when is non-conformity constructive and when is it destructive?

3. In a society that pre-determines what is perfect, how is a person's character development and individuality formed? In *Divergent*, crisis prompted action and served to solidify identity. Have you seen this same pattern in your own life?

Prompts for Classroom Discussion

1. Although students may feel ambivalent about the importance of racial representation when analyzing YA dystopian literature, the lack of racial diversity may provide an opportunity for instructors to discuss the role and implications of the invisibility of race in the genre.

2. The inspirational nature of many dystopian stories will serve as a launching pad into discussion. Consider the inspirational acts and ask the students for evidence of similar acts in today's news or within their own personal experiences.

Ask the students to demonstrate how their real world systems and interactions with others are mirrored in the fantasy world of the text being discussed.

Conclusions

The otherworldly nature of these dystopian stories may not be realistic enough to serve as relatable texts for some student; however, research is demonstrating that there is a strong relatability with many college students, as well as a potential to engage students who have not been previously familiar with the genre. Adolescent life is filled with themes that have been developed within dystopian literature (Ryan 1). Yet, at times, instructor inspiration may be needed in order to engage students who do not intuitively grasp the composition assignment prompts. With a little vision casting, the relatability should become apparent for most critically thinking students (Kizilkan 4).

Popular dystopian fiction is reaching consuming audiences and more specifically consuming students through the consideration of current socio-cultural conditions that appeal to the students' propensity toward critical literacy. However, dystopian literature also provides new types of representation based on familiar relationships and roles. This literature addresses a developing twenty-first century view of multiculturalism; as a result, YA readers are adopting a new perspective that accepts a racially diverse society where "the other has become the norm" (Kaplan 23). Since dystopian literature is establishing new norms, traditionally underserved populations, such as African Americans and first-generation college students, may discover greater agency in a classroom where discussion and writing address a literature where systems can be challenged and new identities formed.

WORKS CITED

Ames, Melissa. *ENG 5010–001: Studies in 20th Century American Literature & Culture: Remediating 9/11.* Eastern Illinois University, 2012. http://thekeep.eiu.edu/cgi/viewcontent.cgi?article=1125&context=english_syllabi_fall2012. Accessed 20 May 2014.

Boyraz, Guler, Sharon Horne, Archandria Owens, and Aisha Armstrong. "Academic Achievement and College Persistence of African American Students with Trauma Exposure." *Journal of Counseling Psychology*, vol. 60, no. 4, 2013, pp. 582–592.

Carano, Kenneth, Robert Schueller, and Matthew Hettwer. "Fantasy Sports, Dystopian Literature and Word Clouds: The Art of Teaching Civics." *Oregon Journal of the Social Studies/Back to the Source: Bringing Social Studies to Life,* vol. 1, no. 2, 2013, pp. 46–55.

Charles, Camille, Gniesha Dinwiddie, Douglas Massey. "The Continuing Consequences of Segregation: Family Stress and College Academic Performance." *Social Science Quarterly,* vol. 85, no. 5, 2004, pp. 1353–1373.

Connors, Sean. "I Was Watching You, Mockingjay: Surveillance, Tactics, and the Limits of Panopticism." *The Politics of Panem: Challenging Genres,* vo. 85, no. 6, 2014, pp. 85–102.

Cox, Rebecca. *The College Fear Factor: How Students and Professors Misunderstand One Another.* Cambridge: Harvard University Press, 2011.

Dimock, James, Chad Kuyper, and Peggy Dimock. "A Rationale for Incorporating Dystopian Literature into Introductory Speaking Courses." *Communication & Theater Association of Minnesota Journal,* vol. 36, 2009, pp. 88–110.

Elbow, Peter. "Opinion: The Cultures of Literature and Composition: What Could Each Learn from the Other?" *College English,* vol. 64, no. 5, 2002, pp. 533–546.

Franklin, Kelly. "Conceptualizing Identity as Performance in Young Adult Dystopian Literature." *Eastern Illinois University: The Keep.* Masters Thesis. 2013.

Huynh, Virginia, and Andrew Fuligni. "Perceived Ethnic Stigma Across the Transition to College." *Journal or Youth and Adolescence,* vol. 41, no. 7, 2012, pp. 817–830.

Kaplan, Jeffrey. "The Changing Face of Young Adult Literature: What Teachers and Researchers Need to Know to Enhance their Practice and Inquiry." *Teaching Young Adult Literature Today: Insights, Considerations, and Perspectives for the Classroom Teacher.* Edited by Judith Hayn and Jeffrey Kaplan. Lanham, MD: Rowman & Littlefield, 2012, 19–40.

Kizilkan, Dicle. "An Exploration of Dystopian Fiction in the High School English Literature Curriculum." *Extended Essay on English,* vol. 3, no. 1, 2014.

Lederer, Richard. "Shaping the Dystopian Nightmare." *The English Journal,* vol. 56, no. 8, 1967, pp. 1132–1135.

Reeve, Phillip. "The Worst Is Yet to Come." *School Library Journal.* 1 August 2011, 35–36. http://www.slj.com/2011/08/collection-development/the-worst-is-yet-to-come-dystopias-are-grim-humorless-and-hopeless-and-incredibly-appealing-to-todays-teens/.

Ryan, Devin. "Emerging Themes in Dystopian Literature: The Development of an Undergraduate Course." *ScholarWorks at WMU.* Honors Thesis, Paper 2466, 2014.

Spisak, April. "What Makes a Good … Dystopian Novel?" *The Horn Book Magazine,* 27 April 2012, 55–60. http://www.hbook.com/2012/04/choosing-books/recommended-books/what-makes-a-good-ya-dystopian-novel/.

Wissman, Kelly. "Spinning Themselves into Poetry: Images of Urban Adolescent Writers in Two Novels for Young Adults." *Children's Literature in Education,* vol. 40, 2009, pp. 149–167.

Young Adult Literature and Otherness

Empathy as a Rhetorical Tool

TARA STILLIONS WHITEHEAD *and*
RICHARD JAMES WHITEHEAD

Young adult literature (YAL) in the twenty-first century has seen its fair share of out-group protagonists whose unique identities has made them relatable outcasts: Katniss Everdeen, a stoic tribute from the poorest constituent in a deeply impoverished dystopia; Percy Jackson, a dyslexic, ADHD-riddled demigod; Auggie Pullman, who suffers from a congenital face deformity; Harry Potter, an orphaned wizard targeted by the Dark Lord; Arnold Spirit, Jr., a part-time white and part-time Indian stranded between identities. And now, one of the most compelling protagonists to enter the young adult arena: Starr Carter, "the witness" to her longtime friend's murder by a white police officer, an alien in her own skin, a young woman subject to so many different definitions of black that it is "exhausting."

Because recent YAL is rife with protagonists who either physically or psychologically exist outside of the established norms of the diegetic world. Because of the genre's increasing popularity, especially with its target demographic, it seems that now, more than ever, YAL can serve various pedagogical needs, including increasing students' perspective taking abilities, which can be difficult to teach in first- and second-year composition classrooms. As instructors know, many reasons account for such difficulty. For example, some students struggle to identify with stories outside of their life experiences, while students who can might still be "more inclined to resist persuasive messages" (Vezzali et al. 117). However, it is important to stress to all composition students, not just those leery of persuasive messages, that taking another's perspective does not mean surrendering to another's ideology. Rather, perspective taking is central to becoming an informed and intelligent writer and critical thinker. As Kasl and Yorks explain, "empathy opens pathways between different worlds" (4), and if increased perspective taking leads to greater cognitive and affective empathy, what better way to connect narrative and reader worlds than through an understanding of shared emotion? And since a writer's ability to identify audience and make formal choices to suit that audience, as well as form a clearer picture of the ongoing conversation about a given topic, are reliant upon the writer's ability to empathize, using appropriate texts that help increase perspective taking—*the vehicle by which empathy occurs*—could help instructors elevate person-centered thinking in the classroom, which fosters a greater understanding of the rhetorical value of identity and ideology in writing.

But what constitutes an "appropriate" text in a first- or second-year writing classroom? The obvious drawback to using a blanket term like "appropriate" is that we all teach different demographics of students with varying levels of competency and, more importantly, we teach at institutions with unique philosophies regarding the composition classroom and what kinds of texts should be used there. Thus, "appropriate" has a wide range of interpretations; knowing the constraints for text selection is an important step, but taking inventory of the uniqueness of the classroom demographics is probably more critical. Most writing instructors would agree that appropriate always relates to audience and context, so there is a common denominator here. The strongest writing comes from writers who understand, acknowledge, and interact with all perspectives, including voices outside of the mainstream, and this means interacting with texts that represent divergent perspectives.

The best of YAL's protagonists are nearly always situated as out-group persons at odds with the sociological, political, or cultural norms of their fictional world (often abstracted from a "real" world known to the author); therefore, it is our belief that well written forms of YAL can evoke empathetic responses from diverse groups of readers, regardless of the degree to which readers identify with the protagonist.

While myriad themes can enable perspective taking in diverse classrooms, it is our stance that young adult narratives dealing with otherness can be especially effective in teaching high school and college composition students about the power of effective rhetorical strategies in voicing ideas, particularly those that are oppressed by the privileged culture. Secondary benefits of developing critical reading and writing activities around young adult narratives that center on otherness include real-world empathy among classroom participants, especially increased racial consciousness in individuals (Kasl and Yorks 9–18); for this essay, however, we plan to focus on the measurable learning outcomes associated with empathy-facilitated perspective taking and how those outcomes create an awareness in the reader that can then be transformed into a learned behavior, one that can be used as a rhetorical tool in the composition classroom.

Defining Empathy

Defining empathy in any context is tricky, and many dedicated researchers in the area of psychology and literary theory have made solid cases for their respective definitions of the otherwise elusive and unexpectedly controversial concept. We acknowledge the psychology and sociology research that clearly defines affective and cognitive empathy as separate processes that interact with one another, and therefore, we understand that evaluating one of those processes involves, to some degree, acknowledgment of the other. That said, the cognitive process is most useful to our discussion of empathy as a rhetorical tool because it involves conscious interpretation of another's emotional experience but does not always *require* that a person, in this context, a reader, experience an emotional response. That said, the emotional response is often part of the empathy package, so working with a well-researched definition will help up in our quest to discuss cognitive empathy and narratives. One of the most accessible and well-supported definitions of empathy out there comes from Cuff et al, who scrutinize what they consider a plethora of confused, convoluted, or otherwise misrepresented definitions of the term. From a psychological axiology that is also aware of the value of many interpretations of the term, they proffer a more distinguished definition of empathy as "an emotional response … similar to one's perception (directly experienced or imagined) and understanding (cognitive empathy) of the stimulus emotion, with recognition that the source of the emotion is not one's own" (Cuff et al. 150). If this is the central definition to be used in discussing empathy across disciplines and in varying contexts, including empathy resulting from encounters with imagined people and narratives, it allows for a greater latitude of application in the composition classroom.

Because perception, a nonlinear process involving selection, organization, and interpretation of stimuli (Wood 44), is subjective, the intensity and accuracy of resulting empathetic responses will be varied and not subject to a common standard. This means that writing instructors need not be concerned with the intensity of empathetic response in their readers so much as the fact that a response happens at all. If instructors realize that our "capacity for primitive empathy … suggests that human beings are basically similar to one another, with a limited range of variations" (Keen "A Theory" 212), assessment of empathetic outcomes becomes a more holistic process. Thus, if a student meets the minimum threshold of response, understanding, and recognition (Cuff et al. 150)—all of which can be gauged through focused reflective writing exercises or discussions, which we will outline later in our text-specific suggestions for practical considerations—the student exhibits the ability to interpret his or her response and evaluate it in terms of perspective taking. Acknowledgment of a threshold and not a common standard is hugely important because it accommodates different emotive styles and accounts for the limitation of language when it comes to articulating complex cognitive and affective processes to an authority figure, such as a teacher, or to a group of non-intimate peers.

However, let's take a step back. We just made the claim that empathy occurs not only in person-to-person interactions, but also in a fantasy setting, for instance, during interaction with a fictional narrative. Believe it or not, a significant amount of empirical evidence supports this claim about experiencing empathy through imaginative means, even if the conclusions researchers come to are incongruous. Empathy can be elicited without the physical presence of another person—via imagination—and psychology researchers at Coventry University assert that "there is little functional difference between empathy for a real, fictional, or absent person" and that "the key element to consider in the presence of an emotionally laden stimulus is that of perception and understanding in the observer, rather than the emotionality in the target" (Cuff et al. 148).

Perspective and Fiction

The truth is, we are more comfortable embodying alternative perspectives through literature because of the clear separation between diegesis and "reality." For adolescent and young adult readers in particular, accessing differing perspectives through fiction can feel much safer (Guarisco and Freeman 58). Therefore, it seems only natural that fictional narratives can be used to effectively increase exposure to alternative ideologies, particularly those oppressed perspectives not subject to ready disclosure because of a reader's willingness to emotionally engage in a narrative that does not pressure him or her to take specific action as a result of feeling. However, as we will discuss later, narrative presentations need to be purposed specifically and strategically to engage students and not alienate them. The line between diegesis and reality has to be maintained, or else a reader's capacity to empathize becomes jeopardized. The result can be emotional contagion, where the understanding of the emotions as being the source of relating to another person's experiences becomes obfuscated, or it can be removal from the narrative altogether. And as Tyler Dodge illustrates, "when a reader is positioned outside of a story, perceived agency may reduce the reader's sense of identification with characters and therefore reduce the effectiveness of the characters as social models" (293). Perceived agency is a violation of what Suzanne Keen describes a social contract between reader and character; the absence of that contract can be the primary factor in preventing prosocial behavior ("A Theory" 212).

Ultimately, it should not be the composition instructor's objective to seek social behavior modifications as the result of analyzing and interpreting a text that is politically, socially, or culturally controversial. Most educators understand the dangers of using a novel or other work of fiction to radicalize students; yet it should also be noted that less extreme, but equally ambitious, objectives, such as resisting students' ideological stances or scrutinizing a student's self-concept as a means of forcing social, political, or cultural altruism, also represent unrealistic, if not unethical, pedagogical goals. Later in this essay, we will discuss suggestions for avoiding the dangerous pedagogical fallacy of *prescription*, or what Freire famously termed "the imposition of one individual's choice upon another, transforming the consciousness of the prescribed into one that conforms with the prescriber's consciousness" (47). Empathy cannot exist in an authoritarian classroom because perspective taking cannot be forced upon the reader; we cannot demand an emotional response from our students. We can only select texts, writing activities, and classroom activities that facilitate perspective taking.

Narrative empathy research has grown substantially over the past few years, and empirical studies in particular have been able to link fiction reading to increased perspective taking and reduced attitudes of prejudice towards marginalized groups (Vezzali et al. 116). While attitudes do not always result in behavior changes, awareness of those attitudes and shifts can be considered a tool to be used consciously by the reader when he or she is called upon to take another's perspective, or at least acknowledge that a difference in perspectives exists. After curating a collaborative study involving a sixth-grade English teacher and a psychologist from a liberal arts college, Martha S. Guarisco and Louise Freeman of Mary Baldwin College build substantively upon prior pedagogy-related empathy research and conclude that perspective taking (one subset of the Interpersonal Reactivity Index, which is used to measure general empathy) can increase in a classroom setting that provides activities focused towards empathy and perspective taking (58–60). Guarisco and Freeman, who selected R.J. Palacio's young adult novel *Wonder* specifically because it deals with a protagonist who is emotionally relatable but alienated as the result of his physical deformity and is likely to be considered by readers an out-group "other," emphasize that "seeing the perspectives of other characters [shows] students they are not alone in their possible discomfort"; they are quick to note, however, that in order to catalyze prosocial behavior and bolster a text's ability to precipitate empathetic responses, focused classroom activities, such as responsive writing and structured discussion, are key (63).

Whether empathetic responses to fictional narratives definitively enable prosocial behavior is, controversially, still up for discussion (Keen "Reader's Temperaments" 297). However, the deniability of an increased likelihood for prosocial behavior as the result of increased cognitive empathy (perspective taking in particular) should not be beyond debate. Results from two cross-sectional studies that examined the effects of fantasy characters on reducing prejudice in high school and university students found that reduced prejudice towards stigmatized groups was the result of readers identifying with the "positive character" (in this case, Harry Potter), and concluded that "participants … may have learnt to take the perspective of discriminated group members and, in turn, applied this enhanced ability to understand disadvantaged groups to real-world out-group categories" (Vezzali et al. 115–116).

Understandably, educators may worry about a particular text's emotional potency or fear that a chosen narrative might push student readers beyond empathetic understanding and into the realm of personal distress; however, Keen draws clear distinctions between personal distress, which happens in real-life instances of empathetic response and empathy produced through reader responses to fiction, noting that "because novel reading can so easily be stopped or interrupted by an unpleasant emotional reaction to a book … personal distress has no place in a literary theory of empathy" ("A Theory" 208).

Strategy and Praxis

Of course, text selection is critical when it comes to maximizing student engagement, and classroom diversity often determines how complicated that selection process might be. Pronounced ideological division in the classroom has the capacity to result in a hostile environment (latent or otherwise) and prevent open discussion of the text. In their article, "Do I Really Know You? Do You Really Know Me? Empathy Amid Diversity in Differing Learning Contexts," Kasl and Yorks contend that "the greater the diversity among participating learners and the stronger the emotional valence of the issues being addressed, the more radical the constituent program elements need to be" (17). This means that composition teachers looking to incorporate novels that use the perspective of a protagonist from a marginalized group need to select texts that consider a diverse readership and create units that address the novel from in-group and out-group perspectives.

For example, when considering incorporating a text like Angie Thomas' bestselling *The Hate U Give*, the instructor must also consider how to skillfully address its controversial reigning themes—police brutality and the systematic oppression of African Americans—in a simultaneously "open" and "controlled" environment. Ideally, we want students to be able to express their opinions, ask questions when they do not understand the character or narrative, and feel safe discussing their own views on the themes, which are relevant and emotionally charged. But how do we go about striking this balance? Teaching is a human act, and thus, the ideological obstacles are not exclusive to students. We, as instructors, need to "develop hyperawareness of self as part of the learning system … [and] examine hegemonic embeddedness as it relates to learners" (Kasl and Yorks 18). If we feel strongly connected to the material, if not polarized by it, we should first take inventory of those emotions and be careful not to push students into our camp. Holding back can be difficult when the text seems to us to have "clear" political, cultural, or social implications that, if interpreted altruistically, should lead the student towards the prosocial way of thinking that we so hope they will adopt. As Terry Dean points out, "when we teach composition, we are teaching culture…. For students whose home culture is distant from 'mainstream' culture, we are also teaching how, as a people, 'mainstream' Americans view the world" (24). At its core, mainstreaming counteracts individuality, reinforces and validates hegemony, and speciously prohibits meaningful discourse from marginalized groups. We have to find a way to teach the necessary elements of academic discourse while discouraging "alienation from the values and relationships of the home culture" (Dean 26) and other aspects of the self. What a daunting task! How, then, can we go beyond self-awareness as instructors? What pedagogical/practical measures can we take?

While there are many ways instructors can avoid anti-empathetic practices or prohibiting student-facilitated perspective taking, we will focus on two groups of strategies: teaching through inquiry and low stakes assignments. These strategies are catered specifically towards young adult novels dealing with current social, political, or cultural issues, novels focused the central theme of otherness, and novels told from the first-person perspective of an out-group protagonist. Specifically, we chose two novels with protagonists whose identities are complicated, invented, or fragmented by the dominant culture's constructs of race and ethnicity: Sherman Alexie's National Book Award-winning young adult text, *The Absolutely True Diary of a Part-time Indian,* and Angie Thomas' explosive debut novel *The Hate U Give.* Because of the novels' similar themes, the suggestions we give each novel in the practical considerations sections could be used for either text.

Teaching Through Inquiry

In his discerning article about reading as a civic duty to be taught, "Reading for a Better World: Teaching for Social Responsibility with Young Adult

Literature," Steven Wolk examines what he calls "the living curriculum" approach to teaching young adult literature, which involves units comprised of inquiry questions as opposed to exams and rote recitations that fail to fully engage students in a dialogue with the texts they read (665). This practice, Wolk emphasizes, is "unlike transmission teaching, [as] these questions do not have single correct answers, so students are immersed into a classroom experience that values listening to multiple perspectives and thinking for themselves" (666). Teaching students to value *the act* of listening to multiple perspectives is different from instructing students to accept and value the perspectives themselves. Teaching value places upon the student the responsibility of making the decision to go beyond valuing the perspective and relate to another's experience empathetically. This "cognitive" act signifies a learned behavior, an intentional act of identifying with alternative views, and when this learned behavior is dispatched in the composition classroom, rhetorical abilities increase significantly.

The key to building rhetorical tools through perspective taking and empathy? Narrative timeliness and character identification. If the story has currency, and if the protagonist is relatable, rhetorical effect can be achieved with a wider readership. Novels that employ what Suzanne Keen calls "broadcast strategic empathy [or that which] calls on the reader to feel with members of a group by emphasizing our common vulnerabilities and hopes" ["A Theory" 224] would likely be the best texts to use in the first- and second-year writing classroom because they can accommodate the rhetorical aims of the instructor and the cognitive needs of the readers. Consider the student demographic of a two-year college in an urban setting, or a rural four-year university, or an elite private college situated just outside of a cultural epicenter. As noted previously, student populations contribute to the definition of "appropriate" when it comes to texts; however, expectations that those students cultivated during their experiences in secondary education also define what attentive educators consider not only appropriate but revolutionary or valuable rhetorical texts.

As Wolk points out, many students enter college with a distorted notion of reading: "Living in a democracy poses specific obligations for reading. While a nation of workers requires a country that *can* read, a democracy requires people that *do* read, read widely, and think and act in response.... However, if you ask adolescents why they go to school you will ... hear a response having to do with one purpose: to get a job" (665). This mentality extends to the college classroom, where students are often unaware of institutional hegemony and can become complicit in assimilating into the "academic culture" being delivered by the teacher in their classroom (Dean 24). This is why text selection and instructor presentation are so crucial, and this is why teaching through inquiry, where the instructor not only solicits student responses through questions (in this case, specifically geared towards perspective taking), but has students ask their own questions regarding character identity, ideology, and experience, is so effective.

Inquiry and Angie Thomas' The Hate U Give

Angie Thomas' *The Hate U Give* provides a golden opportunity for educators to expand the conversation of police brutality, highlight black oppression, and give insight into black adolescence. The latter point is the most important when discussing the use of perspective taking with this book, because adolescence is a "common" experience that can result in a strong empathetic response. However, as Groenke et al. point out, "youth of color don't truly get to be adolescents. Instead … they are viewed as deviant and abnormal, as sub-human" (36).

At the novel's outset, Starr Carter's identity is already controlled by two personas, each of which is largely determined by the given social setting's construct of race and what it means to be black. From the expensive white prep school where her reformed, ex-gangbanger father sends her, to the gunshot overtures of her deeply oppressed home in Garden Heights, or "the ghetto" as she lovingly calls it, Starr acknowledges that "being two different people is so exhausting" (Thomas 301) and that she can never fully identify with each identity—because they are personas determined by hegemonic constructs of "blackness." However, once Starr's longtime friend Khalil is unlawfully murdered by a white police officer (referred to by his badge number, One-Fifteen) in front of her eyes, Starr must reconcile yet another label placed upon her: "the witness." Even more complicated is Starr's realization that "the witness" alienates her from both her home turf and the sheltered Williamson Prep where she and her wealthy white boyfriend go to school:

> I get out of the car. For at least seven hours, I don't have to talk about One-Fifteen. I don't have to think about Khalil. I just have to be normal Starr at normal Williamson and have a normal day. That means flipping the switch in my brain so I'm Williamson Starr. Williamson Starr doesn't use slang—if a rapper would say it, she doesn't say it, even if her white friends do. Slang makes them cool. Slang makes her "hood." Williamson Starr holds her tongue when people piss her off so nobody will think she's the "angry black girl." Williamson Starr is approachable. No stank-eyes, side-eyes, none of that. Williamson Starr is nonconfrontational. Basically, Williamson Starr doesn't give anyone a reason to call her ghetto.
> I can't stand myself for doing it, but I do anyway [Thomas 71].

Thomas' unapologetic narrative about racism and police violence bears witness to the #BLACKLIVESMATTER movement in a way that no other text has, from the perspective of a teenager who has experienced unspeakable tragedy and whose identity is controlled by a longing to belong to the tribe without having to suffer the labels that have been placed upon her and those like her. When described generally, like this, Starr's vulnerabilities and hopes appear universal, relatable, easy to empathize with. However, Starr's experiences are anything but universal. Her experiences are specific to her status as an adolescent black girl deeply affected by institutional and systemic racism, from both sides of the color divide. Beyond the central conflict, we learn a lot about Starr, that her father is an ex-gangbanger trying to provide for his family, that it's not unusual to hear gunfire before bedtime in Garden Heights, that her family, in spite of systemic and institutional oppression and racial inequality, is a loving family, a hopeful family. But Starr's experiences are singular, and when we consider that urgency and the importance of the conversation Thomas enters with her novel, we find a book ripe for rhetorical analysis of voice, audience, and theme.

Practical Considerations for the Composition Classroom

How can a reader empathize with Starr if he or she has never witnessed a murder? Has never lived in the "ghetto"? Is not a youth of color? Or does not attend a privileged prep school? Through inquiry.

Groenke et al. developed an excellent series of questions regarding youth of color and adolescence that could help readers gain perspective, realize ideological and identity differences, and ultimately, empathize with Starr. Some of those questions are: "How is adolescence depicted in this text (e.g., story, song, movie)? Does this depiction of adolescence feel true to you? Why or why not? What is 'adolescence' in a fiction for youth of color? Do youth of color get to be teenagers? Does adolescence look/feel the same for youth of color as it does white youth?" (39).

Different units focusing on different sub-themes connected to Starr's otherness could also create a higher capacity for empathetic response. Incorporating other texts from marginalized voices dealing with similar conflicts—black adolescence, police brutality, and systemic oppression—and creating cross-question inquiries could achieve more complex rhetorical outcomes through perspective taking, depending on the texts selected. Since Thomas already creates intertextual dialogue with black cultural icons, such as Huey Newton and legendary rapper Tupac Shakur (the novel's title is in reference to his THUG LIFE tattoo), incorporating inquiry-based assignments involving select passages from both figures' works could help readers identify with Starr and understand the cultural context informing *The Hate U Give*. Shakur's song "Changes" would be a great text for inquiry because it is both a touchstone for Thomas and has its own reference to Newton in the lyrics.

Examples of effective cross-questioning would include asking students to reflect on the similarities and differences among Newton's, Thomas,' and Shakur's depictions of the black experience. Expanding the conversation to include Will Smith's experience in *The Fresh Prince of Bel Air* (Starr and her white boyfriend Chris consider the show's theme song *their* "song") and having students address the significance of Thomas' allusions to the hit sitcom would be another cross-questioning method of inquiry that could help build rhetorical analysis tools through perspective taking.

Ultimately, inquiry is an effective approach to using YAL to elevate awareness of and empathetic responses towards experiences of otherness. Inquiry is also elastic and can frame a variety of texts for cross-questioning, to broaden the reader's understanding of the context shaping our identities and individual experiences.

Low-Stakes Assignments and Sherman Alexie's The Absolutely True Diary of a Part-Time Indian

Low-stakes writing activities are great tools for getting students to share their ideas without the pressure of a significant effect on the overall grade. While some instructors may refer to these assignments as informal, exploratory, low-stakes, or non-graded, the purpose is to explore students' ideas in written form (Bean 120). Minimal point value and minimal marking allow many students to express ideas without the fear of being right or wrong and places the emphasis on generative writing and ideation as opposed to assessment. These low-stakes activities can be almost any type of assignment: journaling, in-class free writing, reader response, or prompt-driven writing, and they are a great way to encourage perspective taking and generate narrative empathy.

One novel that we feel is a good choice for low-stakes assignments aimed at enabling perspective taking is Sherman Alexie's *The Absolutely True Diary of a Part-Time Indian*, which tells the story of Arnold Spirit, Jr., a Spokane Indian who feels like he does not fit in at the all-white school he attends, or on the reservation in Wellpinit, Washington, where he has lived and stayed his whole life. He is the only student of color at Reardan High, and he is unlike the other kids his age on the reservation—born hydrocephalic, with too many teeth, and with a stutter. Junior is constantly picked on for these differences, by both "rez" and white kids. Like Starr Carter, he is trapped between identities, oppressed by a hegemonic idea of normalcy. While not everyone has been the other and felt the uncomfortable feeling that comes with that, Alexie poignantly describes Junior's realization that he is an outsider:

"They stared at me like I was Bigfoot, or a UFO. What was I doing at Reardon, whose mascot was an Indian, thereby making me the only *other* Indian in town? … Reardon was the opposite of the rez. It was the opposite of my family. It was the opposite of me. I didn't deserve to be there. I knew it; all the kids knew it. Indians don't deserve shit" (38). (Alexie's use of italics for the word "other" should not go unnoticed.) The novel is fraught with scenes of acknowledged otherness like this one, as Alexie's goal seems to be creating a dialogue between cultural differences, informing readers through language, irony, and character interiority.

Practical Considerations for the Composition Classroom

Because he is so intent on creating dialogue, Alexie includes a discussion guide in the paperback edition, and many of the questions are aimed at facilitating perspective taking, namely for in-groups to better understand Junior's out-group oppression. Depending on how the instructor decides to build the unit, he or she could incorporate that discussion guide in the form of low-stakes, generative/reflective writing. The discussion guide questions are very discerning and valuable, but nothing should stop the instructor from developing his or her own low-stakes prompts. A sample prompt we created to facilitate a discussion of identity and context reads: "When Junior attends Reardan High School, he notices that he is the only student of color, and this shapes his self-perception in a negative way. In your writing journal, reflect on a personal experience where you felt like you were the 'other' or 'outsider' and it shaped your self-perception. How did you feel? Why?" An exercise like this can be used as a warm-up for small group discussions geared towards understanding the different social, cultural, and political experiences of marginalized groups and call upon readers to question what they define as "normal" experience. As a low-stakes assignment, we graded it holistically, on the basis of participation, and this in turn alleviated student concerns regarding "right answers" and the less desirable "write what the teacher wants to read" responses.

Another low-stakes assignment that is effective with Alexie's novel, but that could also be used with Thomas or Palacio or any other YAL novel commenting on otherness is the epistolary assignment, where the reader writes a letter to one or more characters. Giving the letter a specific purpose that involves both analysis and reciprocity—such as consoling a character by giving personal examples relating to his or her experiences or adversities—exercises rhetorical skills while simultaneously valuing each student's uniqueness. Presenting this assignment as a low-stakes, participatory exercise, reduces the hegemonic pressures of "correctness" long associated with reader-text

relationships in academia and emphasizes the role of the reader in constructing meaning.

Conclusion

   Empathy can be a powerful rhetorical tool, and new YAL narratives
dealing with varying forms of otherness and current social themes should be
first choice of college writing instructors looking to enhance awareness of
divergent perspectives and teach students to value the act of listening to multiple perspectives (Wolk 666). It is our jobs as writing instructors to be equally
aware, for us to consciously model perspective taking with our students so
that we may empathize with them through the learning experience and so
that they see the importance of their unique experiences as well. We cannot
ignore the value of emerging, marginalized voices in YAL. If "a new crop of
young adult novelists" seem to be able to grasp the fact that "writing is a
form of activism" as Angie Thomas reports to the *New York Times* (Alter),
then YAL enthusiasts and educators themselves should be able to apply
the narrative of activism to general reactions to film and novel narratives
dealing with adolescents experiencing otherness, or the theme of being an
outsider.

WORKS CITED

Alexie, Sherman. *The Absolutely True Diary of a Part-Time Indian*. New York: Little, Brown, 2009.
Alter, Alexandra, "New Crop of Young Adult Novels Explores Race and Police Brutality." *The New York Times*. The New York Times, 19 Mar. 2017, nytimes.com/2017/03/19/books/review/black-lives-matter-teenage-books.html?_r=0. Accessed 22 Mar. 2017.
Bean, John C., and Maryellen Weimer. *Engaging Ideas: The Professor's Guide to Integrating Writing, Critical Thinking, and Active Learning in the Classroom (2nd Edition)*. Hoboken: Jossey-Bass, 2011.
Cuff, Benjamin, et al. "Empathy: A Review of the Concept." *Emotion Review*, vol. 8, no. 2, Apr. 2016, pp. 144–153, doi: 10.1177/754073914558466.
Dean, Terry. "Multicultural Classrooms, Monocultural Teachers." *College Composition and Communication*, vol. 40, no. 1, Feb. 1989, pp. 23–37.
Dodge, Tyler. "Effects of Interactivity on Children's Cognitive Empathy Toward Narrative Characters." *International Journal of Instructional Media*, vol. 38, no. 3, Sept. 2011, pp. 287–294.
Freeman, Louise. "The Wonder of Empathy: Using Palacio's Novel to Teach Perspective Taking." *The ALAN Review*, Fall 2005. *ResearchGate*, researchgate.net/publication/282861944.
Freire, Paulo. *Pedagogy of the Oppressed: 30th Anniversary Edition*. Continuum International Publishing Group, 2005. msu.ac.zw/elearning/material/1335344125freire_pedagogy of_the_oppresed.pdf.
Groenke, Susan L., et al. "Disrupting and Dismantling the Dominant Vision of Youth of Color." *English Journal*, vol. 104, no. 3, 2015, pp. 35–34.
Kasl, Elizabeth, and Lyle Yorks. "Do I Really Know You? Do You Really Know Me? Empathy Amid Diversity in Differing Learning Contexts." *Adult Education Quarterly*, vol. 66, no. 1, 2016, pp. 3–20. *SAGE*, doi:10.1177/0741713615606965.

Keen, Suzanne. "A Theory of Narrative Empathy." *Narrative*, vol. 14, no. 3, Oct. 2006, pp. 207–236. *JSTOR*, jstor.org/stable/20107388.

_____. "Readers' Temperaments and Fictional Character." *New Literary History*, vol. 42, no. 2, Spring 2011, pp. 295–314. *JSTOR*, jstor.org/stable/23012545.

Thomas, Angie. *The Hate U Give*. New York: Balzer & Bray, 2017.

Vezzali, et al. "The Greatest Magic of Harry Potter: Reducing Prejudice." *Journal of Applied Social Psychology*, vol. 45, 2015, pp. 105–121.

Wolk, Steven. "Reading for a Better World: Teaching for Social Responsibility with Young Adult Literature." *Journal of Adolescent and Adult Literacy*, vol. 52, no. 8, 2009, pp. 6646–673, doi:10.1598.

Wood, Julia T. *Communication Mosaics: An Introduction to the Field of Communication*, 7th ed. Boston: Cengage Learning, 2013.

Identity Performance in a Virtual World in Cory Doctorow's *Little Brother*

Kelly F. Franklin

In the media-driven, social network culture of today, young adults often communicate with one another, and even know one another, solely through virtual identities that exist within imagined communities created in cyberspace. These identities are generated and function solely outside of physical reality; screen names and profile pictures have become virtual representations of corporeal personas. Technology provides young adults and adults with the opportunity to create new identities for themselves, identities that allow them to interact and perform not only on the social network but also in emails, online gaming, and blogs. However, if one were to ask an adult if he/she plays characters in these situations, more than likely the answer would be no. Perhaps this is because many people unknowingly, and seamlessly, sculpt profiles online and then portray them in their day-to-day lives. Thus, performance has become an essential facet of day-to-day survival.

Today's adolescents, and now more and more adults, have grown up in, and currently live in, a society that has been heavily impacted by virtual reality and technology. Performance theorist Elizabeth Bell suggests that technology, like performance, provides methods in which humans create, know, form opinions about, and critique the world (234). Cyberspace also provides many adolescents with opportunities in which they can form new identities that arguably serve as more honest representations of who they would like to be, or possibly who they feel they truly are. Therefore, as performance scholars Bonnie Marranca and Gautam Dasguta suggest, "Cyberspace has become a performance space" (2). Historically, books have provided people with characters that afford moments of escape and the opportunities to vicariously live in "created" personas. Social media is able to take this a step further and provides people with a platform to create and then perform these identities—sometimes even assume these new designed personas as their sole identity. Simply put, in this highly technological time identity performance is relevant, relatable, and happens almost unconsciously.

These concepts can be seen in Cory Doctorow's novel *Little Brother* which includes many characters who assume virtual identities in order to represent facets of their personalities that they cannot safely perform in the physical world. Marcus Yallow, the 17-year-old hero of *Little Brother*, performs three identities throughout the novel: he becomes known to the audience first as Marcus, a typical teenage boy; as W1n5t0n, a hacker who frequently hacks the files of local truancy officers and school administrators; and M1k3y, the character who would lead a rebellion against the Department of Homeland Security (DHS). Marcus is forced to create these secret and virtual identities to survive in the post–9/11 dystopic conditions of Doctorow's futuristic San Francisco setting.

The notion that modern day is in fact a dystopia has often been argued by scholars (Ames). Indeed, many dystopian characteristics are present in current society such as surveillance, advanced technology, and resistance. Dystopic elements such as these can promote a climate of unease, impacting how people conduct their everyday lives and construct their identities. Identity formation in an atmosphere of paranoia is not solely relegated to a post 9/11 climate, as youth have been coming of age in times of war and terror for centuries. However, modern technological advances have made it harder to determine who the enemy actually is. Should citizens be wary of foreign terrorist attacks, or a government who has the power to tap phones, hack personal web searches, and monitor bank accounts? It seems that in this modern age, the ability to pinpoint a single terrorist, or threat, is nearly impossible. The story of Edward Snowden is representative of this trend: the enemy depends upon perspective.

In *Little Brother*, Marcus is coming of age in futuristic, and highly surveilled, San Francisco. As stated earlier, Marcus creates multiple virtual and alternative reality identities for himself in order to navigate and survive San Francisco, post-terrorist attack. Perhaps the most important factor in Marcus's ability to successfully construct identity in a time of terror is the fact that he has always been a part of imagined communities. Marcus's participation in Live Action Role Playing (LARP), online gaming, and interactive Alternative Reality Gaming (ARG) enable him to participate in large social networks that afford him the feeling of belonging even when he is performing a different persona. Although Marcus exists solely in fiction, many of the situations he experiences are relevant for youth in the world today. By using Marcus as a case study (exploring how he handles surveillance, trauma, and how he interacts with authority figures) it is possible to understand how many of today's youth are constructing identity in a post 9/11 climate. Exploring Marcus in this way is certainly revealing of modern youth, but it also can provide for rich discussion in the composition classroom. Marcus's story is an example of creating an identity that represents an argument, and how to then support that argument. As such, *Little Brother* can be used in a composition course not only as a piece to write about, but also as a close study of how communication is closely connected to identity performance—and that in order to write convincing texts, writers must fully believe in the role they are playing.

Literature Review

Though *Little Brother* is set in the not too distant future, the setting seems similar to that of San Francisco today; although this version of San Francisco is embedded with more futuristic, high-tech inventions in use to monitor the public. Marcus Yallow and his friends, Darryl and Van, are average teenagers who are keenly interested in sneaking out of school and playing the alternative reality game (ARG) known as Harajuku Fun Madness (HFM). While on the quest to solve a clue in HFM, the trio are caught in an unexpected terrorist attack and mistaken as terrorists. The three are held prisoner by the DHS at a secret location, treated as the enemy, ruthlessly questioned about their supposed involvement in the attack, and eventually let go (with the exception of Darryl). Upon their release, the DHS warns Marcus that they will be watching him. Marcus, who has always fought the heavy surveillance his school administrators and local police enforced, becomes enraged that his rights have been so infringed upon and vows to fight for not only his right to privacy, but the rights of other U.S. citizens as well. Marcus begins using the Xnet (an Internet-connected gaming system) in order to spread his message of freedom, and through the creation of M1k3y (his rebellion leadership persona) he becomes a symbol of resistance and a reluctant hero who must stay on constant guard in order to resist capture and also to defeat the DHS.

Little Brother has not yet been written extensively about, but scholarly articles do exist that discuss the dystopic elements of the text as well as how this text can be used to study adolescence in fields other than literature. In the article "*Feed* vs. *Little Brother*: The Same Only Different" Jennifer Miseck states that

> while both authors work from the premise that technology can be productive or destructive, Doctorow does not long for a time when we did not have technology.

Instead, he considers how technology can corrupt, but how it can liberate, too, and it is technology-savvy teens who are the heroes of the story.... While Anderson longs for a time without technology, Doctorow endeavors to promote a critical eye toward our technology-centered society [73].

Dystopian texts are often written in such a way that technology represents an evil, but Doctorow encourages his characters, and perhaps even his readers, to engage with technology in order to secure our rights and freedoms. A realistic ideology to argue in a world that is tech savvy, if not tech obsessed. Although Doctorow's text does feature technology being used negatively, to monitor and spy on citizens, in general technology is used positively in *Little Brother* as a way to defend freedom. It should not be surprising that media studies scholars are also intrigued by *Little Brother* and the effects high technology has on young adults.

Scholars interested in cultural and media studies are also concerned with the current culture that many adolescents are coming of age in. Annette Wannamaker and Ian Wojicik-Andrews argue that

Little Brother ... constructs adolescent characters and readers who, because they are clever and more media savvy than many of the adults in their world, are able to resist and subvert totalitarian governmental control by creating their own communications networks and media identities ... the dichotomies suggested by *Little Brother's* views of a National Entertainment State give us useful terms and concepts for beginning a discussion regarding the relationships among young people, new media, and history and the way these three areas have converged to produce unsettling questions about children's culture [415].

Youth coming of age today are doing so in a world very different than it was even ten years ago; cyberspace and the social network have completely changed how people live their lives. Frequently, people are only known to each other as Facebook friends or online gaming buddies, and engage with one another in imagined communities.

Imagined Communities

In a 1983 publication, Benedict Anderson coined the term "imagined communities" in his study on nation states. Anderson proposed that nations are in fact "*imagined* because the members of even the smallest nation will never know most of their fellow-members, meet them, or even hear of them, yet in the minds of each lives the image of their communion" (6, emphasis in original). Although Anderson's theory of imagined communities was directed toward the national level (and written during the Cold War/Regan Era), the concept is still relevant today. Arguably, imagined communities continue to exist in this moment in various sizes and media forms. Due to the current cultural trend of sharing personal information with others (on a grand scale), imagined communities have expanded beyond Anderson's original argument. In fact, an imagined community can be found anywhere people interact: social networking (such as Facebook), online gaming groups, Sunday morning coffee groups, book clubs.

Anderson's theory, although not originally written to encompass the social network, remains relevant (perhaps more so) today, a fact that Arjun Appaduri proposes in his book *Modernity at Large: Cultural Dimensions of Globalization*. Anderson argues "…all communities larger than primordial villages of face-to-face contact (and perhaps even these) are imagined. Communities are to be distinguished, not by their falsity/genuineness, but by the style in which they are imagined … [imagined communities exist] as indefinitely stretchable nets of kinship and clientship" (6). Perhaps the only difference is that in regard to social networking, many people were at one time face-to-face friends and knew each other personally, whereas in today's culture people often only meet and interact through virtual discourse communities.

Current scholarly arguments suggest these types of communities are indeed far from positive, often persuading users to not only behave in ways they normally would not without social networks (Fogg 24), but according to Anderson, negative and positive aspects are irrelevant to what imagined communities are. Instead, style is significant in imagined communities, as well as the content that these communities manage. Anderson stresses that style can be interpreted as how a community governs itself or simply the physicality of the community (for example: an internet community). In the case of Marcus Yallow, many of the imagined communities he belongs to are virtual; thus, solely existing in cyberspace, and despite the physical limitations of these virtual communities, they are real to Marcus, and have played a very important role in the creation of his many identities. Appaduri further suggests that media and imagined communities are vital for identity formation, stating:

> They are resources for experiments with self-making in all sorts of societies, for all sorts of persons…. Because of the sheer multiplicity of the forms in which they appear (cinema, television, computers, and telephones) and because of the rapid way which they move through daily life routines, electronic media provide resources for self-imagining as an everyday social project [3–4].

Therefore, according to Appaduri, imagined communities provide people with the opportunity to safely, and vicariously, experience identities that would have been previously unavailable to them. The virtual atmosphere of social networking provides youth with the perfect stage for important developmental role-playing. Although the characters in Doctorow's young adult

(YA) novel are indeed fictional, they frequently create cyber identities that are considered deviant by some, the DHS, and exhibitionist to others. *Little Brother* counters claims made by scholars who argue that the social network, and cyber space itself, is harmful for youth. Instead, the book champions the use of these technologies to interact with others and to create identities that allow youth to realize all aspects of their characters.

Applying Performance Theory and Psychology

In terms of performance theory, cyberspace can be considered a stage; indeed, it provides a setting in which people perform characters (identities). Elizabeth Bell claims that online settings provide rich spaces for sociality and allow people to perform identities that can be considered slippery "morphing the 'stable' categories of gender, age, race, sexuality, and even species and humanness" (257). Although Marcus never performs any non-human characters (aside from his LARP vampire character) in the text, he is able to use the internet as a stage for his character M1k3y. In order to meet with reporters, and possible DHS spies, Marcus sets up a chat in the virtual gaming world of Clockwork Plunder. This space allows Marcus to safely assume the identity of M13ky and to also broadcast his message:

> My name is M1k3y and I'm not the leader of anything…. All around you are Xnetters who have as much to say about why we're here as I do. I use the Xnet because I believe in freedom and the Constitution of the United States of America. I use Xnet because the DHS has turned my city into a police-state where we're all suspected terrorists. I use the Xnet because I think you can't defend freedom by tearing up the Bill of Rights…. The DHS does not govern with my consent [Doctorow 235].

Marcus' last words, and most of his message, are considered rebellious and treasonous by the DHS. Thus, the virtual world acts as a safe place in which Marcus can actively engage in public dissension of the DHS. Clockwork Plunder does not exist in physical reality, but Lance Gharavi, performance theorist, argues, "All video games, by being interactive, also have at least some degree of liveness to them" (355). Therefore, according to Gharavi, the interactions that take place in Clockwork Plunder are still considered live and real—that cause real life and real time consequences. Performance theorist Jon McKenzie suggests that interaction in a cyber world is a "hybrid performance in which human users perform 'real interactions' within continuous 'real time' and 'real space' (3-D) computer environments" (85). As such, the roles that Marcus plays while online, W1n5t0n and M1k3y, are indeed real and also adaptable.

Because many online games allow for performers to chat with one another, or leave one another messages, feedback is readily available which allows a performer to adjust his performance accordingly. Kurt Lindemann argues that cyberspace allows for people to "…utilize the computer screen as a new space for the narration of the 'desired self'" (359). Thus, cyberspace operates very similarly to Psychologist George Kelly's fixed role therapy.

George Kelly, known for research involving role play, believed people perceive and organize their world of experiences by formulating hypotheses about the environment and testing them against the reality of daily life. Although Kelly may have never envisioned virtual reality and cyberspace when creating his theories, his ideas are particularly applicable in the computer-driven world of today. Through social media and gaming, today's youth are able to formulate a hypothesis regarding an experience (real or not) and then test this hypothesis and learned knowledge to everyday life. Theories and research by Anderson, Appaduri, and Kelly make it possible to understand how the character of Marcus is able to successfully develop a strong sense of self and navigate a traumatic experience in *Little Brother*. Thus, Marcus can be used as a case study in order to understand identity performance and construction in the real life youth of today.

Performance, Paranoia and Identity Formation

The feeling of paranoia, basically the sensation of being watched, can be compared to what young adults often feel in regard to their own parents and their house rules. Indeed growing up with parental rules can be difficult, and youths often rebel against the desires of their parents, even though restrictions are meant to keep them safe. Much of the same sentiment can be applied to how citizens feel about their government. Governments are also established to ensure the safety and prosperity of their citizens, yet people often grumble about the amount of governmental control in their lives. It is common for many adolescents to rebel, because parents often establish rules that are either unfair, or simply unreasonable (much like governments). Adolescent psychologist David Elkind states:

> When I talk to parents about being adults to their children and about setting rules and limits with love and caring, some parents respond by saying, "It doesn't do any good, they do what they want anyway." On further exploration, I often find that these parents have set rules that they could not enforce and which their teenagers broke with impunity [244].

A similar sentiment can be applied to the relationship between the government and United States citizens. Marcus, pre-terrorist attack, frequently rebels against school administration rules, simply because to him they appear unnecessary, and are also unenforceable due to Marcus's hacker status. Lillian and Drew, Marcus's parents, appear to not create nor enforce any rules for Marcus until after the terrorist attack—and Marcus believes these rules are unacceptable and refuses to follow them as well.

Sharing a characteristic of many YA novels, Doctorow's *Little Brother* features relatively absent parents. Though Marcus' parents do indeed attempt to appear somewhat strict and controlling, post–terrorist attack, the life of Marcus appears to be virtually rule-free. Doctorow instead provides Marcus with a much larger and terrifying enemy to grapple with, the Department of Homeland Security—a real life authoritative and controlling force known for its use of high tech surveillance (that the youth of today do not often think of in a negative light). In a 2008 interview with the *Chicago Tribune,* Doctorow said, "The authoritarian agenda has been expanding. I tell kids that if you think you're going to graduate into being free adults when you finish school, you'd better think again. But I tell adults that what you're allowing to happen to your kids today is a test laboratory for what's being done to you" (Johnson). Indeed, Doctorow seeks to educate his readers, of all ages, about the amount of surveillance that exists in everyday life. As such, his decision to use the DHS as the dystopic controlling force in his novel serves as a lesson for both adolescents and parents.

Practical Considerations for the Composition Classroom

School can be considered another controlling force that is present in the lives of adolescents, and has been described as a dystopia. In the article "Living in a Real Teenage Dystopia: The Classroom," Isamu Fukui states, "We need not speculate what a dystopia might look like in the here and now. All we have to do is go back to school." Fukui's own high school was one in which a dictator-like principle monitored students through video surveillance, mind-boggling security measures, and restrictions on entering and exiting the school—very similar to Principle Benson in Doctorow's novel. Fukui suggests that high school stifled his independent spirit, rather than encouraged it, and fears that youth today will simply fall in line with preposterous rules, rather than resist and question them, and be incapable to stand up for their rights.

Although, as stated earlier, Doctorow's novel is fictional, it appears realistic due to the real world nature of the predicaments Marcus finds himself in, which result in overbearing and seemingly senseless restrictions as well as governmental-approved surveillance, which in turn spark virtual performances that are performative and instrumental in Marcus' identity formation.

YAL is often referred to as coming of age literature, literature that helps young people form a sense of identity. However, what YAL appears to do, as evident in *Little Brother*, is endorse the performance of multiple roles in order to allow characters to express personal power and control of their environments. Marcus plays many roles in Doctorow's novel: a student, a captive, a hacker, a freedom fighter, a LARPer, ad an ARGer. All of these roles make Marcus who he is, and they also enable him to successfully survive a traumatic experience.

It can be argued that educators are keenly aware of the dystopic nature of high school, but this same connection can be made in higher education—most specifically within a college composition classroom. Here, instructors teach their students how to write for academia. Students attempt to learn a skill, create an assignment, receive comments, revise, and then hope for the best. For many of them, the act is just a hoop to jump through or a general education course that has to be completed. More than likely, very few students are aware of the identity performance they enter into within their classroom community—submitting work for an imaginary community (as teachers typically ask students to write for a specific audience that then never reads their work).

Certainly, the conditions in a composition classroom are not as dire as they are for Marcus in *Little Brother*, yet the notion of performance is every bit as relevant. A close study of this text allows for many possible lessons that an instructor could design for their students: an analysis of role performance and a critical study of surveillance in their own life just touch the surface. What follows is an example unit that an instructor could follow in a composition classroom using *Little Brother* as a primary source (designed for a Monday, Wednesday, Friday, 55-minute course).

Unit 1—Voice, Identity and Setting

Monday—Start class with clip of Key and Peele "The Phone Call" which is an example of code switching. Have students come to board and write down how many codes they use in their day-to-day lives. After a brief discussion of this activity, break students into groups and inform them that Ted is Dead. Ted can die however the group wants him to die, but the group is charged with the responsibility of informing: his boss, his wife, his children, and the insurance company. The Ted exercise is a close study in tone and audience, and is typically fun. End class with students writing a five-minute reflection about how tone/audience impact their writing.

Wednesday—Begin class by asking students what codes they had used today, so far. Then distribute a two person play to students and break them into groups. The play should read as follows:

PERSON 1: Why did you do this?
PERSON 2: Because it had to be done.
PERSON 1: I am so freaking out.
PERSON 2: I knew you would, so I brought a candy bar.
PERSON 1: Right now? A candy bar?

It does not really matter what the script is, but it should be short. Give the students a setting or genre for each group (drama, mystery, action, romance, western) and then have the groups act them out. Not only is this a fun way to start class, but it allows for the community to grow within the classroom and also provides another rich discussion of performance—we perform a role to suit the setting. This point can then directly be applied to writing. Students need to be aware of how important setting, and how that setting affects the performance. Next, segue to *Little Brother* and ask the students if they have ever performed an identity to survive. Ask them to keep this in mind as they read the first half of the book by Friday. Allow time for a five-minute journal where students discuss what they learned or how their thoughts have changed.

Friday—Begin class discussion by asking students to talk about what Marcus looks like. Have they been given a physical description? Or do they know more about his character traits? Then ask students what Marcus's friends look like. They will be quick to discover that characters who are not white are given ethnic signifiers (author tells the reader the character is Korean or gives the character a stereotypical Mexican name). This will lead into a discussion of how identity, how we perform it and how people perceive it, affects most everything. Break students into small discussion groups giving them five questions to discuss. At the end of the small group discussion, elect one member from each group to be a spokesman for the group to answer the questions they were assigned (different questions for each group). Ask students to return to their seats and teach short lesson on what DHS and Homeland Security are—show clip of 9/11 and discuss things that came to pass after that (in law). In the last bit of class, during journal time, ask students to write about if they have ever felt watched—and if they had to behave differently because they were being watched. Tell students to finish the book for Monday.

Unit 2—MLA Format/Works Cited/Citations

Monday—Ask students to retrieve their journals and write for five minutes about the text—whatever they like. After this time, require students to go to the board and write their favorite quote from the book (with page number beside it). Small discussion should happen as a group. Move from discussion to quotes, and tell the students you are going to be working with the quotes on the board. Show them how to create the Works Cited citation for *Little Brother* using either the Purdue OWL or their text, then walk them through how in-text citations work. Require them to write a one-page response about the book, whatever they want to write, but they have to paraphrase one quotation from the board and then direct quote something from the board. Allow class time for work. Ask students to come on Wednesday ready to create a dystopia.

Wednesday—Walk through the quoting/citations from Monday—provide students with their work and comments. Show some fantastic work for the class to see. Then move to a dystopia creation. Each group must design a dystopia, and within this dystopia there are characters who are trying to "win." Make sure each group designs different personas for each character, allowing for role performance. Then, ask each group to create an imaginary profile for their characters, complete with a full day of status updates. Give the group time to work on this in class, and present for the last fifteen minutes of class. Tell students Friday you will introduce their first writing assignment.

Friday—Provide students with the writing assignment for the unit and the rubric. For this assignment, students will be able to choose from a variety of topics, using *Little Brother* as primary source.

LITTLE BROTHER ASSIGNMENT

In this unit of study, you have all become to think about identity, voice, setting, and role performance. You have had the opportunity to work closely with the story of Marcus Yallow, and consider how his dystopia is represented in your own lives. For this assignment, you will be using Little Brother as your primary source and writing a 4–6 word argumentative, MLA style, paper, worth 100 points, that addresses the following: performance and young adults, identity formation and created profiles, surveillance and human rights, and finally navigating virtual and physical communities through performance. If you would like to write about another topic discussed in class, that can reference the book, please speak with me and we will figure something out. Please adhere to the schedule below for due dates for this assignment:

- *Monday—1st memo (reflect on what you want to do in the paper) written in class*
- *Wednesday—Bring written argument to class—Argument Workshop (ethos, pathos, logos)*
- *Friday—Bring quotes to class that can be used as support in paper— small group work*
- *Monday—Bring rough draft to your scheduled conference*
- *Wednesday—Bring revised rough draft to your scheduled conference*
- *Friday—Peer Review bring second version of draft*
- *Monday –Formal version of paper is due to class—Write Reflective Memo about experience within this unit*

This is just one example of a unit of study that could be employed while using Doctorow's important piece. The book could also be used as a compare contrast piece where students discuss modern/classic dystopias (bring *1984* into the mix). Instructors could also require students to use this book as evidence of stereotyping, and how people perform identities to break these stereotypes. There are multitudes of lessons that could be thought that would not only improve student writing, but also provide fantastic discussions that will allow for personal reflection.

Conclusion

In this current cultural climate of heightened paranoia, young people are constructing their identities together—via Facebook and other imagined communities. And although this idea can at first appear frightening, according to the research of many theorists and scholars, it should not be. The more chances that the youth of today have to interact with different social groups (virtually or physically), the more opportunities they have to develop identities that assist in the successful navigation of difficult situations. Applying performance theory to YAL dystopian texts is especially important in this current era, which has been referred to as aggressively performative. Arguably, young adults have begun performing new roles by creating online identities in response to the current climate of war and terror. Dystopian YAL endorses this current performative trend, and has for decades. *Little Brother* features characters performing identities in a virtual environment, free from many of the societal rules and regulations that are present in dystopian fiction and present day, which provides real young adults with examples as to how they can also safely determine what roles best suit them. By using Marcus as a case study, it is possible to understand how performance in YAL empowers fictional characters as well as real people. The performative nature of dystopian YAL positively impacts young adults as well as the people who study them, and sheds a light on the behaviors and identities of the future governing generation which when used in a Composition classroom allows for student academic and personal growth.

WORKS CITED

Anderson, Benedict. *Imagined Communities*. London: Verso, 1983.
Appaduri, Arjun. *Modernity at Large: Cultural Dimensions of Globalization*. Minneapolis: University of Minnesota Press, 2003. Print.
Bell, Elizabeth. *Theories of Performance*. Thousand Oaks, CA: Sage, 2008.
Doctorow, Cory. *Little Brother*. New York: Tor Teen, 2008.
Elkind, David. *All Grown Up and No Place to Go*. Boston: Da Capo Press, 1998.
Fogg, BJ. "The New Rules of Persuasion." *RSA Journal*, vol. 155, 2009, pp. 24–29.
Fukui, Isamu. "Living in a Real Teenage Dystopia: The Classroom." *Tor/Forge's Blog*. www.

torforgeblog.com/2012/11/12/living-in-a-real-teenage-dystopia-the-classroom/. Accessed 13 Nov. 2012.

Johnson, Steve. "Hypertext." *Chicago Tribune.* http://featuresblogs.chicagotribune.com/technology_internetcritic/humor/. Accessed 23 Mar. 2013.

Marranca, Bonnie, and Guatum Dasguta. "Editorial: A New PAJ Platform." *PAJ: A Journal of Performance and Arts,* vol. 24, no. 1, 2002, pp. 1–4.

Schultz, Duanne, and Sydney Ellen Schultz. *Theories of Personality.* 8th ed. Washington, D.C.: Thomson, 2005.

Wannamaker, Annette, and Ian Wojicik-Andrews. "Introduction." *Children's Literature Association Quarterly,* vol. 35, no. 4, 2010, pp. 415–417. *Project Muse.*

Dreaming the Green Man

Toward a Pedagogy
of the Resonant Mythological

CHRISTI L. COOK *and*
LEEANN OLIVIER

> "You're only young once, they say, but doesn't it go on for a
> long time? More years than you can bear."
> —Hilary Mantel, *An Experiment in Love*

This epigraph at the beginning of Patrick Ness's young adult (YA) novel, *A Monster Calls*, eloquently sums up the pain of adolescence. Adults who look back upon these years with nostalgic yearning most likely have forgotten, or at least minimized, the struggles for power and feelings of marginalization inherent in the lives of most young adults. As 15-year-old protagonist Angela Chase states in the television series *My So-Called Life*, "My parents keep asking how school was. It's like saying, 'How was that drive-by shooting?' You don't care how it was; you're lucky to get out alive." This quote could be applied to the protagonists of many young adult novels, and it is certainly applicable to Conor, the 13-year-old hero of *A Monster Calls*. In dealing with a terminally ill mother, an absent father, school bullies, indifferent classmates, terrifying nightmares, and a literal *monster* that appears in his life, Conor's adolescence does indeed seem to go on for more years than he can bear. However, through the use of mythological archetypes and the power of storytelling, Ness supplies Conor with tools that he can use to work through his pain and begin to heal.

In this essay, we share both a theoretical framework behind and pragmatic teaching strategies for including resonant mythological and psychological archetypes as a driving force when teaching *A Monster Calls* by Patrick

Ness, one particular YA novel that exemplifies the *Entwicklungsroman* sub-genre. In *Disturbing the Universe*, Roberta Trites takes great care to define this subgenre of the bildungsroman, the classic coming-of-age tale. Trites asserts that the *Entwicklungsroman*, the novel of growth or development over a truncated period of time that does not culminate in the adolescent's enfranchisement into the adult world, would not have developed if adolescents did not possess a threatening power that adults felt the need to regulate. Power is one of the central motifs of *A Monster Calls*. Teaching this as the only YA novel in the Composition II (literary analysis) classroom has enabled us to utilize contemporary literature to introduce ancient mythology informed by a psychological perspective to college students in order to explore several issues of importance to the emerging adult, including matrices of power. Even though our essay will focus on our usage of *A Monster Calls* in particular, this approach of utilizing the resonant mythological in the contemporary college composition classroom can be applied to any number of texts. Our hope is that this essay will aid other college instructors in encouraging students to find archetypes that resonate with them in various young adult novels and to allow these archetypes to explode in students' own lives and writing—thus connecting the ancient to the contemporary and literature to students' lived experiences.

Conor, the protagonist of *A Monster Calls*, rails against several matrices of power throughout his journey which, like those typical in *Entwicklungsroman,* does not result in his enfranchisement at the end of the tale. He is a thirteen-year-old boy whose mother is dying of cancer. At the beginning of the novel, the yew tree outside of Conor's window transforms into a "monster." When Conor asks the monster/tree who he is, he replies: "*I have had as many names as there are years to time itself! … I am Herne the Hunter! I am Cernunnos! I am the eternal Green Man!*" (emphasis in original) (Ness 34). The monster then informs Conor that he will tell the boy three stories, and in return, the monster expects to hear Conor's story—Conor's "truth." This mythic Celtic "Green Man" figure is central to some of the novel's themes, as we will explore further below. As students research, discuss, and connect the "Green Man" archetype to popular culture artifacts through activities we will detail in this essay, they discover a deity who embodies nature itself.

As Conor listens to each of the monster's stories and eventually tells his own nebulous tale, he learns to accept his mother's death and begins to heal his own damaged psyche. Pedagogically, dreams are a driving force that is compelling to students. Conor's final truth involves the revelation of a recurring nightmare, and the appearances of the monster himself may be more dream than reality. Because mythological and psychological archetypes are so closely interwoven in readers' collective and individual psyches, in this essay, we detail our use of psychological criticism (both Freud's interpretation of dreams and Jung's archetypes) to explore the psychic terrain of the novel. Highlighting this terrain are Jim Kay's striking black-and-white illustrations, which present a contrast to the thematic gray area that permeates the novel. The illustrations give visual learners the opportunity to explore the power of images. This method of storytelling appeals to visual learners and gives art instructors an opportunity to discuss Kay's techniques and the effect of his graphics on readers. These illustrations also provide a concrete connection to the nonexistent "black-and-white" world for which Conor longs. The monster's moral ambiguity and the nebulous nature of the tales the monster tells trouble Conor. The illustrations, then, serve as a contrast to this gray area. And even though Conor is displeased by this new gray, adult world in which he finds himself, he himself is a morally ambiguous character. His acts of destruction in his grandmother's house and his extreme violence against his oppressor, Harry, reveal that Conor himself has a dark side. Giving students a writing prompt that asks them to analyze the theme of moral ambiguity that pervades the novel and juxtapose it with the black-and-white illustrations provides opportunity for analysis of visual rhetoric.

In addition to delving into ancient myth and visual rhetoric when analyzing *A Monster Calls*, students also explore the stages of the grieving process and the cathartic power of storytelling—two areas that are of significance to college-age students. Many students are able to enter the narrative based upon their own personal experiences such as having lost a family member due to illness, having a family member who is currently ill, or having an absentee parent. We have found that a majority of students will connect to the novel on an emotional level due to the ubiquity of these scenarios in their lives. As students read about Conor moving through Kubler-Ross's five stages of grief: denial, anger, bargaining, depression, and acceptance, but spending the majority of his time in denial and anger, students tend either to feel tremendous sympathy and empathy for Conor or to be irritated with his immaturity. Regardless of their approval or disapproval of Conor, students are intrigued by the character, and most find themselves captivated by the YA novel.

The significance of psychology in this novel is paramount. Campbell saw myths as operating on four levels simultaneously: (1) Cosmological; (2) Metaphysical (the spiritual dimension); (3) Sociological; and (4) Psychological (Dunn). In order to delve deeper into the psychological aspects of the novel, students need to be acquainted at least briefly with Freud and Jung. We teach students about psychological criticism, focusing particularly on the key Freudian terms of projection, denial, and repression along with the Jungian archetype of the double. Due to Conor's repression and denial of his sadness and anger surrounding his mother's illness, he projects his difficult to handle emotions onto those around him, perhaps ultimately culminating in the psychic creation of the Monster. This, of course, is but one interpretation; there is ambiguity about how to interpret the monster. A primary purpose of the novel is dream interpretation: What do Conor's "dreams"/ the monster's tales mean? A successful related assignment is a dream prompt: Students can freewrite about a particularly vivid dream they recall. Having discussed common dream motifs and possible interpretations, they share in pairs and then with the class their dreams and possible significance. The power of Conor's dreams is often paralleled by these student conversations.

Asking students to identify, research, and write about archetypes in *A Monster Calls* further facilitates this search for meaning. Carl Jung defined archetypes as inborn tendencies or symbols that shape human behavior (Hall 10). Expounding upon Jung's definition, myth scholar Joseph Campbell further explained that archetypes are experienced on a visceral rather than an intellectual level (Campbell 51). Thus, students are able to make a deep connection with archetypes present in the literature that they read. For example, in *The Hero with a Thousand Faces*, Campbell argues that all stories—whether ancient, contemporary, literary, or cinematic—are indeed one story, that of the hero's journey. He refers to this singular story as the monomyth. Teaching *A Monster Calls* allows us to introduce the concept of the monomyth to students. By entering the dream-like world of the monster and playing an active role in the otherworldly realm of the monster's stories, Conor crosses a threshold between the "real" world and the magical one. This likens him to a shaman, a mystical tribal figure who is able to transcend the barrier between two worlds and eventually, after many tests and trials, become master of them both.

Just like ancient multicultural mythic heroes such as Coyote, Odysseus, Beowulf, and Gilgamesh, Conor begins his journey toward maturity with a call to adventure. In this case, it is a literal "call," one issued by the titular "monster." In this stage of the hero's journey, an outside force arrives to shake up the situation, to awaken the hero from a period of complacency or slumber. Once again, this awakening is quite literal as the monster arrives in Conor's bedroom "just after midnight. As they do" (Ness 1). And just like many reluctant heroes, Conor at first refuses the monster's call to adventure. He has no interest in hearing the monster's stories, nor in telling his own. Just as the hero always meets with a mentor, the monster comes to serve as Conor's mentor, finally imparting the power of storytelling to Conor, especially the power of telling one's own truth. After reluctantly accepting the monster's call, Conor enters the hero's phase of enduring tests, forming allies, and confronting enemies. His father's passivity toward him and the bullies who taunt him at school continually test him, but he finds an ally in his childhood friend, Lily. Although Conor does not literally die and experience a rebirth, the nightmare that he finally reveals to the monster and to the reader involves letting go of his mother (both literally and figuratively). The boy who is dependent upon his mother must die in order for an independent young man to emerge. After his journey into the monster's world is over, the reader is left hoping that the "elixir" Conor brings back to his own world will enable him to heal and to grow.

Using Conor as a mythic model, we encourage students to explore the stages of Campbell's heroic journey in their own lives. As an in-class or informal homework assignment, we ask them to write about their own calls to adventure, mentors, tests, triumphs, and rebirths. A majority of our student population is composed of first-generation college students, and many of them cite the desire for higher education as their own personal call to adventure. Many of them rightfully see themselves in the midst of this hero's journey.

The monster who serves as both a call to adventure and a mentor to Conor appears in the form of a giant yew tree, and Ness emphasizes this detail several times throughout the story. For example, even though Conor does not tell his mother about the monster's manifestation in his life, she often gazes out of the kitchen window, reminding Conor, "There's that old yew tree" (Ness 17). Although Conor initially sees the monster as an added nuisance in his life and does not ponder its symbolic significance, it seems to the reader as if his mother has some connection to the tree and knowledge of its power. Toward the end of the novel, the doctors make one last attempt to heal Conor's mother by using a drug derived from a yew tree. This detail is scientifically sound because the drug paclitaxin, which is extracted from the yew tree, is used in modern chemotherapy, particularly in the treatment of breast, ovarian, and lung cancers (Roberts).

According to Tony Roberts, Professor of Philosophy and Religion at Tarrant County College, yew trees are often found in graveyards in England because they have the power to extract toxins from the earth. Roberts created a presentation, shaped by his knowledge of *The Golden Bough*, that helped students understand the religious, cultural, and scientific significance of trees in general and of the yew tree in particular. "The yew is a healing tree," the monster tells Conor. "It is the form I choose most to walk in" (Ness 136). Conor then believes that the whole purpose of the monster's intrusion into his life is to heal his mother. However, the monster emphasizes that he will only be able to heal Conor's mother "if she can be healed" (Ness 137). As Conor and the readers learn over and over in this novel, nature is ambiguous; it has the power to heal or to destroy, but lacks both compassion and malice. Indeed, the tree has come walking to heal, not Conor's mother, but Conor himself. This novel serves up archetypes with a twist. In the monster's tales, the evil witch ends up not being wholly evil; the good, victimized prince ends up taking the life of an innocent victim; and the "evil" apothecary and "good" parson inflict both good and bad on their community. Dualities are not permitted to stand in this novel, while ambiguity is held up above all else. Ness serves readers the Jungian archetype of the double, but with a twist.

Perhaps in part because the reader never finds out if the monster is "real" or "imaginary," his function in the story is largely open to interpretation. This lack of clarity allows students the opportunity to understand the monster's purpose in various ways. Is he an alter ego allowing Conor to act out his anger and frustration in ways that are socially unacceptable for a human boy, providing him with a much-needed voice and outlet? Does he serve as a replacement for Conor's absent father, sternly forcing Conor to face the truth but ultimately supporting him in his acceptance of his mother's death? Or is his function in the novel even larger—connecting Conor not only to the truth he must face in his own life but to universal truths about nature itself? Because Conor's life has no center with no connection to his father and an inability to hold on to his mother, he is existentially adrift, having neither center nor periphery. What better guide for him, then, than a yew tree—the universal center itself (Roberts)? Ness juxtaposes magical chapters in which the monster appears and tells his stories to Conor with realistic scenes that show Conor's struggles with school and home life. This structure forces students to ponder the symbolic nature of monsters in literature. Even though they are not "real," what real situations or emotions might they represent? Encouraging students to discuss and write about what they personally think the monster symbolizes while providing textual evidence for their disparate viewpoints offers an excellent opportunity for persuasive rhetoric and critical thinking.

In addition to drawing scientific and philosophical connections to the novel, students can make cinematic ones as well. Patrick Ness has adapted his novel into a screenplay for a feature film directed by J.A. Bayona (December 2016). Other films also serve as fitting points of comparison to Ness's novel, such as Guillermo del Toro's *Pan's Labyrinth* and Behn Zeitlin's *Beasts of the Southern Wild*. Both of these films feature young protagonists whose sole caregiver is terminally ill along with mystical creatures who invite them to travel on their own shamanic journeys between worlds. Instructors who teach either English or film theory classes could assign essays prompting students to write about the connections between *A Monster Calls* and the films we have mentioned.

As we discussed earlier in this essay, the monster's assertion that he himself is the "eternal Green Man" also provides a framework by which students can begin to identify, research, and investigate mythic archetypes (Ness 34). According to Luke Mastin in "The Enigma of the Green Man," the Green Man archetype appears in some variant in many cultures throughout the world. Most often found carved in wood or stone in medieval European churches and cathedrals, this figure is essentially a face or head sprouting, surrounded by, or even entirely made from leaves and foliage. When students learn that he often represents fertility, rebirth, and the cycle of growth each spring, his presence in *A Monster Calls* becomes clearer. He is there to help facilitate Conor's own rebirth after his acceptance of his mother's death.

As a manifestation of this Green Man archetype, the yew in particular has become a symbol of life, longevity, death, and resurrection—connecting the upper and lower realms (Roberts). This *axis mundi* symbol provides students with an entryway into exploring the significance of the yew tree in Celtic folklore, which in turn helps students connect this contemporary work to older works of British literature. We have assigned older Celtic texts that feature the yew tree or Green Man archetype to read alongside *A Monster Calls* and have asked students to draw comparisons. In the tragic Irish folktale "Deirdre of the Sorrows," for example, the love between protagonists Deirdre and Naoise is only able to thrive after their deaths; as large yew trees grow over their graves, their branches reaching toward each other and twisting upward into a single spire. And in a gesture similar to the one that opens *A Monster Calls*, a monstrous creature arrives at King Arthur's court to issue a call to adventure to knight Gawain near the beginning of the epic medieval British poem *Sir Gawain and the Green Knight*. Scholars believe this figure was also a representation of the eternal Green Man, harkening back to the pagan traditions of the British Isles (*Sir Gawain*). Even though the knight (like the monster in Ness's novel) is intimidating and at first unwelcome, he is actually there to teach Gawain a lesson about Gawain's own character, to help him discover the strength that already lies within him and to set him on the path toward his own shamanic journey.

Because of this ancient symbol's re-emergence in contemporary culture, it serves to show students the connection between mythic archetypes and modern concerns. In her article in the *Jung Society of Washington* journal, for example, Janet Kane shows the connection between the Green Man archetype and our current ecological crisis. Because of our destruction of the ecosystem, we as a culture have cut ourselves off from nature. Honoring the Green Man archetype, however, helps us to re-establish our lost bond with the natural world (Kane). Exploration of this ecological resonance can lead to assignments as varied as having students journal or freewrite about spaces in nature that they find sacred or creating research projects investigating the causes and impacts of climate change.

Practical Considerations for the Composition Classroom

We have found this novel is an ideal choice to assign as part of a campus-wide interdisciplinary program because it provides rich opportunities for students to see connections between their English composition class and other classes they are taking, such as Religion, Philosophy, Psychology, Biology, Art, and Film Studies. We assign students a cumulative research project that enables them to connect to a personal truth by picking a theme or subtheme from *A Monster Calls* that resonates with them and exploring that theme in the "Finding Patterns" project featured below. Students find that same theme or pattern represented in another literary text, film, work of visual art, and a song of their own choosing, thus encountering meaning within their current world and connections between literature and life. Pop culture becomes a common language through which students can explore the ancient. We have found the rich mythological resonances in *A Monster Calls* to extend far beyond the classroom as students create original work that often astounds us with its impact.

Finding Patterns

Research and Multimedia Project Instructions
   for English 1302

We read literature for many reasons, but perhaps among the most important is to find patterns and make a connection between what we're reading and our own lives. The purpose of this project is to extend the idea of making meaningful connections to several different genres we interact with in our daily lives.

First, select specific theme or issue from that *A Monster Calls*. Think critically about your theme; don't pick anything too superficial or simplistic. Then:

- find a work of visual art that relates to the theme or issue.
- find another piece of literature either *not* from the syllabus or from a different section of the syllabus (poem, short story, novel, etc.) that contains the same theme or issue.
- find a song that relates to the theme or issue.
- find a movie that presents this theme or issue [but not an adaptation of the original reading].

1. Paper Component:

Write a 3–4 page essay that explains the connections you have found among these works. The essay must contain the following components:

- an introduction that discusses the reading and the theme or issue you chose and explains why you chose this particular theme or issue. Why does the issue matter? To whom does it matter?
- a body paragraph that explains the work of art and its connection to the theme or issue/ primary work

- a body paragraph that explains the other piece of literature and its connection to the theme or issue/ primary work
- a body paragraph that explains the song and its connection to the theme or issue/ primary work
- a body paragraph that explains the movie and its connection to the theme or issue/primary work
- a conclusion that ties these connections together and explains their significance to the reader, synthesizing the sources
- it must be written in MLA format using Times New Roman 12 pt. font
- it must have a Works Cited page with five sources: reading from course schedule, work of art, other piece of literature, song, and movie

2. *Presentation component:*

You will present the connections you have made orally to the class in the form of a PowerPoint, webpage, video essay, or blog. There must be a visual representation of each individual source in the presentation (i.e., still photos or short clips from your movie, a brief sound recording of your song or a section of lyrics, etc.) Be creative! The sky's the limit!

The presentation will include the following components:

- You must email me your PowerPoint or video essay before class begins on the day you will present. If you create a webpage or blog, you must email me the address before class on the day you will present.
- Your oral presentation must be 5–7 minutes long.
- You will lose points on this project if you do not attend class on the days you are not presenting. You are expected to take good notes over each presentation; these will be taken up as a participation grade.
- If you are not on time and prepared the day you are scheduled to present, there will be no make-up dates under any circumstances. This presentation serves as your final exam for this class.

(Prompt and Rubric written by Author 9a and Lucinda Channon)

We have observed the "Finding Patterns" project to be one students are able to connect with meaningfully and on a personal level since they have the freedom to select a theme that resonates with them and then choose from genres prevalent in their daily lives, like music and movies, to illustrate their chosen themes. We encourage students not to feel limited by selecting the main theme or themes from the novel but rather to choose any theme or sub-theme that appeals to them. Students tend to participate enthusiastically and often to create unique and profoundly moving visual components for their presentations. Although they sometimes struggle toward the beginning of the process since this is an atypical essay prompt, we have found that the end product definitely justifies any challenges along the way.

Finding Patterns Rubric

Name: _____ Portfolio/Presentation submitted on time _____ Portfolio complete _____

The chart below reflects my evaluation of your portfolio as "Excellent," "Satisfactory-Plus," "Satisfactory," or "Unsatisfactory" on each criterion. Portfolios that satisfy the criteria earn a C. To earn a B, the portfolio must score overall a Satisfactory-Plus—you must go beyond fulfilling the criteria. To earn an A, the portfolio must be rated Excellent in most of the criteria. The criteria are listed in order of importance.

Excellent, Satisfactory-Plus, Satisfactory, Unsatisfactory.

FINDING PATTERNS ESSAY–10%

- Identifies the issue and explains the rhetorical situation.
- Describes at least four different media and connects to the issue and to a primary text, supporting each perspective with substantial evidence that demonstrates critical thinking.
- Explains your interest in the issue and makes a claim that states your position.
- Integrates sources properly and explains their significance. Paraphrases properly by communicating the authors' ideas without using their vocabulary or sentence structures.
- Synthesizes theme/primary work throughout paper
- Material is coherent and well-organized.
- Sentences are complete, clear, and relatively error free.

Formatting meets assignment guidelines: MLA Format (including a Works Cited page), 3–4 pages, typed, double spaced, 12 point Times New Roman font, with 1 inch margins on all sides.

Portfolio Grade: _____
Excellent, Satisfactory-Plus, Satisfactory, Unsatisfactory.

FINDING PATTERNS PRESENTATION—10%

- Presentation is well-prepared and organized.
- Presenter makes eye contact, speaks clearly, and is engaged with the audience.
- Presenter is ready to present on time and then stays within time limits (5–7 minutes).

- Presenter fields questions effectively.
- When not presenting, student pays attention, takes notes and asks thoughtful questions of peers' presentations.

FINDING PATTERNS VISUAL AID—5%

- PowerPoint, webpage, video essay, or blog is emailed to instructor before presentation
- Visual aid is well made (not text-heavy, visually appealing, interesting, organized, etc.)
- Visual aid is incorporated into presentation effectively.

Presentation Grade: _____
Visual Aid Grade: _____
Overall Grade: _____

Additional Comments: In addition to the "Finding Patterns" project, *A Monster Calls* offers numerous opportunities for reflective, creative, and scholarly writing. Below we have included several writing prompts that could work in a variety of college classroom situations:

Essay Prompts

- Revisit the novel, paying close attention to Jim Kay's illustrations. Describe the mood/imagery of the illustrations. How do you think they enhance the story?
- Conor is troubled by the monster's moral ambiguity as well the ambiguous nature of the tales that the monster tells. He wants the monster to present a more "black-and-white" world to him (perhaps like the world of the illustrations?). However, Conor himself is morally ambiguous and is neither "all good" nor "all bad." Discuss this theme of uncertainty that pervades the novel.

Before they begin the novel, have students answer the following questions (verbally or in writing—you could even use this as an essay prompt): What is your definition of monstrosity? What does it mean to *be* or to *have* a monster? What do monsters symbolize in literature and film? Then after they have read the novel, ask them to discuss and/or write about the following questions: What kind of monster is the monster in *A Monster Calls*, and what function does he serve? Does he fit your original description of what a "monster" is or should be?

Research Project Prompts

- Research the various stages of grief as described by psychologist Elisabeth Kubler-Ross, and explain how Conor navigates these stages.

- Based upon our readings about Jung's concept of the "double" as well as our research into modern psychological disorders, what condition(s) might Conor be suffering from? Pay attention in particular to the scene in which Conor confronts and then beats Harry. Explain/elaborate upon your "diagnosis."
- Explain how Conor navigates several (or all) of the stages of the monomythic "hero's journey" as introduced by Joseph Campbell in *The Hero With a Thousand Faces*.
- Research the various mythic allusions the monster cites in answer to the question "Who are you?" He mentions the Green Man, Cernunnos, Herne the Hunter, and later alludes to the Uroboros. Discuss the importance of myth and folklore to the monster's stories in the novel and to the function of literature as a whole. (Prompt created by Curtis Fukuchi, Professor of English at Tarrant County College Northwest Campus)
- Conduct some research on the healing power of the yew tree. How has it been used in ancient as well as contemporary medicine?
- Write an analysis comparing *A Monster Calls* to either *Pan's Labyrinth*, directed by Guillermo del Toro or *Beasts of the Southern Wild*, directed by Behn Zeitlin.

How does *A Monster Calls* serve as a meditation on the importance of nature? How does this topic resonate with you personally? Include some findings on the causes and impact of climate change.

Creative Writing, Journaling and Discussion Prompts

- Freewrite about a particularly vivid dream that you recall. Share your dream with another student and discuss possible interpretations and significance.
- Discuss a hero's journey that you have experienced in your life. What was your call to adventure, for example, and how did you navigate one, a few, or even all of the stages of the journey?
- Freewrite about a space in nature that you find sacred. Describe your space in detail, using concrete language that appeals to the five senses. Include a subjective description that captures the essence of the place and what it means to you on a personal or spiritual level.
- Write a narrative about Conor several years in the future. For example, "It's been years since Conor has seen the monster in the shape of a yew tree, but every night at 12:07, he still looks out his bedroom window, hoping to see its lumbering form. When his mother died, he didn't lose only her; he also lost the tentative friend he had in the monster. One day in his university mythology class, Conor's professor gives a lecture on the Green Man, and Conor,

wanting one last conversation with the monster, attempts to summon him walking…"

Conclusion

Whether they view this novel through a personal, mythic, or ecological lens, college students are able to find a connection to Conor and his heroic journey. Drawing upon their own experiences with dream interpretation and/or the grieving process allows them to apply central motifs of *A Monster Calls* to their own lives and enriches their analysis of the novel. Exploring Jungian archetypes such as the monomythic story pattern, the Green Man figure, and the yew tree broadens students' understanding of Ness' narrative and allows them to connect Conor's journey (and indeed, their own personal journeys) to more timeless, universal themes. Finally, tying the mythic and psychological archetypes in the novel to immediate concerns for the environment shows students the ability of literature to have an impact, not only on their own lives, but also on the future of their world.

Works Cited

Campbell, Joseph. *The Hero with a Thousand Faces*. Novato, CA: New World Library, 2008.
Campbell, Joseph. *The Power of Myth with Bill Moyers*. Ed. Betty Sue Flowers. New York: Doubleday, 1988.
Dunn, Joseph R. "Mythology in Psychotherapy." *Psych Journal*, vol. 3, no. 2, 2002.
Hall, James A., M.D. *Jungian Dream Interpretation: A Handbook of Theory and Practice*. Ontario: Inner City Books, 1983.
hooks, bell. *Feminist Theory: From Margin to Center*. London: Pluto Press, 2000.
Kane, Janet. "Re-awakening the Green Man." *Jung Society of Washington*, pp. 181–82.
Mantel, Hilary. *An Experiment in Love*. London: Picador, 1995.
Mastin, Luke. *The Enigma of the Green Man*, 2011, www.greenmanenigma.com. Accessed 30 October 2014.
Morris, Tim. *You're Only Young Twice: Children's Literature and Film*. Urbana: University of Illinois Press, 2000.
Ness, Patrick. *A Monster Calls*. Somerville, MA: Candlewick Press, 2011.
Roberts, Tony. "*A Monster Calls* Presentation." Tarrant County College, Fort Worth. March 2013. Lecture.
Sir Gawain and the Green Knight: The Literary Masterpiece Behind the Legend, Arts Magic Ltd., 2008.
Trites, Roberta. *Disturbing the Universe: Power and Repression in Adolescent Literature*. Iowa City: University of Iowa Press, 2000.
Younger, Beth. *Learning Curves: Body Image and Female Sexuality in Young Adult Literature*. Lanham, MD: Scarecrow Press, 2009.

Reading Young Adult Dystopian Fiction in the Indian Classroom

PADMA BALIGA *and*
NAMRATA HARISH

In India, "a country of continental diversity, especially in its linguistic landscape" (Amritavalli 21), English composition classes need to be structured carefully, as English is a second language to most students. Of 230 million children enrolled in school, 20 million children study English from the first grade (Mukherji). Most school students learn an Indian language such as Tamil, Kannada, Bengali, or Hindi from the first grade, with English being introduced as a second language from sixth grade. They study subjects such as mathematics, science and social studies not in English, but in their mother tongue. To such students, English is an unfamiliar language which has no place in their everyday world, but is associated with classrooms and examinations. In many schools, the language is taught using outdated, exam-oriented methods of teaching that emphasize rote learning and memorization. The curriculum includes a mix of poems, short stories, essays, and extracts from plays, and the examination system requires the student to answer questions on these texts based on content recall. The student's acquisition and mastery of the language is shaped by environmental exposure (which can be limited) and outdated pedagogy. Upon finishing school, most move on to do a three-year college course in the pure sciences, social sciences, or commerce and accountancy, before taking up a job. Along with their core subjects, they are also required to study English and another language of their choice for a period of two years. We find that, once they enter college, students have to unlearn the notions that language can be acquired by memorizing set answers to set questions, or by writing essays on set topics, and instead, other pedagogical approaches must be applied.

To help students learn to use the language comfortably and profitably and become critical thinkers at the college where we teach, we emphasize a pedagogy that focuses on reading and writing. Since English classes are not optional, but mandated, students are often reluctant to read or write. When compelled, they use a variety of shortcuts such as reading plot summaries, and copying and pasting their assignments from the Internet. Also, since some struggle with the English language, the idea of reading canonical texts with their archaic vocabulary and formal sentence structures seems formidable to the average student. We have found that using a mix of graphic novels, film texts, and young adult literature (YAL) leads to better and more eager responses. Students generally prefer texts that use linguistic registers closer to the ones they use, are populated with characters closer to them in age and ways of thinking, and depict situations with which they can connect. When reading such texts, the students learn skills of comprehension, analysis and argumentation through a writing program that does not make use of disparate writing exercises, but demonstrates the act of writing in specific contexts.

In this essay, we plan to explore the ways in which Indian college students relate to American YAL, especially dystopian fiction, through an analysis of students' responses to YA dystopian themes. YAL is a recent entrant in Indian literature and not many YA novels by Indian authors are available in India. Poulomi Chatterjee, managing editor of Hachette India, says, "Fiction until a few years ago, was restricted to 'literary' fiction…. But more people are reading home-grown popular fiction now—younger generations that would not have read fiction perhaps" (Pal). Much of the Indian YAL belongs to the genre of romance, and dystopian themes are not favored by writers of Indian YAL in their work. However, the bleak narratives of American YAL such as *The Hunger Games* and the *Twilight* series are popular among Indian youth. YA dystopian fiction uses tropes of an authoritarian world, exemplifies the blurring between the self and the technological Other, and envisions a time when there is no difference between human and android. In Lois Lowry's *The Giver*, the citizens are brought up to feel no emotions, to be extremely precise in their language, and to aim for sameness rather than individuality. What does the freshman college student, who has newly graduated from a fairly rigid school system, think of such societies? Reading such texts provides opportunities for the college student to read dominant texts critically and analyze them for their implicit ideologies. This can be achieved when the students can see their contemporary political situations mirrored in the dystopian futures of YAL.

A Government of India study, the National Employability Report-

Graduates 2013, which surveyed 60,000 college students in the final year of their undergraduate course states that "a significant proportion of graduates, nearly 47 percent, were found not employable in any sector, given their English language and cognitive skills" (qtd. in British Council 2). The Planning Commission's (Government of India) Approach Paper to 12th Plan underscores the importance of acquiring fluency in English stating, "Special emphasis on verbal and written communication skills, especially in English would go a long way in improving the employability of the large and growing mass of disempowered youth" (106). We need to move away from an examination-oriented "one size fits all" pedagogy that does not encourage independent thought or writing, and instead, require students to engage with texts in ways that will render the classroom experience meaningful to their everyday lives.

Against this background, we see that text selection for the Indian classroom can be a contentious issue, especially keeping in mind a right-wing political scenario, the national education policy, the debate around higher education, and the pressure to offer courses that make the student "job-ready." There is also an inherent bias working in favor of tried and tested classics, texts that stand for (in some inexplicable manner) "good writing," and texts that don't raise uncomfortable questions. However, a book like *Mockingbird* by Walter Tevis, set in a dystopian world in which people do not read or write nor aspire to do so, is a reminder to the teaching community that disseminating the ability to read, and through that, to think critically, never ceases in importance. Students respond better when a text resonates with them, when it does not appear disjointed, disjunctive, or disparate from their lives. If the text is about issues that matter to them, about characters they can relate to, characters who speak, dress, play, think, and move like they do, their emotions come into play; their thought processes are quickened, and they find it easier and desirable to respond critically. Rather than present the text as a means to improve one's vocabulary or to learn about sentence structures, by enabling the student to respond to the text, it can become a means of engaging with the world. In order to think critically, a student draws upon existing knowledge and understanding of the matter at hand. A carefully thought-out reading and writing program for eighteen and nineteen-year-olds should make use of YAL as part of a constantly expanding selection of texts.

In her article, "Teaching Writing through Literature: Toward the Acquisition of a Knowledge Base," Roseanna M. Mueller asks, "If we concede that critical thinking skills are based on both knowledge and experience, what knowledge and what experience does the average freshman bring with him to the college?" We believe that American dystopian fiction with its themes of rebellion, its tropes of totalitarian societies, authoritarian lawmakers, constant surveillance and policing, and absence of community is the answer. Dystopian fiction serves to underline many of the fears young people have for themselves and their future. Faced with a barrage of laws, many of which they either do not know or do not understand, a distancing between the self and the community, and an increasing sense of alienation from the corporatization of education and society, young readers look to dystopian novels to express their fears. Students who struggle with steadily rising college costs and an inflationary economy are able to apply the oppressive scenario of the dystopian novels to their lives.

Literature Review

In her article, "The Appeal of Young Adult Literature in Late Adolescence: College Freshmen Read YAL," Gail Zdilla attempts to redefine the traditional readers of YAL demographic. According to Zdilla, adolescence now stretches into the early 20s: "Our cultural conception of adolescence has redefined this period of life. Continued dependence on parents in order to meet their needs marks many 20-somethings as not quite ready for the demands and responsibilities of adulthood" (191). Zdilla's contention is that contemporary YA fiction pushes the envelope in terms of sexual content and other "more mature and emotionally difficult issues" (192). She also writes that finding similarities between themselves and the characters they were reading about was a huge motivation for young readers to choose YA books.

In their book titled, *From Hinton to Hamlet: Building Bridges between Young Adult Literature and the Classics*, Herz and Gallo advise teachers to give thought to their students' choices in YAL. They see the genre not as a replacement of the classics, but as a bridge to the curriculum. Herz and Gallo explain,

> To engage today's students in reading, we need to consider quality adolescent literature as a means to meet the needs of those individuals in our English classes who are not reading—especially students of average or high ability who choose not to read, and students who have not developed any interest in reading literature since they were in middle school [12].

They pinpoint a serious problem in education: the inability of the texts in the curriculum to hold the interest of the students. In an in-depth examination of reading habits and tastes, Herz and Gallo arrive at the conclusion that nearly half the junior and senior high school children in USA do not like the texts they have to engage with in English classrooms. Most of the respondents considered pieces of classic literature that they read for their classes to only be mandatory work, and could only memorize details and themes and not relate to the characters or the situations they faced (16).

In tracing their students' stages of literary appreciation, Herz and Gallo write, "The first step involves helping them to become readers, to enjoy the act of reading, and to realize that reading is experiential. Through their reading experiences they can begin to understand the nature of human relationships; they can begin to conjecture and to explore some answers about their primary question—Who am I?" (19). Three vital points are made here. First, that reading is experiential. Next, the students have to come to the books themselves, either through word-of-mouth, social media, or even watching the film adaptations first. Finally, understanding the nature of human relationships is complex and is tied up with questions of identity. Alvermann, Moon and Hagood claim that for students "to be literate in today's highly complex and technologically advanced society, it is important to read the signs of our times with a critical awareness that is equally applicable to school-sanctioned texts and those of contemporary culture" (10). They argue that ideas of what construes a text have to change because students are constantly reading the world around them for what it says about themselves, and therefore, approaching their "school-sanctioned texts" very differently from what pedagogues of earlier generations might have envisioned.

Alvermann, Moon and Hagood, while initially concerned about breaking the barrier between the formal space of a classroom and the informal space of popular culture, seen as an "individual pleasure," are eventually led to questions of which examples of popular culture are "actually admissible in the classroom? How do we determine which of the many forms and examples of popular culture are appropriate for exploration?" (22). There cannot be a tailor-made answer to this question. Differences in the teacher's and students' contexts and difficulty in understanding each other's perceptions of popular culture create hurdles to interpreting texts in the classroom. The approach that the three writers finally agree on is one of balance:

> Grounded in feminism, postmodernism and cultural studies, this aggregate approach attempts to address the issues of analysis, pleasure, positioning and audience so that a balance is created in the classroom. Teachers acknowledge several crucial points: the expertise that students bring to the learning environment, the pleasures that popular culture produce for students, and the multiple readings that students produce from popular culture [27].

An approach such as the one mentioned above ensures that students feel comfortable with the text, approach it with confidence, and embark on their writing tasks with enthusiasm. Students are more likely to read a text, reflect upon it, and write about it if it concerns an issue that interests them. If the college teacher can travel to where the student is and orient the teaching process to the students' language levels, she is more likely to get the student interested in reading and writing.

Thematic Exploration of Young Adult Literature in the St. Joseph's English Classroom

Teachers of undergraduate English classes in St. Joseph's College, Bangalore, India, have been using dystopian YAL as texts in both compulsory and recommended reading lists for the last three years. Below is a list of some of the recommended texts with a brief description of themes and issues discussed by the teachers and students in class over the years 2012–2015.

Selections from	Themes explored
The Hunger Games by Suzanne Collins	Significance of the female protagonist, class divisions, oppressive state apparatuses, leadership
Divergent by Veronica Roth	Factionism, identity formation, oppressive state apparatuses, ideology
Maze Runner by James Dashner	Survival, teamwork, leadership, oppressive state apparatuses
The Giver by Lois Lowry	Leadership, identity formation, sacrifice, mentorship
The Host by Stephanie Meyer	Identity formation, belongingness, body image, questions of the soul and spirituality

The most popular YA dystopia among the students at St. Joseph's College, Bangalore, is *The Hunger Games* trilogy, finding fans from both genders. Many of our students are from the Northeastern states of India, which are ethnically very different from the rest of India. They travel over 2000 miles to come to Bangalore to earn a college degree. Reading dystopian fiction for them is one way of coming to terms with the geographical, linguistic, cultural, and gastronomic displacements they undergo. The themes of loss of control over one's choices and human rights violations in these YA dystopias significantly resonate with the migrant as well as local students.

Choosing *The Hunger Games*, the first book in the trilogy, as a benchmark text, we asked 300 undergraduate students, ages 17–20, in St. Joseph's College English classes, to respond to the text in terms of the themes they observed. Their responses can be broadly categorized in three areas: relatability to the protagonist, problems of authority and control, and dystopian future versus real world contexts.

Relatability to the Protagonist

Almost 90 percent of the female student respondents saw Katniss not only as a leader or someone to follow, but as a young woman whose protectiveness over her sister Prim and emotional response to younger peer Rue's death gives her more credibility. One first-year student said, "The love that Katniss displayed for Prim throughout makes her a very strong character. That is an important quality for a leader." Another student admired her qualities: "Katniss valued human life over everything else; that may have made her sentimental but it gave her something worth fighting for."

The female students also believed that it was important that Katniss develop as a person in her own right and not dependent on any of the men in her life. These Indian girls are growing up in a society where women are keenly scrutinized, labeled, regulated, and, harassed by the male majority on the streets. New Delhi, the nation's capital, has an average of 6 rapes and 15 molestations each day, and 65 percent of the female victims are 15–30 years of age ("2015: Average of 6 rapes, 15 molestations each day"). A majority of female college students in India have to deal with questions of arranged marriage as soon as they graduate, and some even before—the median age for marriage among women as of 2011 is 19.2 ("Sample Registration System Baseline Survey 2014"). Being confined in a patriarchal society, they see Katniss as the mythical liberated woman who can take up a cause beyond home and family.

Katniss as protagonist fared better than her counterparts from other books; Tris from *Divergent*, Thomas from *Maze Runner* and Jonas from *The Giver* were often dismissed in undergraduate English classes as being privileged, not only because they enjoy the benefits of living in the Western world, but also because "they are white and we are not," as a second-year student Chinoy[1] put it. Antero Garcia, in his book *Critical Foundations in Young Adult Literature: Challenging Genres*, feels that representation within YAL is polarized. "A large portion of YAL is focused on the interest of white, affluent teenagers. It depicts the culture and life choices of America's affluent even in controversial texts that are seen as challenging, provocative, difficult. What's more, in depicting a specific set of cultural practices, YA–in general–defines and reinforces these practices over time" (5). Garcia attempts to look closely at whose voices are represented through YAL literature and what those voices tell their readers about the world they inhabit. He looks at the cover photos of contemporary young adult novels—not just the dystopian ones—and finds that the readers themselves are racialized as white. "That is, though not all readers may necessarily be white, they are assumed to be interested in consuming books for and about white experiences in schools" (39). The white teenager's high-school experiences are important is the message represented in YA fiction, mirrored in a post-apocalyptic world where drama is restricted to how it plays out for that demographic.

Therefore, if a "culture" is created for the youth, to what end is it being done? At first glance, one would say that it would be to bring all experiences of youth—even those of young people of color—under the same generalized banner. However, movements across the publishing industry in the West have been working to bring diversity in voices to YAL. We Need Diverse Books (WNDB) is one such movement. The WNDB website also gives links to a whole gamut of other sites for foundations, libraries and journals committed to bringing diversity to the mainstream in children's books and YAL ("Where to find diverse books"). In 2014, mainstream publishers in the U.S. published 47 LGBT YA books, a 59 percent increase from 2013 (Lo). However, this wave of positive action has yet to reach India. The YA section of the Hachette India catalogue leaves you with an option to choose between Stephanie Meyer's *Twilight* series and L J Smith's *Vampire Diaries* series—both featuring white protagonists. On Indian online shopping site Flipkart.com, *The Hunger Games* trilogy boxed set costs less than Sherman Alexie's *The Absolutely True Diary of a Part-Time Indian*. You can get accessories based on *The Hunger Games,* but nothing on Nnedi Okarafor's *Akata Witch. Eleanor and Park* by Rainbow Rowell—a popular LGBT YA novel with a Korean protagonist—is relegated to the Chick-Lit and Romance section of many walk-in bookstores. The Indian YA reader is saturated with books about the white American teenager set in dystopian futures. So, while the female student reader sees in Katniss a role model for defiance, there is also the belief that she can rebel only because she is a First World woman, and not subject to the same patriarchal boundaries of her Indian reader.

Problems of Authority and Control

In *The Hunger Games*, political hierarchies are clearly delineated in its twelve districts, and young adults are forced to come to terms with power imbalances and whether or not to question them. They explore the worlds of fascist control and must find a place for themselves within it, or modify it to fit their identities. The undergraduate English students at St. Joseph's College see their own struggle with identity formation mirrored in Katniss, Gale and Peeta's struggle in standing up for what they believe in. One second-year student William wrote, "Authority is both constructive and destructive. It depends on the person who wields it to use it fairly." This statement doesn't show a shunning of power, but rather the understanding that effects of power displays depend on the nature of the person wielding it. The student has looked beyond the scenario presented and looked at the various characters in the novel, even placed them in power equations. They appear to implicitly understand that identity formation is not on an individual level, but in relation to the world around them: "Everyone is born free and to snatch away their freedom is a crime. The story depicts a state of inhumaneness, a state where the poor and the weak are suppressed by the rich," wrote Kedi, another second-year student. The mystery and wonder of adolescence is turned on its head in YA dystopian fiction. An adolescent's important concerns are about fear, or the conquering of it, of choosing a side or a stand and showing, above all else, how you're willing to do the right thing at any cost.

In *The Hunger Games*, Collins ends her trilogy with Katniss feeling ambiguous about leadership at any level, and therefore choosing to kill both President Snow and rebel faction leader President Alma Coin, effectively doing away with authoritarian figures in total. Veronica Roth's heroine Tris, in the *Divergent* series, is allegiant to the cause that she fights for, rather than being a leader who can pave the way. The teenaged reader transiting into adulthood can relate to Katniss' and Tris' conflicting feelings of lack of control and the dilemma of a hard choice. When Katniss and Tris make the right choices, they aren't just the right choices for themselves, but the right choices in a moral, altruistic, and social sense. When Kedi talks about what constitutes a crime, she is speaking not just of what she individually believes in, but of how she sees herself in relation to society, the state and oppressive state apparatuses.

Dystopian Future Versus Real-World Contexts

Young men and women are waking up to the fact that the world is not as rosy as the books of their childhood made it out to be. They are increasingly more aware of conflict, war, disaster and violence as it occurs around the world.

A first-year student, Manu, explains,

> The authorities in *The Hunger Games* can be compared to the Taliban, ISIS and other dangerously active terrorist groups who threaten people, take hostages for ransom, and even videotape the beheading of their hostages for the world to see. A few individual terrorists blow themselves up killing many innocent people in the name of God to mainly gain attention and create fear among the citizens and the ruling governments.

His friend in the same class writes,

> Innocence used to be a good characteristic trait, but in this world full of wickedness there is no room for an innocent person. In our society, innocence is weak and wickedness is strong. The phrase "survival of the fittest" can be applied here; only the wicked survive easily. Just like the slaughter of innocent people in *The Hunger Games* entertained the society in the Capitol, wicked people all over the world have no qualms in killing hundreds of people for their own purposes.

This bleak view of the world is more realistic than we would like to concede, and the youth are sensitive to issues that happen in a wider community than their own circle. Rocio Davis sees it as an articulation of the developing individual's constant conflict with society:

Young adult dystopian fiction can be read as a response to today's mass media culture's often pessimistic and/or catastrophic vision of the world. Through all kinds of social and public media, adolescents are being trained to view humankind as inherently wasteful and oblivious to the consequences of their actions on the earth. Dystopian YAL blends the traditional developmental narrative with a heightened concern with issues regarding the individual against society (generally in the form of strict political organization), often in the context of a post-apocalyptic world [48].

So, not only is the individual student constantly in conflict with society in terms of identity, but also in terms of what society has degenerated to. In the Indian situation, this kind of negativity is not unfounded. Of the 444 million children in India under the age of 18, 25 percent are not in school. In Classes 10 and 12, there is intense pressure to attain high marks in qualifying examinations and fear of failure in examinations was the second highest cause of suicides in children in 2014 ("Statistics of Children in India"). As they look to the future, they are met with alarming unemployment rates in the country—the highest being in October 2016 at six percent ("Unemployment Rate in India").

These are but a fraction of problems students see around them. They have seen the refugee influx from Bangladesh and Tibet and the challenges that emerged; as they widen the scope, they witness conflict with Pakistan. They hear hate-speech in the name of religion and they see religion and race-based violence in Syria and various other parts of the world. A second-year student confirms,

The Hunger Games is an exaggeration of the present world scenario. Religion, banks, major pharmaceutical companies, famous leaders use their authority in a similar but more clever way. If one starts questioning everything and does a bit of research, one would know how all humans are enslaved. We are forced to work for companies, believe in religion and buy expensive medicines. If you don't work, you'll die of poverty. If you question religion, you'll get killed; if you want to live and want your family to survive, you have to abide by the law.

So, when the Indian students see the dystopian future in The Hunger Games, they see their own world around them in the present.

Analyzing a dystopian setting is rich fodder for the writing talents of a Third World student, and these students are populating classrooms all over the West too. U.S. schools play host to many immigrant and even refugee students. Understanding how the Third World student reads and responds to American dystopian YAL can inform the American teacher in setting composition exercises in a symbiotic manner; it will not only help migrant student connect their experiences to the text and its place of origin, but will also bring diverse and fresh perspectives to the American classroom.

Practical Considerations for the Composition Classroom

Some of the questions raised here can be used as discussion and writing prompts in college classrooms:

1. Shifting from the comparatively optimistic world of children's literature to the darker themes of YA dystopian fiction: Teachers can get students to explore specific points in narrative that differ greatly in treatment from children's literature. Are certain taboo topics openly discussed in YAL? Why is there no shielding of the reader from all the negativity in the dystopian future? Why, in fact, is there a hyperbolic representation of everything bad—evil, cruel, malicious—in YAL? The glaring shift from innocence to maturity in YAL will help put the real-life situation faced by many immigrant and other Third World families in perspective for the whole class.

2. Relating to the protagonists' struggles with their immediate surroundings: Students can be encouraged to relate to one of the characters—it need not be the protagonist. That relationship can be explored; do the students see themselves as heroic, or as one among the downtrodden, relegated to the role of observer in the conflicts around them? Asking the students to make a clear choice in this question will help the hesitant or indecisive student to form opinions of their own. If they struggle, the teacher can draw parallels with the protagonist's own struggle with being categorized or pigeon-holed. Differences in race between the protagonists and the student population in the diverse English classroom can be explored. In most cases, Third-World students may respond defiantly against stereotyping and generalizations when answering such questions, but it can also be an ice-breaker for students who haven't had a chance to get to know each other before.

3. Identifying and learning to negotiate with figures of authority and control: Teachers can encourage students to identify points in the narrative where freedoms are afforded or denied to the characters. Further discussions can be held on where in the world such freedoms considered obvious, and where they have to be earned. Conversations on power structures and ideology can also be attempted, with references to personal experiences and anecdotes. Ideas of leadership can be explored; oppressive state apparatuses can be deconstructed and questioned.

4. Mirroring of real-life political situations through the plot-lines of dystopian YAL: Once the teacher is able to lay enough groundwork for the students to compare and contrast ideas, they can be invited to use those ideas in analyzing political, military, legal, and human rights

issues of the present. Students can be encouraged to find parallels in dystopian YAL and comment on possible outcomes of conflicts in the contemporary world. "What would Katniss do in North Korea?" is a possible composition prompt. Students can then be prompted to use their ideas of power structures and ideology in writing about the problems of contemporary civil society such as race, religion, caste, gender, etc.

Conclusion

The English classroom in St. Joseph's College has been a site for experimentation and much learning, even on the part of the teachers. As the world becomes smaller and the East communicates with the West, it is fruitful to look beyond the dystopian YAL writer's immediate sphere of influence for responses. Composition exercises created for the Third World student can not only help immigrant and refugee students assimilate to their English-speaking classrooms, they also open up the English classrooms to wider areas of questioning and debate; Dystopian YAL enables this two-way transaction in its ability to create unique and concentrated narratives of conflict and resolution.

NOTE

1. Student names in the essay are pseudonyms.

WORKS CITED

Alvermann, Donna E., et al. *Popular Culture in the Classroom: Teaching and Researching Critical Media Literacy.* Newark, DE: International Reading Association, 1999.
Amritavalli, Raghavachari. "An English for Every Schoolchild in India." *English Impact Report: Investigating English Language Learning Outcomes at the Primary School Level in Rural India,* edited by Vivien Berry. London: British Council, 2013. 21–6.
"Children's and YA Fiction." Hachette India. http://www.hachetteindia.com/Children/Default. aspx. Accessed 25 Nov. 2016.
Collins, Suzanne. *Catching Fire.* New York: Scholastic Press, 2009. Print.
_____. *The Hunger Games.* New York: Scholastic Press, 2008. Print.
_____. *Mockingjay.* New York: Scholastic Press, 2010. Print.
Dashner, James. *The Death Cure.* New York: Delacorte, 2011.
_____. *The Fever Code.* New York: Delacorte, 2016.
_____. *The Kill Order.* New York: Delacorte, 2012.
_____. *The Maze Runner Series.* New York: Delacorte, 2009
_____. *The Scorch Trials.* New York: Delacorte, 2010.
Davis, Rocío G. "Writing the Erasure of Emotions in Dystopian Young Adult Fiction: Reading Lois Lowry's *The Giver* and Lauren Oliver's *Delirium.*" *Narrative Works: Issues, Investigations and Interventions,* vol. 4, no. 2, 2014, pp. 48–63.
English Skills for Employability (ESfE) Think Tank. British Council, 2015. www.britishcouncil. in/sites/default/files/english_skills_for_employability.pdf. Accessed 10 Nov. 2016.
Garcia, Antero. *Critical Foundations in Young Adult Literature.* Boston: Sense, 2013.
Herz, Sarah K., and Donald R. Gallo. *From Hinton to Hamlet: Building Bridges Between Young Adult Literature and the Classics.* Westport, CT: Greenwood, 1996.

Lo, Malinda. "2014 LGBT YA by the numbers." *Malinda Lo*, 10 Dec. 2014. http://www.malindalo.com/2014/12/2014-lgbt-ya-by-the-numbers/. Accessed 24 Nov. 2016.

Lowry, Lois. *The Giver*. Boston: Houghton Mifflin, 1993.

Meyer, Stephenie. *The Host*. New York: Little, Brown, 2008.

Mueller, Roseanna M. "Teaching Writing Through Literature: Towards the Acquisition of a Knowledge Base." Annual Meeting of the Mid-West Regional Conference on English in the Two-Year College, St. Louis, 13–15 Feb. 1986, conference paper. https://ia802701.us.archive.org/35/items/ERIC_ED273963/ERIC_ED273963.pdf. Accessed 12 Sept. 2015.

Mukherji, Anahita. "2 Crore Indian Children Study in English-Medium schools." *The Times of India*, 2 Mar. 2012. timesofindia.indiatimes.com/india/2-crore-Indian-children-study-in-English-medium-schools/articleshow/12105621.cms. Accessed 10 Nov. 2016.

Pal, Deepanjana. "The Hunt for the Next Chetan Bhagat." *DNA India*, 15 July 2012. http://www.dnaindia.com/mumbai/report-the-hunt-for-the-next-chetan-bhagat-1715210. Accessed 10 Sept. 2015.

Planning Commission, Government of India. *Twelfth Five Year Plan (2012–2017) Social Sectors, Volume III*. New Delhi: Sage, 2013. http://planningcommission.gov.in/plans/planrel/12thplan/pdf/12fyp_vol3.pdf. Accessed 7 Nov 2016.

Roth, Veronica. *Allegiant*. New York: Katherine Tegen, 2013.

_____. *Divergent*. New York: Katherine Tegen, 2011.

_____. *Insurgent*. New York: Katherine Tegen, 2012.

"Sample Registration System Baseline Survey 2014." *Census of India*, Government of India Ministry of Home Affairs, 2014. http://www.censusindia.gov.in/vital_statistics/BASELINE%20TABLES07062016.pdf. Accessed 22 Nov. 2016.

"Statistics of Children in India." *Child Rights and You*. http://www.cry.org/issues-views/statistics-on-children-in-india/. Accessed 22 Nov. 2016.

Tevis, Walter. *Mockingbird*. New York: Doubleday, 1980.

"2015: Average of 6 Rapes, 15 Molestations Each Day." *The Indian Express*, 5 Jan. 2016. http://indianexpress.com/article/cities/delhi/2015-average-of-6-rapes-15-molestations-each-day. Accessed 24 Nov. 2016.

"Unemployment Rate in India." *Centre for Monitoring Indian Economy*. http://unemploymentinindia.cmie.com/. Accessed 22 Nov. 2016.

"Where to find diverse books." *WNDB*, We Need Diverse Books. http://weneeddiversebooks.org/where-to-find-diverse-books/#. Accessed 22 Nov. 2016.

Zdilla, Gail. "The Appeal of Young Adult Literature in Late Adolescence: College Freshmen Read YAL." *Young Adult Literature and Adolescent Identity Across Cultures and Classrooms*, edited by Janet Aslup. Abingdon-on-Thames: Routledge, 2010. 191–203.

Teaching Creative Writing as Composition

Kekla Magoon's How It Went Down, *Social Justice Texts and Expanding Student Narratives of Difference Through Use of Engaged Pedagogy and Significant Learning Goals*

Jenny Ferguson

When creative writing classes serve as part of the general education composition sequence in liberal arts institutions, new concerns for student engagement arise. Some of these concerns are artistic ones and some of these concerns are the kind all composition instructors face regardless of students' level of preparation or students' desire to take the course. When creative writing meets composition, the creative writing as composition classroom becomes one where multiple disciplines need attending to in order to meet institutional general education learning goals, and to help students develop both their artistic and general communicative writing skills.

While creative writing as composition and the inclusion of literature in the composition classroom is gaining ground, detractors to this method of composition instruction remain. This uneasiness comes from creative writing teachers and composition teachers alike. In "The Place of Creative Writing in Composition Studies" Douglas Hesse suggests that

> [f]rom a disciplinary perspective, then, it might seem best to have composition and creative writing continue to fork their separate paths. The former could maintain its serious practical focus on argument and idea, explanation and analysis, with the overt goals of shaping how people think and act. The latter could celebrate the aes-

thetic artifact, produced and read for pleasure—sometimes trifling, often serious—the artifact important for how it's made and experienced, important as much or more for what it is as what it does, written because its act of writing satisfies a creative, expressive desire that finds time spent writing preferable to time spent otherwise [42–3].

Yet, in maintaining these perhaps entirely artificial boundaries, students, writers, and the discipline of writing are harmed. That's why Hesse calls for "composition studies [to] unilaterally explore the place of creative writing—of creative *composing*—in teaching, in scholarship, and in our expanded sense of ourselves as text makers." Integrating creative writing into the field of composition, especially in liberal arts colleges, under general education requirements allows students and teachers to explore creative composing while writing texts that may, at times, blur the boundaries between the serious, the practical, and the aesthetic. For the purposes of this essay, I'd like to set aside these institutional and discipline concerns to a focus on students who find themselves in the creative writing as composition classroom and teachers who seek to integrate creative writing, social justice, and engaged pedagogy into their teaching.

In every classroom—whether face-to-face or online—our students always impact the challenges we face. While course content can change semester to semester—we can shift our texts, and design our courses to react to new topics and themes currently of interest—it is the students who populate our courses who influence shifts in teaching for basic concepts as well as more advanced ones. Every group of students is different; therefore classroom pedagogy must be able to change accordingly.

It has been my experience at a small-size, flagship liberal arts university in the Midwest that many of the students who end up taking a creative writing as composition course have little interest in becoming writers. Instead, they find themselves in my classroom to fulfill what they consider a cumbersome general education requirement in the easiest way possible. I do wonder where and when and who it was that told these students creative writing is "easy," but I will reserve that discussion for another time. As a result, student apathy and disengagement is one of the first challenges to be faced in the creative writing as composition classroom. Many of my students actually dislike writing and will be upfront about both their reasons for taking my course and their strong feeling about general education, the composition sequence, and writing—creative or otherwise. For a teacher, at best, this can be demoralizing.

Student apathy raises another set of particular issues in the creative as composition classroom, and it insists on a pedagogy that engages students in important, real-life questions from day one. According to the 2015 survey conducted by the Association of Writers and Writing Programs (AWP), continued growth across undergraduate and graduate creative writing programs has been noted, with undergraduate programs growing most in this most recent survey (2). Specifically, "[o]ver the past five years, AA programs grew from 0.4 students to 13.5, BA from 12.3 to 22.0, and BFA from 20.0 to 30.0" ("AWP Releases Its 2015 Survey of Creative Writing Programs"). While the survey does not distinguish between creative writing courses that fall under general education writing requirements and those that only serve majors and minors, the growth trend suggests that more students than ever before are enrolling in creative writing courses. Therefore, questions about how to best teach creative writing, how to design creative writing courses, as well as how to engage writers who are perhaps reluctant writers "waiting in the wings" are important ones. Concurrently, the market for young adult literature is growing, and there are more readers—both adults and children alike—who are buying and reading young adult literature (YAL) books than ever before. For example, in 2014, the bestseller's list for the year was populated by 17 titles meant for youth and children out of the possible 20 spots (Gilmore and Burnett). As creative writing programs continue to flourish, students in these programs want to study the literature they grew up loving, and where the market for young adult novels is also growing, the creative writing as composition course opens up fertile opportunities to recruit students who never though they could be writers, and to invite them into a community where social justice is approached through art, through the young adult (YA) novel, and through engaged pedagogy.

In this essay I outline YAL social justice texts as a form of engaged pedagogy aligned with L. Dee Fink's Significant Learning Goals, discuss how reading YAL social justice texts affects students' writing and their narratives of difference, offer some practical applications teachers in the classroom are invited to actively co-opt, adapt and share, as well as suggest how to engage creative writing as composition students in service learning initiatives.

Young Adult Social Justice Texts as Engaged Pedagogy

I define YAL social justice texts as novels, story-cycles, novels-in-verse, graphic novels, or collections of essays that implicitly through their characters, plot, and/or themes address issues of social justice and of race, ethnicity, class, religion, sexuality, ability, and especially, texts in which intersections and intersectionality are privileged. While some critics dismiss these novels as "issue books" and therefore suggest that they are didactic, not entertaining, not high concept, or worse, without artistic value, YA social justice texts are thematically compelling and raw. In their rawness they explore the human element that news clips often ignore while questioning society's assumptions across differences. As such, YAL social justice texts tend to end up on "banned" or "challenged" books lists. For example, according to the American Library Association (ALA), Sherman Alexie's *The Absolutely True Diary of a Part-Time Indian* was the #1 challenged book in 2014, #3 in 2013, and #2 in 2012 ("Top Ten Most Frequently Challenged Books Lists"). However, it is particularly this reaction from parents and community members—that these texts are too real, too graphic, or simply an ephemeral "too much"—that engenders student engagement in the classroom. For learning to occur, student engagement and student give-a-care are absolute musts as learning is an active, not passive, experience. At the university level, I engage with freedom in learning; I focus on what materials will excel students' learning experiences, both inside and outside the classroom, as well as focus on the development of the whole person as valued by the liberal arts curriculum. I recognize that additional problems may arise for K-12 teachers; however, I recommend teachers in these institutions teach social justice texts as well. All students deserve to engage with materials that speak to human experience across a wide variety of intersections.

Although many definitions of engaged pedagogy exist, I am working with a model that says, for one, the pedagogical approaches I use must, at the front engage students in active learning, and through student engagement with the material, the assignments, and each other, long-lasting learning can happen. In order to be sure that learning is long-lasting, I employ L. Dee Fink's concept of Significant Learning Goals at the course design level and therefore in the classroom on a daily basis. Fink says: "The central idea of this phrase—'significant learning'—is that teaching should result in something others can look at and say, 'That learning experience resulted in something that is truly significant in terms of the students' lives'" (7). Therefore, significant learning goals are not about memorizing material and regurgitating it, for example to answer questions on an exam. Instead, significant learning is learning that will last at least one year, and ideally many more. Furthermore, Fink identifies that classrooms framed around significant learning goals employ pedagogical moves that result in engaged students and courses that can be described as high energy (8). I suggest that teaching YAL social justice texts such as Kekla Magoon's *How It Went Down* (2014) aligns with L. Dee Fink's Significant Learning Goals and therefore serves long-term learning by connecting students to values that matter beyond the classroom, and, frankly, for life.

Magoon's *How It Went Down*—a recipient of the Coretta Scott King Award Honor in 2015, an award that highlights African American authors writing remarkable books about the experience of African Americans for young readers—is a recent novel that models what YAL social justice texts can do in the creative writing as composition classroom. The three key phrases on the award sticker are telling: Peace, Non-Violent Social Change, and Brotherhood. However, many other fine social justice texts currently in print, can be adapted to serve the same purpose in a classroom where engaged pedagogy is key. I decided to teach Magoon's *How It Went Down* for two main reasons that align with the significant learning goals and pedagogical approach used in my creative writing as composition classroom. One, Magoon's novel fictionalizes a shooting death of an African-American youth by a white adult and provides very needed perspectives that my primarily rural, middle-class, white students feel are "cinematic" or "only on the news" and therefore, not part of their own lives. Two, Magoon's novel is formally innovative and allows my creative writing students to practice the genre of flash fiction, while also studying a longer text to see how elements of craft are developed in small and large scopes. As this course fulfills part of the composition sequence, there is also a research component and an explanatory writing component. Magoon's novel serves both of these needs as well, opening up research opportunities. Yet before students can begin to write creatively and critically in the creative writing as composition class, students' reactions to and comfort level reading social justice texts needs to be attended to.

Reactions to social justice texts in the classroom speak to students' prior life-and academic experiences, reading habits, perceptions regarding what I expect from them—note that these assumptions are often false—and their reactions to how their peers will judge them for voicing an opinion on possibly divisive issues. In teaching social justice texts across composition classrooms of all levels—including the creative writing as composition classroom—I've observed a variety of student reactions. These range from outrightly racist comments (especially on online discussion boards where students feel anonymous), to equally harmful micro-aggressions, to liberal exhibits of shock and outrage over violent acts "actually happening" in their country, to strong vows to learn more about topic X, Y, or Z and a general wish to "be better" in their every day lives. Often these reactions come from students who have not experienced racism or violence or micro-aggressions in their own lives. While none of these reactions are ultimately unexpected, they can often blend and shift, and also silence other students in the classroom. Early in the semester, there is greater need to teach students how to learn from social justice texts, as well as greater need to remind students how to engage with views that differ from their own.

I have found that discussing what academic discourse looks and sounds like, and by modeling this in my interactions with students vastly changes how students react to social justice texts. To ground this, early in the semester I ask students to tell me a story about something funny that happened to them during the week. They will narrate the event, and the class will nod or maybe smile. Then, I ask students to tell that story again in the manner they'd tell it to their best friend. The story shifts. This time, the class often breaks out laughing. This quick exercise can demonstrate how audience changes how we tell our stories, and how we make our arguments, without alienating students by centering this kind of discussion on "hot" (read: social justice) topics. However, I can quickly shape what students take away from this activity to, for example, a discussion on micro-aggressions or stereotypes. This activity acts as gentle approach, and asks students to think about their narratives in relation to others. From here, the class can become a space where students learn that gut reactions or values they are not willing to question are dangerous to critical and creative thought. Furthermore, reminding students that racist discourse and uncritical discourse does not meet the rigorous standards of academic research or liberal arts values, and by discussing how audience changes tone, levels of formality, and what kind of discourse is being used, students can begin to have discussions that matter and to learn how to write both critically and creatively.

In a recent creative writing class, several of my students began calling themselves "non-racists" in their creative non-fiction essays. This term is one they gravitated towards, and one they were willing to own. Its power comes from how the term implicates the writer in racist systems and acts by differentiating "I'm not a racist" from "I'm anti-racist." This moment for many students was revelatory, and one that changes the lens students are able to use when they approach social justice issues that they feel they do not contribute to. Finally, by leading students to form a community in the classroom, one that is not based on shared values, but on a shared exploration of values, and by asking students to position themselves in light of their experiences, beliefs, values, and perceptions early in the semester, productive discourse and students writing abilities—and the kinds of stories they tell—develop.

Effect on Students' Writing

One of the major effects on students' writing I've observed is that beginning creative writing students were more likely to take risks in their form and content after reading YAL social justice texts. While not all of the student writing produced may have been deemed "successful," in the creative writing as composition classroom, experiments in craft areas and a focus on revision is more important than producing "successful" stories, poems, creative non-fiction essays, and hybrid texts. While the term "successful" is inherently problematic, in typical composition classes, and in many other creative writing classes, "successful" pieces of writing are those that "fit" the model of the genre being studied, and by fitting the model they mimic the model's structure, tone, and style. There's nothing wrong with this. But for creative writers, experiments lead to discoveries, and discoveries stumbled upon on the page can and should be revised. The concept of revision and the writing process is central to both the composition classroom and goals of creative writing programs. When these goals come together in the creative writing as composition classroom, they are among the easiest to serve: revision, after all, is a technique many students have experienced and the creative writing as composition classroom opens up discussions about revision that benefit all kinds of writing, not only creative work. Therefore, when the pedagogy I use focuses on experiments, discovery, and risk-taking alongside a study of YAL social justice texts, students can develop a stronger relationship with revision as a process. Specifically, here, I will look at how student writing developed after reading and studying Kekla Magoon's *How It Went Down* in terms of two major craft issues whose lessons can be translated to serve more general composition classrooms needs as well, addressing both artistic and communicative writing needs: the concepts of voice and structure.

For beginning creative writing students, understanding the concept of voice generally, and understanding what their voice as a writer sounds like on the page can be a struggle. This is a different, but related, issue to beginning creative writing students learning to develop voices for their characters through dialogue. Magoon's *How It Went Down* privileges voice, and furthermore, privileges a multiplicity of voices as it explores gun violence, violent crimes committed against a black teenage boy by a white man, gang culture, and life in high-density, urban neighborhoods versus life in more gentrified parts of the city.

Magoon uses multiple first person narrators in *How It Went Down* and by doing so models a wide range of voices and the craft choices that develop those voices in one novel. For example, Will (AKA eMZee) is a teenager who has moved out of the "ghetto," uptown with his mother and stepfather. His voice is plainly that of a teenager, as he employs fairly conventional sentence structure with the word-play typical of youth. He accuses his stepfather of being "a total ghettophobe" and through his narration develops his character's values and voice (Magoon 42). Yet Will (AKA eMZee)'s voice is starkly different from members of the Kings gang. Brick, the leader of the gang, talks in sentences that are shaped to reflect a voice that worries less about sentence structure and word play and embraces the terse strength of facts and declarations: "Damn right Tariq was wearing red and black. Like any good King. Straight up" (52). And Tina, the younger sister of the teenager who was killed, speaks only in verse: "Siren song / Out the open window / Siren Song / *Weee-ooo-weee-ooo*" (7). Discussions of craft choices that develop voice are clearer when a text allows multiple voices to exist against each other. Through challenges, prompts, and exercises, students can try on many voices, and learn how to shape voice on the page. Ultimately, throughout the semester, they may begin to hear their own voice as a writer, and begin to see what craft and grammatical choices make their voice differ from those of their peers. For young writers, establishing a voice that suits their writing style and their narrative and thematic concerns is important to invite them into the community of writers, and in reframing their perception of self to include "writer" as a descriptive element, whether they ever thought that was something they could claim, or not.

Specifically, the formal structure of *How It Went Down* highlights voice and, at the same time, asks students to take risks in their formal writing choices by modeling such choices. Magoon's novel works on several formal levels. For one, it is a novel. More specifically, it is a formally innovative novel, where the story is composed using hybrid narratives: flash fiction sections; inserted text like a 9–1–1 Call Log and newspaper headlines; as well as verse. While the creative writing as composition class I am currently teaching as I write this essay focuses on the prose genres of flash fiction and flash nonfiction, students are including verse in their prose, making formal decisions that structure stories in different ways (by pouring content into unexpected forms), and by-in-large taking risks with the materials and manner in which they tell stories. When composition courses can get students to consider what form is best for what content and for what audience at the start of the writing process, and ask students to make choices between forms, students develop their critical thinking and writing skills. Creative writing is not so far off from traditional composition that these same concerns about form, content, and audience cannot serve both creative writing classroom and composition classroom needs simultaneously.

Effect on Students' Narratives of Difference

One of the popular conversations about the benefits of reading literature, specifically, and a liberal arts education, generally, is how these experiences promote the development of empathy and increase performance on theory of mind exercises. Those of us in the liberal arts have known this all along, but are happy to see scientific studies supporting why reading and studying in the liberal are important. In David Comer Kidd and Emanuele Castano's 2013 study, the results of which were published in *Science*, they discuss this first issue and begin to frame my discussion on YAL social justice texts' ability to effect students' narratives of difference in the creative writing as composition classroom. Kidd and Castano state the connection between reading and empathy or theory of mind: "Cultural practices [such as reading fiction] […] may function to promote and refine interpersonal sensitivity throughout our lives" (377). They follow Miall and Kuiken's argument "that through the systematic use of phonological, grammatical, and semantic stylistic devices, literary fiction defamiliarizes its readers" and through this defamiliarization theory of mind is improved (377). Kidd and Castano summarize their findings as such:

> Our contention is that literary fiction, which we consider to be both writerly and polyphonic, uniquely engages the psychological processes needed to gain access to characters' subjective experiences. Just as in real life, the worlds of literary fiction are replete with complicated individuals whose inner lives are rarely easily discerned but warrant exploration. The worlds of fiction, though, pose fewer risks than the real world, and they present opportunities to consider the experiences of others without facing the potentially threatening consequences of that engagement. More critically, whereas many of our mundane social experiences may be scripted by convention and informed by stereotypes, those presented in literary fiction often disrupt our expectations. Readers of literary fiction must draw on more flexible interpretive resources to infer the feelings and thoughts of characters. That is, they must engage ToM [Theory of Mind] processes [378].

Reading social justice YAL directly confronts "the experiences of others" and asks student writers to consider through theory of mind, empathetic understanding, and critical and creative thinking processes large-scale questions about the human experience, connecting students to real-world questions that engage students in the classroom.

Furthermore, the concept of mirror neurons expands the discussion of theory of mind, reading and students changing narratives of difference while studying YAL social justice texts in the creative writing as composition classroom. Vilayanur Ramachandran in his 2009 TED Talk "The Neurons That Shaped Civilization" explains how mirror neurons work:

> [A] subset of these neurons, maybe about 20 percent of them, will also fire when I'm looking at somebody else performing the same action. [...] And this is truly astonishing. Because it's as though this neuron is adopting the other person's point of view. It's almost as though it's performing a virtual reality simulation of the other person's action. [...] [A] subset of [these mirror neurons] will fire even when I watch somebody else being touched in the same location. So, here again you have neurons which are enrolled in empathy. [...] In other words, you have dissolved the barrier between you and other human beings.

Additionally, Ramachandran claims "mirror neuron system[s] underlies the interface allowing you to rethink about issues like consciousness, representation of self, what separates you from other human beings, what allows you to empathize with other human beings, and also even things like the emergence of culture and civilization." YAL social justice texts—as well as social justice texts targeted to children and adults—use narrative and art in order to connect to readers' hearts and minds. Mirror neurons and theory of mind suggest that studying YA social justice texts has the ability to change students' narratives of difference throughout the semester, and through that shift, change students' abilities to empathize across differences as well.

Anecdotally, in my creative writing as composition classrooms where I employ significant learning goals and create a community of engaged students through active and engaged pedagogies, students' narratives of difference develop as they learn to empathize with diverse characters, with anti-heroes, and with people in the classroom—and beyond—who hold different values and whose life experiences may be radically different than their own. In the classroom, students who expand their narrative of difference expand the possibilities for their writing, for their lives, and for the lives of all those they meet. As lofty as that final statement is, I stand behind it. My pedagogy stands behind it. In the next section, I would like to draw back to practical applications instructors can use while teaching Kelka Magoon's *How It Went Down*, or use to adapt for the teaching of another YAL social justice text.

Practical Considerations for the Composition Classroom

In this section, I offer practical applications for instructors of creative writing as composition classrooms.

1. Modeling: using productive social dynamics implicit in team-based learning and project-based learning in the classroom, ask students to respond to each other's writing-in-process. While in traditional composition classrooms, it is difficult to ask student to co-write a research paper, this exercise allows students to practice a team writing effort while maintaining creative control over their own sub-sections of the project without having to worry about cohesion or a singular voice. In this assignment, I ask students to collaboratively co-write a dramatic "incident" that follows Magoon's model found on the first page of *How It Went Down*. Students' incidents should be described generally, in journalistic terms. Individually, students then compose flash fiction narratives from different points of view surrounding and exploring the incident. This assignment asks students to write collaboratively and individually. It also asks students to consider elements central to the composition classrooms such as audience, tone, and argument, as well as elements of creative crafts such as voice, plot, character arcs, setting, and point of view. This assignment works best in face-to-face classrooms, but can be implemented through online learning management systems as well. I do, however, recommend giving students ample time in class

or during a suitable synchronous time in online classes to work on team-based assignments.

2. Mapping: this assignment asks students to develop a creative map of Magoon's novel focusing on one element of craft. This assignment works equally well in teams as it does individually. One variation that allows students to learn from each other and combine their knowledge is to ask students to form a team and map different elements on an individual basis, which can be combined and exchanged afterwards so that the team learns what each individual does. Another variation asks students to map one component individually and come together as a team to create a mega-map addressing multiple craft concerns. Class presentations may follow, if they meet your curriculum and program needs. Students might choose to map one character's motivations throughout the novel, or map the setting, or students might opt to map a trope, or a theme, a series of images, or a single word. The key here is for students to think about the structure of the text and one craft element. Once they have mapped their craft element, an additional creative writing assignments can be added on. One such assignment is described below.

3. Creative Responses to Mapping: once students have studied an element of craft closely, they can then devise their own short creative writing texts where they actively attempt to use what they have learned from their mapping experience. I like to ask students to continue to work in compact forms, such as flash fiction, flash nonfiction, or prose poetry as these forms are complete yet brief. Students should be working in a form and in a style and genre of writing that they want to work in. This is a wonderful assignment to have students workshop in class and debrief as a whole class at the end of the unit where you teach Magoon's novel. This assignment can be expanded to rift off of multiple craft concerns developing students skills exponentially.

While many other assignments can be developed to compliment the novel, I want to conclude this essay by transitioning to some out of the classroom applications for teaching YA social justice texts in a creative writing as composition curriculum.

Young Adult Social Justice Texts in the Creative-Writing-as-Composition Classroom, Now and Beyond

The creative writing as composition classroom comes with increased challenges in student engagement, but offers significant opportunities to develop a parallel set of writing skills—both of the artistic and communicative kind—while encouraging students to see writing as impactful in the world outside of academia and meaningful in their lives and the lives of others. One kind of assignment I have used in the traditional composition classroom but have not yet implemented in the creative writing-as-composition-classroom where YA social justice texts are studied is service learning. As service-learning opportunities "serve as threshold spaces where hospitality is enacted" (Barrett 70) students in the creative writing as composition class-room can extend the kinds of assignments that are possible when reading social justice YA texts by stepping into spaces where they can enact hospitality and reciprocity between people as part of the learning experience. While Kenna Barrett, quoted above, is discussing how service-learning projects in the professional writing classroom can enact hospitality, her argument trans-lates to the creative writing as composition classroom and to any classroom where students are engaged with social justice issues. In fact, by instituting service-learning opportunities in the classroom, that classroom becomes con-nected to social justice concerns through service to others.

I invite teachers to connect their students to their local communities, and to strangers, and to life experiences beyond students' current scope by reading and studying YA social justice texts, by designing courses that insist on engaged pedagogies, and by developing assignments that meet the needs of the creative writing classroom, the larger composition program, the stu-dents, and the wider community through initiatives such as team-based learn-ing, project-based learning, and service learning.

WORKS CITED

"AWP Releases Its 2015 Survey of Creative Writing Programs." *Association of Writers and Writing Programs.* www.awpwriter.org/magazine_media/writers_news_view/3989/awp_releases_its_2015_survey_of_creative_writing_programs. Accessed 20 Feb 2017.

"AWP 2015 Survey of Creative Writing Programs." *Association of Writers and Writing Pro-grams,* 2016. www.awpwriter.org/application/public/pdf/survey/AWPMFA Survey15.pdf. Accessed 20 Feb 2017. PDF.

Barrett, Kenna. "Where Professional Writing Meets Social Change: The Grant Proposal as a Site of Hospitality." *Composition Studies,* vol. 41, no. 1, 2013, pp. 70–83.

Fink, L. Dee. *Creating Significant Learning Experiences: An Integrated Approach to Designing College Courses.* 2nd ed. Hoboken: Jossey-Bass, 2013.

Gilmore, Natasha, and Matia Burnett. "Crunching Numbers at the Nielsen Children's Book Summit." *Publisher's Weekly.* www.publishersweekly.com/pw/by-topic/childrens/childrens-industry-news/article/65068-kids-are-thriving-reading-and-hungry-for-more-crunching-numbers-at-the-nielsen-children-s-book-summit.html. Accessed 23 Feb 2017.

Kidd, David Comer, and Emanuele Castano. "Reading Literary Fiction Improves Theory of Mind." *Science* 342, 18 Oct. 2013.

Ramachandran, Vilayanur. "The Neurons That Shaped Civilization." The Future Beckons, TEDIndia 2009, 4–7 Nov. 2009, Mumbai, India. TED Talk.

"Top Ten Most Frequently Challenged Books Lists." *American Library Association.* www.ala.org/bbooks/frequentlychallengedbooks/top10. Accessed 20 Feb 2017.

"I can't always be Lois Lane....
I want to be Superman too"

Twilight, *Gender Studies and Encouraging Analysis in the College Composition Classroom*

JENNY L. HOWE

Towards the end of Stephenie Meyer's young adult novel *Twilight,* the protagonist, Bella Swan, insists to her vampire boyfriend Edward, "I can't always be Lois Lane.... I want to be Superman too" (Meyer 474). This moment occurs just after Bella awakens in the hospital to discover that Edward had saved her from James, a rival vampire who had threatened her life. But maybe more importantly, her statement introduces one of the many conversations Bella and Edward have over the course of the series concerning whether or not she should be changed into a vampire. For Bella, until she too is a vampire, Edward will always need to come to her rescue. They aren't "equals" (473–74). From Edward's perspective, protecting Bella from vampirism is the best way that he can "save" her, and especially, preserve her soul.

Whenever I assign *Twilight* in my classes, my students are quick to point out the irony in this scene. If anyone is almost always "Lois Lane" (i.e., the "damsel in distress"), it is Meyer's Bella Swan. They note her perpetual clumsiness, the way she always seems to be in the wrong place at the wrong time, and her stubborn, often-questionable decisions as reasons why she repeatedly needs to be rescued. But our conversations around this scene also open up discussions about paranormal romance and the many ways in which Bella's humanity and Edward's vampirism are coded with constructions of gender.

My students' astute observations about Meyer's gender politics in *Twilight* demonstrate to me the useful role gender studies and young adult literature can play in the development of college-level writing. Mark Richardson has noted about the role of literature in the first-year writing classroom that "one way to make writing about literature a more successful experience for first-year students is to open it to the kinds of information that students already command, allowing them to bring to their writing the confidence and conviction that flows from knowledge" (Richardson 291). I would argue that both young adult literature and gender studies offer the kinds of familiar lenses Richardson discusses here. For instance, students tend to enter our courses with their own assumptions about gender, as well as opinions about the usefulness or authenticity of the gender roles that they see perpetuated by popular culture. They similarly have usually encountered some amount of young adult fiction before entering college, either in their high school English classes or while reading on their own. And even if they haven't, the prominent themes in young adult literature—growing up, coming to terms with who you are, dealing with parents while trying to assert some independence, understanding how you fit into the world, leaving worlds you know for ones that seem scary and unfamiliar—are accessible and relatable to our students.

Peter Elbow points out "the culture of literary studies feels to me to work against students' impulses to involve themselves personally with literature and feel they are making personal connections with characters and authors" (Elbow 538). Often, this is because, as Elbow, Richardson, and others have argued, students are asked to approach the literary text with a distance or reverence that makes it difficult for them to invest personally in the story.[1] But analyzing young adult literature encourages this kind of personal identification. It asks readers to engage with adolescent experiences. It allows our students to explore what they already know.

This essay will use Meyer's *Twilight* to consider how the intersection of gender studies and young adult literature in a college composition course can bolster students' critical thinking by tapping into the knowledge bases they bring to our classrooms. In my experience teaching college composition, I have found that students often understand that their claims must be supported by strong, relevant evidence, but they have not yet honed the skills to identify such evidence. Offering students the opportunity to practice these skills by engaging with texts they connect to, the types of "literacies," as Richardson calls them, in which students already participate, allows them to develop and fine-tune these skills, fostering a stronger foundation in analysis and argumentation crucial for effective academic writing (Richardson 282).

Pop Culture Versus the Classics: Literature in the Composition Classroom

The role of literature in the college composition classroom has been the subject of steady debate in composition studies since the 1990s. Those who oppose using literature in college-writing courses tend to cite, among other things, a tension between the student-centric approach fostered in most first-year writing programs and the lecture-based structure often assumed in literature courses. Erika Lindemann, for instance, in her oft cited essay "Freshman Composition: No Place for Literature," paints a picture of the literature classroom that allows no space for student voices:

> Moreover, many literature courses are not humanistic. They present the teacher's or the critic's truths about the poetry, fiction, and drama being studied. They rarely connect literature with life. If students get to write a paper or two, they must assume the disembodied voice of some abstruse journal as they analyze the ingrown toenail motif in *Beowulf*. Such assignments silence students' voices in the conversation literature is intended to promote. In other words, literature teaching offers the writing teacher no model worth emulating [Lindemann 314].

Lindemann sees the study of literature as a discourse where expertise screams loudest. Students must ventriloquize scholarly voices they do not connect with and may not even yet fully grasp, leaving no room for their own exploration and development as writers. In fact, Lindemann suggests that the literature classroom does not value students as writers at all.

It seems to me no accident that Lindemann cites *Beowulf* as her paradigm for literature. An iconic "classic" text, one students often encounter in high school and even more often fail to find engaging, *Beowulf* embodies the formal, rigid, and even elitist portrait of literary study that Lindemann constructs in contrast to the dynamism of composition classrooms. But it also underscores a question I see persisting beneath the surface of these disagreements about literature's role in college-writing programs: *if you must teach literature in college writing, what kind of literature do you teach?*[2]

Lindemann assumes that instructors will gravitate towards classics like *Beowulf*. In some cases, this proves true. Richardson and others such as Daniel Mangiavellano have demonstrated ways in which classic literature can be used to encourage student-centric, writing-focused discussions in a college composition classroom. In "Who Killed Annabel Lee," Richardson's experience with a reticent group in his writing class stuck on how to analyze Edgar Allan Poe's famous poem demonstrates how approaching classics from different angles can help engage students in the writing process and encourage thoughtful, developed analytical writing (Richardson 282–92). Mangiavellano, conversely, argues for ways that classic literature like *Pride and Prejudice* can be used in composition courses not only to invite deeper discussion and more meaningful analysis, but to open up conversations about writing and process. Focusing on the ways in which *Pride and Prejudice* reflects upon different modes of writing, as well as on the many challenges of the writing process, he illustrates how the text helps him to "strike a healthy balance between skill-based writing instruction and encouraging students to recognize themselves as academic writers with worthwhile contributions to make" (Mangiavellano 551). Both Mangiavellano and Richardson show that classic literature can be broken from the authority of scholarly expertise and instead used to help our students explore the process of writing and develop as academic writers.

Others have argued for the introduction of non-canonical literature into the writing classroom. Jeanne Marie Rose makes a compelling case for the ways in which literature that represents "non-standard dialects" can serve to "foster a more inclusive view of language" (Rose 1). For Rose, introducing texts like John Edgar Wideman's "Doc's Story" into her writing classroom allows her to demonstrate the multiplicity of literacies and to dismantle hierarchies of rhetorical styles often linked to U.S. socio-political structures of class and race. For students who are not, to use her phrase, "linguistically dominant," encountering various dialects within literature can help them to view themselves as legitimate writers and also validate their modes of expression (1).

While Rose sees non-canonical literature as a way to forge a more inclusive writing classroom, Jerome Evans believes that using pop culture can help students to more effectively decode and engage with classic literature (Evans 33). Like Richardson, Evans understands pop culture as a way to tap into literacies that students already possess. "Artifacts of pop culture," he argues, "can serve as advanced organizers for students, who can then connect new material ... to their own experiences with literature" (33). Pop culture texts become a gateway through which students can develop the skills necessary to more effectively approach difficult writing and analytical tasks later in the semester.

Non-canonical literature and pop culture, these authors all suggest, have a productive place in the composition classroom. Engaging with these types of literary texts validate student identities and experiences, and help them to feel like the kind of "experts" that Lindemann suggests literature in a composition classroom shuts down. Even Richardson, whose discussion of literature in the writing classroom focuses more narrowly on classic literature, points out that he uses pop culture to help students gain access to these classic texts: "When I interrogated students about the sources of their insights, it quickly became apparent that there were three: TV ... movies ... and their own life experiences and those of their friends. These are the literacies—the kinds of 'text' that students are already familiar with and know how to read ... when they come to college" (Richardson 285–86). Activating students' existent literacies through pop culture thus helps to maintain the student-centric approach so important to composition classrooms. Instead of relegating inquiry and analysis to experts, working with popular culture and non-canonical literature encourages students to see themselves in the texts the class reads and to use those points of access to hone both writing and reading skills.

Young Adult Literature and Gender Studies as Modes of Student Literacy

At the end of his last "Teaching Young Adult Literature" column in *English Journal,* Mike Roberts rationalizes the use of young adult literature in the classroom:

> High-achieving students in your class can dissect YAL for the literary elements contained within the pages. Proficient students will be able to make text-to-self connections. Finally, struggling students will benefit because they will be able to read and understand the story line easily enough to truly enjoy the book, something that they often aren't able to do with the classics [Roberts, "YA Belongs in the Classroom" 90].

This practical assessment of how young adult literature can provide important access for students of all levels makes a strong case for the value of YA, especially for the high-school and middle-school teachers that he addresses.

Roberts also sees YA as accessible in the ways in which Richardson and others talk about the utility of literature in the college-writing classroom. "Today's world is filled with new and unique challenges," Roberts says, "and students need a place where they can connect with characters that struggle with the same issues they battle every day" (90). He argues that young adult literature functions as a mode of meaning-making for students, a way for them to make sense of the world. Characterized this way, young adult literature can be seen as a form of student literacy, similar to the non-canonical texts and pop culture that Rose and Evans advocate for inclusion in classrooms.

YA writer Susan Beth Pfeffer describes young adult literature's usefulness as in stark opposition to the role of classic literature. "Unlike Shakespeare and Dickens," Pfeffer writes, "YA novels aren't worshiped for their perfection" (qtd. in Roberts, "YA Belongs in the Classroom" 89). She goes on to add, "it's okay to rip YA to shreds" (89). Students, she suggests, would be less willing to "rip to shreds" Shakespeare. They don't feel they have the knowledge or expertise necessary to make claims about classic texts, much less criticize them. But young adult literature feels less "sacred." Put another way, students feel like they have some authority over the text. They feel comfortable making value judgments about young adult books and criticizing them. This is an important first step to strong analytical claims: feeling like you have something to say, and the right or authority to say it.

Young adult literature's accessibility for students makes it a strong vehicle through which to navigate more complex concepts. Roberts advocates for the use of YA across disciplines, including science and math (Roberts, "YA Novels across the Curriculum" 92). Similarly, Jacqueline Glasgow uses YA in her classrooms as a way to jumpstart discussions on social justice. As she argues, "young adult literature provides a context for students to become conscious of their operating world view and to examine critically alternative ways of understanding the world and social relations" (Glasgow 54). Glasgow chooses young adult books for her curriculum that "cause [students] to question the ways that systems (e.g., race, privilege, gender dominance, social class advantage) are implicated in specific actions, events, or situations," and these books serve as gateways through which students choose and explore more deeply a specific form of systemic oppression (55). For both Roberts and Glasgow, YA novels are not simple feedback loops that reproduce or reinforce student worldviews. Instead, they offer accessible, familiar ways into topics that are difficult and may even be uncomfortable.

I would argue that gender is one of these complex social structures. While students usually possess their own assumptions around what it means to be a man or a woman, understanding the performative or constructed nature of gender is sometimes challenging for them. Using young adult novels as points of entry into gender studies can help to expose the ways in which culture defines masculinity and femininity. Laura M. Robinson notes that many YA novels depict "the adolescent's struggle to define him-or herself against normative culture" (Robinson 209). Studying the tension between the main character's sense of self and what the world tells them they ought to be can be a starting point to revealing the constructed nature of gender.

Pairing YA with gender inquiries can be productive in a college-writing classroom as well. In my experience, even if students do not have a sophisticated grasp of gender theory, they are comfortable having conversations about masculinity and femininity. In past years, I have included writing assignments in my composition courses where students had to analyze advertisements for assumptions about gender in order to practice supporting analytical arguments. To start, students were able to make broad argumentative strokes about what they saw in the ads we studied, claims that we worked together in office hours and workshops to narrow down and complicate. Classes where I displayed ads for us to discuss were often some of the most active discussions in the semester, and even more reticent students piped in with their own interpretations.

Introducing these kinds of analytical discussions to young adult literature in a composition course provides, I believe, ample opportunity to model analysis and practice generating arguments and supporting those arguments effectively. The intersection of YA and gender studies allows instructors to use texts in a composition classroom that tap into students' pre-existing literacies, or, put another way, texts over which students feel they possess some authority, while also providing a narrowed lens through which students might approach those texts, limiting the scope of their investigations and thus helping them to hone their argumentative skills. When students feel they don't need to be experts, or better yet, feel like they, too, *are* experts, they take more analytical risks, leading to more fruitful class discussion and opening up further spaces with which to practice skills-based writing, including making claims and supporting those claims with evidence.

Reading Gender in Twilight: *A Sample Analysis*

Most young adult literature is, at its core, a coming-of-age story. Even YA fantasies like Leigh Bardugo's *Six of Crows* (2015) explore the struggles of figuring out who you are and how you fit into the world. Robinson clarifies this relationship between YA and identity, arguing that "young adult fiction is often about the individual's troubling relationship to the norms of the greater society, and the outcome of such books usually highlights the power of the individual to transform his or her world" (205). "Perhaps," she goes on, "one of the significant regulatory regimes that causes conflict in children's and young adult fiction … is gender" (205). As Robinson makes clear, one of the major ways in which we negotiate the world around us is in adhering to or subverting the normative modes of gender offered to us. With this perspective in mind, most YA fiction could be used in a writing classroom to analyze gender.

I have chosen *Twilight* for its persistent cultural recognition (even years after the final film was released, most young adults are at least aware of the series), but, more importantly, because the story seems especially immersed in constructing and promoting particular gender constructions. It is, simply put, a book about gender. Bella Swann's status as "every girl,"[3] the series' pro-abstinence message,[4] and its "old fashioned" approach to romance[5] represent just a few of the many ways that *Twilight* explores masculinity and femininity. For this essay, I will focus on one: how the paranormal aspects of the book (that Bella is human and Edward a vampire) reproduce the traditional gender norms upheld by the story.

Stephenie Meyer takes liberties with her interpretation of vampires in

Twilight, especially by giving them rock-hard skin that sparkles, rather than burns up, in the sunlight. When Edward steps into the meadow to show Bella why he avoids the sun, she says that "his skin, white despite the faint flush from yesterday's hunting trip, literally sparkled, like thousands of tiny diamonds were embedded in the surface" (Meyer 260). "A perfect statue," she calls him, "carved in some unknown stone, smooth like marble, glittering like crystal" (260). Throughout this scene, Meyer piles more and more adjectives onto Edward to solidify this image of him as both beautiful and inhuman. The natural beauty of the untouched meadow "paled next to his magnificence" (261). His chest was "sculpted" and "incandescent," his bare arms "scintillating" (260). These descriptions, chosen, of course, to remind us of Bella's overwhelming attraction to Edward, also work to define Meyer's vampire. As Tammy Dietz aptly puts it, "as a vampire, Edward represents more than a man: he is practically a god" (Dietz 10). "Perfect," Bella will call him, over and over again. Vampires in the *Twilight* series are invulnerable, impenetrable, and, as Edward tells Bella earlier in the story, excessively beautiful in order to entrap their prey. Bella reveres them in the text, and given that Edward's self-critical lens is the only opposition to them,[6] and one that Bella is quick to negate, I think it is safe to assume that Meyer wants readers to admire her vampires as well.

Humans in *Twilight* are not nearly so perfect. Bella focuses for a significant portion of the narrative on how her humanity makes her weak. She describes herself as being plagued with "crippling clumsiness" (Meyer 55). In fact, she answers Edward's demands as to why she didn't run away from the threatening men she encountered in Port Angeles by insisting, "I fall down a lot when I run" (191). Bella's humanity shackles her with an unsteadiness sorely lacking in her vampire boyfriend. Most strikingly, when Edward spends the night in her room later in the novel and encourages her to get up the next morning for some breakfast, she thinks to herself that he meant "to prove … that he remembered all my human frailties" (314). To be human is to be frail. And mortal. It is to age and die (476). By the time the first book has ended, Bella is determined to shrug off her mortal coil and be turned into a vampire. If not by her boyfriend, then, as she reminds him, by someone else (476). This desire to no longer be human and to associate humanity with weakness and frailty casts humanity as a burden and as inferior to vampirism. It is better, it seems, to be a monster.

Bella reminds us of this dichotomy between humans and vampires in her continuous comparisons of herself to Edward. "Look at me," she says. "I'm absolutely ordinary—well, except for the bad things like all the near-death experiences and being so clumsy that I'm almost disabled. And look at you" (210). What she doesn't say out loud is that what she sees when she looks at Edward is "bewildering perfection" (210). He is *so* perfect that she can't quite comprehend it. Perfect versus ordinary. Strong versus weak. Impenetrable/invulnerable versus prone to "near death experiences." Bella sees her humanity and Edward's vampirism as making them opposite in every way.

And while, in Bella's eyes, Edward is invaluable, she sees herself as having no value. Repeatedly throughout the series, Bella puts her life at risk for her boyfriend and the rest of the Cullen family. Though Meyer's series tends to equate love with sacrifice, and being willing to give up your own life for the safety of others is viewed as noble in the book (especially in regards to Edward), because Bella tries to sacrifice herself for immortal beings, the onus shifts from a noble act to the devaluing of herself. Her mortality makes her dispensable, crystallizing the book's reverence of the vampire. In Bella's eyes, she won't be equal to Edward, she won't matter, until she too is a vampire.

Throughout the text, Edward's vampirism and Bella's humanity are fused to their embodiments of gender. This is especially clear in Meyer's treatment of Edward. He is often characterized as paternal.[7] His love for Bella may be romantic, but it manifests itself in a compulsion to keep her safe. He tells her, "it makes me … anxious … to be away from you…. I wasn't joking when I asked you to try not to fall in the ocean or get run over last Thursday. I was distracted all weekend, worrying about you. And after what happened tonight, I'm surprised that you did make it through a whole weekend unscathed" (188–89). Edward's masculinity is predicated on his desire to protect. And his vampire body, impenetrable, inhumanly strong, and impossibly skilled (he can see, smell, and hear better than a human, and his vampiric superpower is that he can read minds) allows him to be the ultimate protector. Masculinity, in Meyer's book, then, is to be strong and protective and invulnerable, to the point, one might argue, that to be a man one *must* be a vampire (which is why Bella is never attracted to any of her school friends like Mike and Eric, who show an interest in her).

But Edward's quote above illustrates not only his intense need to protect. It demonstrates how much he thinks Bella needs protection. He sees her as incapable of taking care of herself. She cannot, it seems, go to the beach without falling in the water or walk down a street without being threatened by passing cars. Though she has managed to survive seventeen years without him, he believes she is only safe when he is around. His extreme paternalism forces Bella (and the image of femininity associated with her) into the position of a child. More than once, the novel literalizes this comparison. When Bella is surprised by Edward's unexpected presence in her room, she describes him moving her to the bed: "he sat up slowly, so as not to startle me again. Then he leaned forward and reached out with his long arms to pick me up, gripping the tops of my arms like I was a toddler" (297). This is not a romantic moment of being swept off her feet: instead he lifted her as he would a child. A few lines later, Meyer links this depiction of Bella as childlike to her humanity by having Bella request to Edward, "can I be human for a minute?" (297). The juxtaposition of this request with the way he carried her like a child associates Bella's feminine weakness with her humanity. Just as Edward's protective nature—his masculinity—is tied to his vampire nature, so Bella's "childishness"—her femininity—is linked to her being human.

Vampire, strength, and masculinity become irrevocably intertwined, in the same way that human, weak, and feminine are woven together by the text. By conflating her narrative's paranormal elements with the gender constructions produced by the romance plot of *Twilight*, Meyer thus reinforces the traditional gender norms of masculine hero/damsel in distress reiterated in so many other ways throughout the book. Bella may claim to want to be "Superman," but her humanity, and the femininity it represents, relegates her for a good portion of the series to the position of Lois Lane.

Practical Considerations for the Composition Classroom

I most often use *Twilight* in my classes as a way to practice analysis for a later paper assignment where my students must analyze a primary source of their choosing to contribute to an academic conversation they've spent the semester exploring. Though they are not required to choose a YA text or to write about gender, many of my students gravitate towards these topics after our class discussions on *Twilight*. This activity happens over the course of two class days, and serves to encourage discussion around what it means to support an argument and how to interrogate examples to find the strongest ones.

Students are asked to read sections of *Twilight* before class and they must write a short discussion forum post on what they see to be Stephenie Meyer's definitions of masculinity and femininity in the novel. This establishes gender from the beginning as the primary lens through which we will look at the novel and also helps students begin to define the terms masculinity and femininity for themselves by looking for evidence within the story.

On the first class day that we discuss *Twilight*, I ask students to work individually to find examples in the text that support pre-determined claims. I scaffold this activity by asking first for support for concrete or factual claims, such as examples that show Bella's feelings for Edward, examples of her clumsiness, etc. Then we will discuss what they found, always focusing the discussion on how the example helps to prove the idea. In the second half of class, I give them a new claim to support, this one more argumentative, such as *Meyer equates femininity with weakness*. Students again work alone to find examples. When they are done, they exchange what they found with a partner, and, working together, they come up with that they see as the strongest support and why. I ask the groups to share their examples with the class. This opens up a space for us to discuss the function and importance of support for an analytical argument, allowing me to demonstrate for them how specific, concrete examples help to strengthen a claim.

On the next class day, students are put into groups and asked to write their own claims about the gender norms constructed in *Twilight*. I also ask them to come up with five examples from the text that support their argument. This activity may not always produce enlightened readings of the text, but because students have their own assumptions about gender and feel some sense of authority on the subject, groups are usually able to produce gender-focused claims without much resistance. Often it leads to lively debates within groups as they determine what to focus on. We spend the second half of class sharing arguments and support and reinforcing the discussions about analysis and evidence opened up in the previous class.

Overall, I've found this activity successful for engaging students in analysis and generating discussions both around *Twilight* and around skills-based writing. Because *Twilight* (and young adult literature more generally) feels familiar to my students, they claim some authority over the text. They are willing to ask complicated questions of Meyer's work, like the one discussed in the opening to this essay, and to look at pieces of the text that may challenge their own relationship to it. Many times students have voiced nostalgic affection for the novel, only to be troubled by it upon a second reading, and I've found them, for the most part, willing and open to interrogating the text in support of these responses.

Using gender as a way to read the novel also helped me to be able to model analytical arguments for the class, and to give us narrow, well-defined ideological spaces through which to find and evaluate support for those claims. When I ask students to look for textual examples that show Bella as weak, they are able to point to moments in the narrative and explain how Bella's clumsiness, for instance, functions as an image of weaknesses. Through these exercises, we are able to discuss how strong support for an argument requires not only relevant, concrete examples, but also analysis of those examples.

These activities accompany the course's final writing assignment, which asks students to enter into an academic conversation around monsters (the course's theme) by making their own argument about a primary source (a novel, film, TV show, etc.), which they select on their own. In their paper, they must use a handful of examples from their primary source and explain in detail how these examples help support their argument, while also considering how their argument relates to what other writers and scholars are already saying about this issue. Our class days on *Twilight* help prepare students for this paper by modeling effective analytical arguments and providing ample practice of evidence selection. Scaffolding the activities in this way places emphasis on defining what makes strong evidence: this encourages effective analysis, and also gives students tools to help them evaluate and vet their evidence for papers rather than settling on what they find first. These kinds of skills extend beyond literary analysis to academic argument in general and help prepare students for the demands of writing throughout their academic careers.[8]

Conclusion

Even when I don't assign *Twilight* as a part of my composition course, students often introduce the text into their own papers. Over the years, I've received essays on *Twilight* and fandom, on Edward Cullen as representative of 21st century masculine ideals or as the embodiment of shifts in conversations about the role of the vampire in popular culture. I even had a student write a paper on *Twilight* as an example of how audience impacts a written text.

My students' engagement in class activities around *Twilight* and their readiness to turn to it as a text to help them figure out what they want to say as a writer reiterates the important role young adult literature and gender studies can play in the college-writing classroom. By giving students the opportunity to engage with literacies in which they already participate, such as *Twilight* and other YA novels, and by providing them with clear, focused lenses throughout which to approach those literacies, we can encourage students to develop their analytical skills and create deeper, more well-supported arguments. In this way our students learn not to pantomime experts, as Lindemann fears, but to interrogate for themselves what it means to support an argument well, skills necessary for academic pursuits in any discipline.

NOTES

1. See, for instance, Peter Elbow, "The Cultures of Literature and Composition: What Could Each Learn from the Other?"; Elizabeth A. Flynn, "Beyond College Composition"; Erika Lindemann, "Freshman Composition: No Place for Literature."

2. See Abigail Scheg's article "My Composition or Yours: What Do We Teach in First-Year Composition?"

3. Tanya Erzen, in her book *Fanpire,* for instance, notes that "thousands of girls are Bellas. The fear of the books is that Meyer has created in Bella a character so unremarkable, yet so desirable, that anyone can project herself onto her" (6).

4. See, for instance, pp. 20–21 of Rhonda Nichol's article "'When You Kiss Me, I Want to Die': Arrested Feminism in *Buffy the Vampire Slayer* and the *Twilight* Series."

5. See Ananya Mukherjea's article "My Vampire Boyfriend: Postfeminism, 'Perfect' Masculinity, and the Contemporary Appeal of Paranormal Romance."

6. This becomes more complicated as the series continues and the vampire world is extended, but in the first book, Meyer's monster figures seem to have almost no flaws.

7. Tanya Erzen, in *Fanpire,* explains that "most of the fanpire girls and women view Edward's control issues as part of his old-fashioned charm. His charisma, icy marble muscles, and undeniable gorgeousness enable them to overlook his paternalism, though it is his paternalism that makes him so appealing to fans" (18). Tammy Dietz similarly notes Edward's "fatherly dominance" (Dietz 5).

8. Though not the focus of this particular essay, using gender as a lens to read literature in college-writing classes also creates spaces for discussion of outside research and the finding and vetting of sources for a paper, by providing a limited framework with which to conduct online research.

Works Cited

Dietz, Tammy. "Wake Up, Bella! A Personal Essay on *Twilight,* Mormonism, Feminism, and Happiness." *Bringing Light to Twilight: Perspectives on a Pop Culture Phenomenon.* Ed. Giselle Liza Anatol. London: Palgrave Macmillan, 2011. 1–14.

Elbow, Peter. "The Cultures of Literature and Composition: What Could Each Learn from the Other?" *College English* vol. 64, no. 5, May 2002. 533–546.

Erzen, Tanya. *Fanpire: the* Twilight Saga *and the Women Who Love It.* Boston: Beacon Press, 2012.

Evans, Jerome. "From Sheryl Crow to Homer Simpson: Literature and Composition Through Pop Culture." *English Journal* vol. 93, no. 3, January 2004. 32–38.

Flynn, Elizabeth A. "Beyond College Composition." *College Composition and Communication* vol. 61, no. 2, December 2009. 474–483.

Glasgow, Jacqueline N. "Teaching Social Justice Through Young Adult Literature." *The English Journal* vol. 90, no. 6, July 2001. 54–61.

Lindemann, Erika. "Freshman Composition: No Place for Literature." *College English* vol. 53, no. 3, March 1993. 311–316.

Mangiavellano, Daniel R. "First Encounters with *Pride and Prejudice* in the Composition Classroom." *Pedagogy* vol. 12, no. 3, Fall 2012. 550–555.

Meyer, Stephenie. *Twilight.* New York: Little, Brown, 2005.

Murkherjea, Ananya. "My Vampire Boyfriend: Postfeminism, 'Perfect' Masculinity, and the Contemporary Appeal of Paranormal Romance." *Studies in Popular Culture* vol. 33, no. 2, Spring 2011. 1–20.

Nichol, Rhonda. "'When You Kiss Me, I Want to Die': Arrested Feminism in *Buffy the Vampire Slayer* and the *Twilight* Series." *Bringing Light to* Twilight: *Perspectives on a Pop Culture Phenomenon.* Ed. Giselle Liza Anatol. London: Palgrave Macmillan, 2011. 15–25.

Richardson, Mark. "Who Killed Annabel Lee? Writing About Literature in the Composition Classroom." *College English* vol. 66, no. 3, January 2004. 278–293.

Roberts, Mike. "Why Should We Have All the Fun? Encouraging Colleagues to Read YA Novels Across the Curriculum." *English Journal* vol. 102, no. 1, 2012. 92–95.

_____. "YA Literature Belongs in the Classroom Because…" *English Journal* vol. 102, no. 5, 2013. 89–90.

Robinson, Laura M. "Girlness and Guyness: Gender Trouble in Young Adult Literature." *Jeunesse: Young People, Texts, Culture* vol. 1, no. 1, 2009. 203–22.

Rose, Jeanne Marie. "Standards of English: Literature as Language Standard." *Composition Forum* vol. 14, no. 2, Fall 2005. 1–9.

Scheg, Abigail G. "My Composition or Yours: What Do We Teach in First-Year Composition?" *Writing Pathways to Student Success.* Ed. L. Craton. Anderson, SC: Parlor Press, 2016.

Writing in the *Afterworlds*

Michele D. Castleman

Scott Westerfeld's *Afterworlds* is a meditation on the process of writing a young adult (YA) paranormal romance novel. Told in two voices, *Afterworlds* weaves the story of Darcy Patel as she moves to Manhattan to revise her first young adult (YA) novel for publication with the account of her protagonist, Lizzie Scofield, who survives a terrorist attack in an airport by crossing into the afterworld and meeting an Indian deity named Yama. After Lizzie returns to the land of the living, she must recover from trauma and aid a ghost from her own mother's past, while also exploring her growing romance with Yama. The dual narrative structure allows the reader to see the ways Darcy draws inspiration from her own life and from those around her to craft the revisions for her novel. This not only explores an author's inspirational process for writing, but provides insight into the young adult publishing world. The reader is with Darcy as she changes the ending of her novel, joins two other authors on tour, goes through copy edits, and signs advanced reader copies of her novel—also titled *Afterworlds*—at Book Expo of America. Beyond the overview of the publishing process, the reader also experiences Darcy's deeper struggle to represent herself as a writer and to represent cultural and religious experiences on the page. As Darcy struggles with the ethical dilemma of having drawn inspiration from her religious faith, teen writers can gain perspective on how to approach writing about similar issues or their own personal experiences in their own research and drafting process.

As Darcy contemplates how to write and revise Lizzie's story, her reflection can serve as a model for teen writers. Nilsen articulates several reasons that YA novels can serve as inspiration for students. Such reasons include "the problems in the books are likely to be ones that readers" have experienced, the "variety of ethnic backgrounds and settings enlarges the chances of students finding stories they can identify with," the dialogue in the novels resembles the speech patterns of teens, the protagonists have the "intellectual and emotional development" similar to that of the teen readers, and the intriguing details in the stories are the same ones "clever and witty teenagers observe and relate to each other—which means they have a head start when it comes to incorporating such details into stories" (81). In the case of *Afterworlds*, teen writers may find inspiration and connection with Darcy since she is pursuing her passion, struggling with living independently and on a budget for the first time, and experiencing her first major romantic relationship with another debut YA author named Imogen Gray.

Writing Identity as an Insider and Outsider

Darcy is also motivated by the desire to play with her identity and reinvent herself, a sense many teen writers may share. Darcy focuses upon her new identity as a writer, fixating on it so much in discussions with her family that her little sister, Nisha, wants to charge Darcy a dollar whenever Darcy mentions her agent more than ten times per a day. With the sale of *Afterworlds*, Darcy finds she is in a financial position to define herself in new ways and she leaves her hometown. When Darcy initially moves to New York City, she avoids telling her new friends her exact age and leaves behind the vast majority of her books and other belongings at her parents' home. She notes that her new apartment "was a blank page" (269) was a space she chose for its potential "to be filled with stories" (143).

Beyond embracing this new identity of writer, Darcy explores her sexual identity as well. Her relationship with Imogen is Darcy's first serious romantic relationship and Imogen expresses concern that Darcy wanted to rewrite herself with her move to New York (269). This tension between the characters reemerges later, as Darcy and Imogen plan to visit the Patel family to celebrate Pancha Ganapati, a five-day celebration "in honor of Ganesha" (451). Imogen argues that Darcy does not want to tell her parents that Imogen is her girlfriend and Imogen eventually questions Darcy about her choices. Darcy defends her reluctance:

> "It's not about being afraid!" Darcy cried. Suddenly all that mattered was that Imogen understand her, completely. "When I sold *Afterworlds*, I didn't just get a book deal. I got a whole new life, one that came with no assumptions about who or what I was. And I know how lucky that is, like winning the lottery. But it's still *my* lottery ticket, and I don't want to give it up! And part of that is not having to define myself."
>
> Imogen was shaking her head. "You define yourself all the time, Darcy. You hold my hand when we walk down the street" [454–455].

This moment serves as the intersection of larger issues of identity and authorship, including Darcy's religion, ethnicity, and sexual identity as well as her attempt to avoid harsher realities of the world by staying in "YA heaven" and being able to write all the time with her girlfriend in her pricey China Town apartment.

Underpinning these issues of a character's struggle to know herself and be known by others is the issue of authorship and a question common to examining multicultural literature: that of who may write from whose perspectives. This question is also relevant to the composition classroom as students and teachers must explore together how much knowledge, research, and personal experience is necessary to represent the subjects students write about. In *Stories Matter*, Fox and Short compiled essays by YA and children's authors exploring the dilemma of who can authentically represent various cultural experiences in YAL and children's literature and related questions: To what extent can an author rely upon imagination? Can only people who have had an experience firsthand represent it in writing? How far can research lead an author who is a cultural outsider to bridge cultural gaps? Fox and Short incorporate the voices of many authors with a variety of perspectives on the topic. Celebrated author Jacqueline Woodson asserts:

> My belief is that there is room in the world for all stories, and that everyone has one. My hope is that those who write about the tears and the laughter and the language in my grandmother's house have first sat down at the table with us and dipped the bread of their own experiences into the stew [Fox and Short 45].

Whether through personal experience, interviews, or visits with subjects, Woodson advocates for an author to have direct interaction with her subject. In the composition classroom, this position lends itself to students solidly placing themselves in the research process, perhaps through a project like an I Search paper, an approach to research-based writing that Ken Marcorie describes and advocates.

In contrast to Woodson, author Kathryn Lasky's stance towards taking on others' cultural experiences focuses on the underlying authenticity or realness of a character's voice:

> It has been said that great stories are told from the inside out and therefore a writer from another culture has no chance of capturing the true voice in which the story must be told. I would agree with the first part of this statement—great stories are told from the inside out, but great artists, even those not of a particular culture, can indeed find the real voice. They can go inside out, even if they have not been there before. That is the whole meaning of being a great artist [Fox and Short 89].

Lasky advocates for a less restrictive approach to writing from others' cultural perspectives. She argues, "the first criterion for publication should always be that the book is good literature" (91). She cautions against assuming that because an author is from an particular ethnic group that his or her book will automatically be good, but rather asserts that great authors will still find an authentic voice to represent experiences that are not their own. In

Afterworlds, Darcy's struggle with this insider-outsider issue arises from her inclusion of the character Yama in her novel. Yama is "the Hindu god of death and judgment," (Uth). He serves as Darcy's romantic love interest for Lizzie. "Along with his twin sister, Yama is considered the progenitor of the human race" (Uth). Yami, his sister, also appears in Darcy's novel. Darcy has fictionalized the origin story for Yami and Yama, creating a death scene for them that was set in the ancient past and that involves a donkey. Darcy reflects:

> The donkey story was one of the few things in the book that she had come up with on her own. It had nothing to do with [Yama] of the Vedas, or her mother's murdered friend. It had come out of nowhere, it seemed, a tale from another era [Westerfeld 257].

Darcy takes pride in the fact that she did not rely upon another part of her life for inspiration. Following Lasky's assertions, Darcy is most concerned with telling a good story by being willing to move beyond religion and experience to create an engaging novel.

In contrast, Darcy's appropriation of Yama from Hinduism as well as the appropriation of the premise of a dead childhood friend haunting her mother both become a key struggle for Darcy throughout the novel. These questions may reverberate with teen writers as well: To what extent do they rely upon personal experiences for story ideas, upon those experiences of their loved ones or their religious or cultural traditions? Darcy contemplates her own choices to use Yama as a romantic lead:

> Darcy wondered when exactly she'd decided to borrow a character from her religion. Maybe those stories from the Vedas had always been in her head. Maybe it hadn't even been conscious.
> But at some point Yama had gotten mixed up with all the other stories in her head, and he had blended with Bollywood actors, manga boyfriends, paranormal romance hotties, and even the handsome princes from Disney movies… [257].

Initially, Imogen and other writers in the novel dismiss concerns over her use of the Hindu religious figure because Darcy appears to be an Indian cultural insider who Imogen assumes is a practicing Hindu. Darcy reacts by noting, "'I guess so' … but that was a tricky one. The only statue of Ganesha in her parents' house sat on her dad's computer, and had magnetic feet, and she'd rejected her family's vegetarianism when she turned thirteen" (85). She later notes, "A character like Yama, someone borrowed from the Vedas, already has his own stories out here in the real world. And every day, Darcy grew more uncertain whether he was hers to play with anymore" (239). In response to these meditations, students could journal and debate whether Darcy's use of Yama is appropriate as they read Lizzie's half of *Afterworlds* and examine the way Yama is characterized.

Darcy's concern over her use of a figure from Hinduism is heightened when two of her friends from high school note a paradox in the way Yama is included into Darcy's novel. She begins by asking if her friend, Sagan, a practicing Hindu, found her appropriation of Yama offensive:

> He shrugged. "It seemed weird at first, but then I figured that it wasn't a problem, because there's no Hinduism in your universe."
> Darcy blinked. "What?"
> "Well, you know when … [Lizzie] Googles all those death gods? At first I didn't get why she never ran into the concept of Yama."
> "Because that would be weird," Darcy said. "I mean, she's been making out with him. And he's not a god in my world, he's a person" [237].

Sagan goes on to explain that the "Angelina Jolie Paradox" applies, meaning that when a well-known actor, like Angelina Jolie, takes on a role as a character, that character is not usually acknowledged as looking like the actor, meaning an alternative reality exists within the movie or other text, in which that actual actor does not exist. He states:

> "Well, given that Lizzie's been researching death gods, and yet somehow never realizes that her boyfriend is an actual death god for, like, eight hundred million Hindus, I assume your book takes place in a universe in which Hinduism does not exist. There's no other explanation."
> …"*Dude.*" Carla laughed and sat beside her punching Darcy on the arm. "You just erased your own religion" [238–239].

Although Darcy's concerns over including a religious figure are never truly resolved, for the reader of *Afterworlds*, it is possible to complicate the matter further by taking a step back to consider that Westerfeld is writing from Darcy's point of view, a character who potentially diverges from his own background in terms of gender, sexual orientation, and culture. Although arguably he is a cultural outsider, however, there are still underlying experiences that connect Westerfeld to his protagonist, Darcy: As Darcy has a relationship with another YA author in the novel, Westerfeld is married to Justine Larbalestier, a fellow YA author with whom he has lived in New York City, among other places (Hiltbrand). While much of a work of fiction is invented, the novel still reveals underlying truth. These potential overlaps with Westerfeld's own lived experiences is one such way that he may reveal underlying truth through fiction, meeting Lasky's expectation that an author find a "real voice." In the composition classroom, this allows for student reflection on the emotional truth of their own writing and how they can work to create real voices for their own characters. Exercises from Rosenfeld's *Writing the Intimate Character* may prove helpful with creating authentic characterizations.

Westerfeld also has Darcy contemplate this concept of incorporating realness when she reflects upon her use of Yama. She narrates:

Whenever she began to type a story, Darcy felt an alternative universe inside her computer taking form. Some parts of it intersected with her own world, real places like San Diego and New York, but other parts were made up ... those connections with reality gave stories their power [239].

In terms of ethnicity and Indian culture, Westerfeld remains an outsider, but he uses Darcy to reveal the realities of a writing career in YAL to young readers who may find value in seeing these ideas revealed through the voice of an eighteen-year-old protagonist who resembles them. Students can discuss whether they feel the realness of Darcy and Lizzie's stories and the techniques Westerfeld uses to attempt to create this realness.

Like Westerfeld, Darcy also writes as a cultural outsider to her own protagonist when she writes Lizzie. While in conversation with two other YA authors, Kiralee and Imogen, Darcy discusses why she chose to characterize Lizzie as white. She informs them:

"It's just, I wanted to have an Indian guy as the love interest, a guy who looks like Muzammil Ibrahim." They both gave her another questioning look, and Darcy felt embarrassed and young. "He's a Bollywood actor, a model, really. He's the hot guy who was never in the paranormals I read when I was little, you know? But I didn't want it to be about *me* wanting him."

"You wanted every girl to want him." Kiralee was smiling again. "So you chose a white girl from California."

Darcy suddenly wished she had drunk less, even as she took another drink.

"Pretty much?" [83].

The male love interest being discussed, Yama, is intentionally positioned to be a viewed as desirable to his white love interest, and by extension, to the readers as well. This effort is poignant given the recent critiques of movies and other media that have historically included very few Asian male leads (Rogers).

The multicultural insider-outsider discussion may also be taken one step further with students by asking them about their own comfort levels with writing about cultural experiences outside their own. After all, such an exercise is not uncommon among school assignments. My personal response as a writing instructor is to always encourage my students to empathize and explore others' perspectives, but if students are interested in formally publishing their explorations of another culture, then that work should be held to a much higher research or experiential standard.

Practical Considerations for the Composition Classroom

As Darcy and Westerfeld must contemplate and choose their position to write from within the insider-outsider multicultural debate, teen writers too must consider their method and approaches for creating authenticity within their writing. They too must deal with the reality of real world audiences engaging with and responding to their writing; whether that audience be a family member, a teacher, or millions of readers. While these large-scale questions loom throughout *Afterworlds*, there are also concrete lessons the novel lends itself to as well, including the use of archetypes to contribute to characterizations, approaching specific writing structures like the query letter, and noting the works and experiences of YAL authors who were themselves published as teenagers.

Reflecting Upon and Writing Archetypes

I have taught *Afterwords* in a course on the use of Classical myth and religion within American culture. The focus of our reading of the novel was upon Darcy's discomfiture at using Yama as a character. In the weeks after reading *Afterworlds*, students prepared their open-ended final assignment in which they wrote their own original myths or incorporated character from myths or religions into their own works of fiction. I wanted them to consider the authorial experience of contributing to myth through writing and reflecting. I required students to examine mythical character archetypes as outlined in Vogler's *The Writer's Journey* and connect the character types to both story lines in *Afterworlds*.

In his writer's guide, Vogler describes both the character archetypes and the stages of a traditional heroic journey that are present in many popular books and movies. For the purposes of *Afterworlds*, the archetypes are more relevant. Vogler recommends considering the archetypes as "flexible character functions rather than as rigid character types" (24). A character can serve in different positions in different parts of a story or can have the qualities of multiple archetypes (see table 1). This complexity is part of the fun in asking students to analyze *Afterworlds* for these archetypes.

Table 1: Archetypes Present in Westerfeld's *Afterworlds*

Character Archetype	*Brief Description of the Archetype*	*Characters That Serve This Archetype's Function Within* Afterworlds
Hero	Focused on the "search for identity and wholeness" and is connected with self-sacrifice (29).	Darcy, Yama, and Lizzie.
Mentor	"Usually a positive figure who aids or trains the hero"(39).	Yama; Nan, Darcy's editor; Imogen; and Kiralee.

Character Archetype	Brief Description of the Archetype	Characters That Serve This Archetype's Function Within Afterworlds
Threshold Guardian	"Powerful guardians at the threshold places to keep the unworthy from entering. They present a menacing face to the hero, but if properly understood they can be overcome, bypassed, or even turned into allies" (49).	Moxie, Darcy's agent; Nan, Darcy's editor; the woman that encourages Lizzie to pretend to be dead over the phone and guides her to crossover into the afterworld; and Darcy's aunt, Lalana.
Herald	A figure that issues "challenges and announces[s] the coming of significant change" (55).	Agent Reyes; Lizzie's mother; Imogen; and Moxie, Darcy's agent.
Shapeshifter	Figures that "appear to change constantly from the hero's point of view" (59).	Darcy and Imogen.
Shadow	Figures that represent "the energy of the dark side, the unexpressed, unrealized, or rejected aspects" (65).	The bad man, Lizzie's father, Mr. Hamlyn and Darcy.
Ally	Figures that serve "a variety of functions, such as companion, sparring partner, conscious, or comic relief" (71).	Imogen; the other YA authors that were debuting in 2014; Mindy the ghost; Agent Reyes; Jamie, Lizzie's best friend; Nisha, Sagan; and Carla.
Trickster	Figures that embody "the energies of mischief and desire for change" (77).	Mr. Hemlyn, Imogen, and Darcy.

Adapted from Vogler.

Examining the archetypal functions that the characters in both storylines inhabit serves as a jumping off point for students to consider the characters they are developing in their own myth. In addition to this, Darcy's contemplation of her use of a religious figure from Hinduism is a potential model for the students' own reflection upon their writing for the course. Beyond the scope of my specific myth assignment, these archetypes can be incorporated into critical response to assigned readings or can be used to ask students what functions do the students' own characters fulfill within their own narratives and how are those functions made clear through dialogue, description, and actions.

Text Structures and More Writing Considerations

There are other models for writing at work in *Afterworlds* as well. In the composition classroom, to complement the focus on characterization and representation of cultural experiences through fiction, a teacher might introduce students to a more formal public form of writing: that of the cover or query letter.

QUERY LETTERS

The opening of the book consists of a description of Darcy's cover letter for her submission that led to her getting her agent. She describes the specific structure of the letter and establishes the dramatic impact a single typed email was about to have on her life. Darcy notes it was "the most important email" that she had ever written (Westerfeld 1). The cover letter is three paragraphs: the first about herself, the second about her novel, and the last was flattery for the Underbridge Literary Agency that would go on to represent her. "The email was not a perfect query letter. But it did its job" (2). She leaves out the fact that "all sixty thousand words of *Afterworlds* had been written in thirty days. The Underbridge Literary Agency hardly needed to know that," demonstrating how Darcy considers her audience in crafting the email (1). The description of the cover letter could be used as one model for high school and undergraduate students on how to write an effective cover letter. By pairing this with cover letter examples for job applications, students could write their own letters. A teacher could also direct students interested in publication to writing guides to books like Burt-Thomas's *Guide to Query Letters*.

The Five Elements of Story

Another passage from *Afterworlds* that lends itself to reflecting upon writing occurs when Darcy joins her girlfriend on a book tour. Darcy, Imogen, and a third YA author named Sanderson, compete in front of 200 high school students by making arguments over which element of fiction—character, conflict, setting, theme, and plot—is the most important. Students could have a similar debate or could contemplate how, depending upon the story, which elements are emphasized for their intended medium and audiences.

Providing Students with Writing Goals

While on tour with Imogen, Darcy also has the opportunity to share with several hundred high school students how she wrote the first draft of *Afterworlds*. She tells them, "A year ago, I was a senior in a high school kind of like this one, and I wondered what would happen if I wrote two thousands word a day for a month. Turns out, you wind up with sixty thousand words" (369). It is not only the fictional audience that receives this message, but the readers of *Afterworlds* as well. This attention to Darcy's youth in *Afterworlds* can serve as motivation for students to write back to the text with their own stories. *Afterworlds* can serve as a lead-in to an in-class challenge to participate in National Novel Writing Month (NaNoWriMo). NaNoWriMo has a young writers program at ywp.nanowrimo.org. The website includes a support page for educators with activity suggestions to guide students through the process of writing a novel. Although generally the expected word count for a writer to reach throughout the month of November is 50,000, the NaNoWriMo Youth Writers Program allows students to self-select a goal that will be both challenging and attainable for them.

A composition instructor can also draw students' attention to authors who were teens when they wrote their first published novels (see table 2). They will see that teens have a valuable and important place in YAL history. Such approaches could prove empowering for a classroom of teen writers.

Table 2: YAL Authors Who Wrote and Published as Teenagers

YAL Author Name	Age of the Author When He or She Wrote His or Her First Book	Book Titles
Amelia Atwater-Rhodes	13 years old	*In the Forests of the Night* and *Demon in My View*
Anne Frank	13 years old	*Anne Frank: The Diary of a Girl*
S.E. Hinton	15 years old	*The Outsiders*
Gordon Korman	12 years old	*This Can't Be Happening at Macdonald Hall*
Christopher Paolini	15 years old	*Eragon*

All of the ages of the authors are reported in the peritext of each of their novels.

From the focus upon inspiration and rewriting, to developing a sense of realness and providing exposure to the publishing industry, *Afterworlds* is a power tool for creative writing instruction. It embodies the idea of using text as a model for students' own writing and of reflecting upon the cultural implications of that writing. The novel is dedicated "to all you wordsmiths, you scribbles … for making writing a part of your reading," connecting the two pursuits. Having finished reading *Afterworlds*, the natural next step for the reader is to pick up a pen or pencil, or to open a laptop or app, and to write his or her own story.

Works Cited

Atwater-Rhodes, Amelia. *Demon in My View.* New York: Delacorte Press, 2000.
Atwater-Rhodes, Amelia. *In the Forest of the Night.* New York: Laurel-Leaf Books, 1999.

Burt-Thomas, Wendy. *The Writer's Digest Guide to Query Letters.* Cincinnati: Writer's Digest Books, 2008.

Cole, Pam. *Young Adult Literature in the 21st Century.* New York: McGraw-Hill, 2009.

Fox, Dana L., and Kathy G. Short, editors. *Stories Matter: The Complexity of Cultural Authenticity in Children's Literature.* Urbana: National Council of Teachers of English, 2003.

Frank, Anne. *The Diary of a Young Girl.* New York: Bantam Books, 1967.

Hiltbrand, David. "Author Scott Westerfeld Found His Niche Writing for Teenagers." *Philadelphia Inquirer,* 7 Sept. 2006.

Hinton, S.E. *The Outsiders.* New York: Speak, 1995.

Korman, Gordon. *This Can't Be Happening at Macdonald Hall!* New York: Scholastic, 1978.

Macrorie, Ken. *The I-Search Paper.* Portsmouth, NH: Heinemann, 1980.

NaNoWriMo's Young Writers Program. National Novel Writing Month, 2015. http://ywp.nanowrimo.org/. Accessed 18 Oct. 2016.

Nilsen, Alleen Pace. "Readers Responding: Creative Writing and YA Literature." *English Journal,* vol. 86, no. 3, 1997, pp. 81–86.

Paolini, Christopher. *Eragon.* New York: Alfred A. Knopf, 2003.

Rogers, Katie. "John Cho, Staring in Every Movie Ever Made? A Diversity Hashtag Is Born." *The New York Times,* 10 May 2016.

Rosenfeld, Jordan. *Writing the Intimate Character.* Cincinnati: Writer's Digest Books, 2016.

Uth, Alexandra. "Yama (deity)." *Salem Press Encyclopedia,* 2016.

Vogler, Christopher. *The Writer's Journey: Mythic Structure for Writers* (3rd ed.). Studio City, CA: Michael Wiese Productions, 2007.

Westerfeld, Scott. *Afterworlds.* New York: Simon Pulse, 2014.

Performing Resistance
in the Epic Theater
of *The Hunger Games*

KELLY F. FRANKLIN

"Where there is Power, there is Resistance..."
—Michel Foucault

In 2008, Suzanne Collins' bestselling novel, *The Hunger Games,* captivated audiences; adults, young adults, and children were reading its gripping
present tense prose with fervor. Collins had rejuvenated dystopian literature.
The story of Katniss Everdeen revitalized the sub-genre, sparking a dystopian
trend in young adult literature (YAL). However, popularity of this type of literature, and *The Hunger Games* series itself, should not be surprising as many
attributes of dystopia can be compared to tropes of adolescence. Carrie Hintz
and Elaine Ostry, editors of *Utopian and Dystopian Writing for Children and
Young Adults,* claim that dystopian writing is perfectly suited for YAL due to
the nature of adolescence, stating:

> Adolescence frequently entails traumatic social and personal awakening. The adoles-
> cent comes to recognize the faults and weaknesses of his or her society. A common
> trope in such literature is the emphasis on the lie, the secret and unsavory workings
> of the society that the teen hero uncovers. Dystopian literature thus mingles well
> with the coming-of-age novel, which features a loss of innocence [9].

Katniss Everdeen's journey from District 12 to the Capitol of Panem is
chock-full of traumatic awakenings, social and personal. Readers quickly find
themselves experiencing the Games through the first person present tense
narrative of Katniss. Collins' writing in this style affects her readers because
they begin to feel as if they are experiencing the games alongside their heroine. Readers witness Katniss performing many roles throughout the novel—

roles that Katniss is sometimes keenly aware that she is playing. In the Gamemakers arena, which can be thought of as a stage (because it is painstakingly designed and produced), Katniss knowingly performs multiple roles, most noticeably that of: hero, killer, lover, and reality television persona in order to assume control of her situation and survive the Games. By writing Katniss in this way, Collins provides audiences with a character who utilizes performance as power in order to achieve social and personal change. This notion is particularly powerful for young adult readers to witness in that it allows them to recognize role performance in their own lives. This recognition can assist young adults in successfully navigating their own social settings. The idea of performance as power to encourage social change is a component of epic Theater; thus, *The Hunger Games* can be compared to epic theater because it is written in such a way that mimics this type of performance. For Katniss, performance is power. Her ability to successfully perform roles that vastly differ from her personality makes her a formidable component, champion, and authority. Collins' series also serves as an example as to how young adults engage in "the art of making do"[1] (Certeau 30) within unjust structures of power—and then successfully perform resistance. Certainly, Michel de Certeau can be credited with the term "making do" which loosely defined means that a person manipulates events in order to transform them into opportunities.

Although the story of Katniss Everdeen is typically married to economic, feminist, and political conversations, her tale is also well-suited for the college composition classroom. When entering college, students find themselves enrolled in composition courses and introduced to another style of writing—academic writing—that feels foreign. In fact, Composition I can be compared to a dystopia: there is a controlling force that dictates format, grammar, tone, and style. Students living in this dystopia must learn to navigate it as best they can in order to "win." The first step to doing this is to understand the types of roles they need to learn how to play for survival. In many ways students in the composition classroom are performing resistance in an academic epic Theater—learning to portray believable characters (or roles) that allow them to "make do." Certainly, this can be thought of as a defense mechanism similar to Katniss's reality television created persona. By encouraging students to be aware of this notion, it is possible to keep them from feeling discouraged by the unfamiliar outside academic voice, and to embrace it as a defensive tactic they can use to "defeat" their dystopic conditions.

Performance and the Games

Dystopian YAL is commonly recognized as a genre that features elements such as strict governmental control, high technology, futuristic settings, and rebellion; *The Hunger Games* includes all four of these genre-specific components—with strict governmental control pulsing at the heart of the story. The text is set in Panem, a country located in the ruins of North America, which is composed of twelve districts and a controlling Capitol. In order to control and wield its power over its citizens, the government holds an annual event known as the Hunger Games. During these Games, citizens who reside in all twelve districts must offer two of their children, ages twelve to eighteen, up as tributes to the Capitol. Tributes engage in a nationally broadcasted fight to the death in an arena designed and controlled by the Capitol, where there can only be one victor. Katniss Everdeen, the sixteen-year-old heroine who offers herself as tribute in the stead of her younger sister, finds herself in the Games attempting to not only survive, but also appear genuine and likable to gain sympathy and support from the citizens of the Capitol. People living in the Capitol find great excitement and joy in the games, and often select tributes to support by sending much desired gifts into the arena in times of need; citizens in the Capitol can be compared to people who cheer for contestants on *Survivor* and other similar reality television shows.

Reality television was one of the inspirations for *The Hunger Games* series. In fact, Suzanne Collins first thought of the concept for her novel while watching a reality show. In an interview with James Blasingame, Collins states:

> The very moment when the idea came to me for *The Hunger Games*, however, happened one night when I was very tired and I was laying in bed channel surfing. I happened upon a reality program, recorded live, that pitted young people against each other for money. As I sleepily watched, the lines of reality started to blur for me and the idea for the book emerged.... I am fearful that today people see so many reality shows and dramas that when real news is on, its impact is completely lost on them [Blasingame and Collins 727].

By situating her novel within the dystopian sub-genre, and by including a televised Hunger Games reminiscent of current reality television culture, Collins provides readers with an opportunity to vicariously experience a character transitioning and performing resistance in a post-modern epic theater.

Epic Theater

As mentioned earlier, Collins was partially inspired by reality television when creating *The Hunger Games* series, but her similarities to epic theater can be thought of as a happy accident. Bertolt Brecht, whom is credited with coining the epic theater term, was a political philosopher, dramatist, and theater practitioner, and is most famous for theories that rejected "realism in acting and Aristotelian dramatic form.... Brecht argued that theater can be a forum for social and ideological change" (Bell 201). Brecht's theory of theater is based in three radical concerns: attention to the realities and assumptions of social relations, most especially class conflicts; commitment to staging and acting techniques that refuse to engage in mimetic representations; and the production of audiences who are critical observers moved to enact social and political change (71). Further explicating his concept of " epic theater," Brecht encouraged actors and audiences to "…remain aware of how any performance is at once bound by historical and social contexts and changing," providing an opportunity for cultural critique and ideally inspiring spectators to exclaim: "This cannot be! Who would have thought this was possible! This treatment has to stop, they offend me, and these behaviors must end" (70–71). Brecht encouraged actors and audiences to "…remain aware of how any performance is at once bound by historical and social contexts and changing" (70). He also believed that although performances are often constructed, they provide powerful ways in which to view life and the world.

Theater that operates in this matter was termed "epic theatre" by Brecht; epic theatre appeals to reason and allows audiences to think in new ways.[2] This type of theater often does the following: arouses the audience's capacity for action, forces the audience to make decisions, presents a picture of the world, makes the audience face something, brings an audience to a point of recognition, and the audience often stands outside the action and studies. Epic theatre is also known as theater that breaks the fourth wall (Bell 203), keeps emotions in check, makes strange, and provides arresting moments.

In *The Hunger Games,* Collins appropriates many Brechtian techniques without forcing her text to conform to the totality of all of Brecht's theories. As such, Collins' text is written in the style of epic theatre which causes its readers to experience similar emotions to those that would have been experienced in a Brechtian production. The Arena, cunningly designed by Capitol Gamemakers, serves as the stage that provides arresting moments which cause some people living in Panem to seek action against the Capitol; the fast-paced horror of the Games also affects readers of Collins' series, causing them to inwardly address atrocities and contemplate the immediate need for social change (in real and fictional worlds).

In regard to the composition classroom, instructors can be thought of as Gamemakers. Though most instructors are not creating assignments that will literally kill their students, though students may claim this metaphor is true, instructors do design rigorous units of study with strict rubrics that allow little room for conversational or personal voice (depending on the assignment). Units of study are typically designed to create the classroom, or in this case the arena, and through a series of activities, assignments, and weeks of attendance, instructors attempt to mold students into what academia wants. It is unfair to claim that instructors are forcing students to become robotic slaves to higher education, but it is possible to argue that many instructors understand what students need in order to survive academia, and their "arena" is one where "tributes" learn how to play the game.

Survival Type

For many students, learning how to separate their personal voice from their academic voice is quite difficult. Typically, people do not speak to one another in academic tone. An example of conversational tone is something like this: "I really liked that movie, it was cool. The graphics were great. We had so much fun! I was on the edge of my seat!" It is an emotional sentence that points toward the speaker, full of gusto and excitement. This can be transitioned to Academic tone in this way: "Arguably, the movie was an excellent representation of how producers can virtually grab an audience and leave them breathless. Though there is no definite reason to its magical hold, it can be assumed that its grip is due to the intricate visuals throughout the film." Both sentences virtually convey the same information; however, one is restrained in its personal level of emotion, which makes readers take it more seriously.

Emotional restraint is not a common characteristic of adolescence, but it is a component of epic theatre, which sheds light on Collins' characterization of Katniss. According to Bell, "Performers separate themselves from the characters they play by keeping their emotions 'in check' and working to stay emotionally detached in performance. This is not to say the performance is void of emotion, but rather that the performer and character do not become one" (203). In *The Hunger Games*, Katniss plays roles in a similar way. There exists a tension between who Katniss thinks and knows she is and who she is performing for everyone else. Due to the death of her father and near catatonic state of her mother, Katniss is required to play different roles from a very young age; she acts as sole provider for the family, stand-in parent(s) to Prim, and nursemaid to her mother. The poverty in District 12 requires Katniss to become quick-witted, a skilled hunter, and a masterful strategist—which allow her to perform in different ways throughout her lifetime. Thus, Katniss indeed separates herself from the many roles she plays.

Due to Collins' use of first person point of view, readers are attuned to Katniss' inner thoughts and feelings, and are easily able to spot when she is performing for the sake of survival. Katniss is not often thought of as a killer, although she does kill many times in the story, she herself is never branded as a killer. This is because Katniss frequently keeps her emotions in check and often appears so composed that some readers have considered her verging on emotionless. Instead of appearing angry with the Capitol, Katniss is able to remain composed and unfazed, allowing her to internally strategize her next move without her emotions giving away her motives.

The critical distance between Katniss and her emotions allows readers to question the construction of not only the characters in the text, but also the dystopic conditions surrounding them. This same maneuver can be used by composition instructors in the classroom setting. It can be quite difficult for students to learn how to control their emotions in writing, and understanding that "loud" writing is often scoffed at as a valuable lesson. In the text, this component of epic theatre used by Collins serves as a powerful agent in how audiences react to and are inspired by Katniss Everdeen. For students, it can be powerful for them to witness the way in which people respond to writing that sounds academic vs. conversational—the awareness of this power removes can remove the sting. If a student realizes how they can manipulate the game without giving up who they are, the game is easier to play.

This element of epic theatre can also be witnessed in reality television, which, as mentioned earlier, Collins used as inspiration for her series. Reality television is aggressively performative and indeed often far from "reality." Characters are often seen in difficult situations, emotionally and physically, but will then be filmed as if they are "talking" to the audience in monologue style—appearing to break the fourth wall.

Brecht is most commonly known for creating the phrase "breaking the fourth wall." In theater, performers break the fourth wall by addressing audience members directly. This technique is particularly interesting in a novel because it momentarily disrupts the action and can, for a moment, give readers a break from the battle at hand. Breaking the fourth wall also gives audiences (citizens of Panem) and readers the opportunity to become aware that they, too, are a part of the action; their actions affect those of the performers and the performers are watching them.

Breaking the fourth wall occurs in the act of composition as well, most especially in narrative works that "speak" directly to their readers. This style of writing requires conversational tone, a stark contrast from academic voice. Indeed, this style is considered more natural, but can still be uncomfortable for students. A true narrative can be quite powerful, but to do it correctly and be taken seriously, students must learn how to write conversationally, but not in such a way that they are not taken seriously. For some students being taken seriously can be a unique problem, as some hail from minority communities whose voices are either silenced or not considered important.

Terri Coleman, adjunct professor at a historically black college near New Orleans, has become accustomed to role performance in writing both in her own writing and in the classroom. Though many may be surprised by this, Coleman suggests that breaking the fourth wall, or narrative work, is much more difficult for minority students because they feel as if their story does not matter. Coleman claims:

> I mean, why should anyone care about their story? When they write in their voices, they are told that they aren't speaking in English. These youth have been speaking in English for years, their language isn't foreign, it just isn't considered white enough to be proper. So, yeah. When it comes to a narrative essay, I'm almost at a loss in seeing fantastic finished products that truly speak. But, when I started making them all aware of their power, of writing as power, of how they could try on a role to be safe, to use it as a defensive mechanism … that's when I started seeing progress. That's when they all decided to volunteer as tribute.

As such, performance in writing can be likened to resistance, and if students can be taught how to properly perform these defiant roles—then they are resisting a controlling force, but the force does not realize it. The force itself, in this case, academia, will accept their work as the required format, but the student will feel more powerful in thinking that she has "fooled" the establishment into accepting her.

Resistance

Much of Brecht's work applies to actual theater and the effect productions have upon their audiences. Performance, however, is not limited to the stage or television and can be found not only in literature but in real life, especially the notion of performing resistance. According to Bell:

> A cursory look at the evening news quickly demonstrates that when citizens are actively engaged in public debates, they often take their concerns to the streets— chanting, marching, waving signs, and staging 'events' for media that broadcast the sounds and images around the world. The aesthetics of these events—orchestrated as spectacle, as drama, as conflict, through media—and the political realities that prompt them demand that resistance and performance belong in the same sentence [199].

Naturally, before there can be resistance there must be a controlling force wielding power. In Collins' novels, the Capitol exercises what Michel Foucault refers to as traditional understandings of power. This type of power can be compared to ancient Roman power structures. Foucault suggests that traditional power is acquired, seized, held or lost; is enacted and enforced by laws that for the most part strictly inform citizens what they cannot do; divides people into groups of either ruler or ruled; is often found in strict class systems; is oppressive and assumes the right to lord over others (94). Traditional power is frequently referred to as repressive power and is viewed as a power that seeks to punish and wound (94).

Though many students would like to claim that academia has the power to punish and wound, its power can be thought of as transformational rather than repressive. However, an inherent component of dystopia is the presence of a controlling force, commonly a government, which separates characters into groups: rulers and ruled. Within these controlling forces resistance generally beats at the heart of the dystopian novel and drives the story; the same characteristics can also be observed in the college classroom with the instructor as the ruler and the students as the ruled. Coleman first noticed the real world dystopia she lived in while attending a school for rich New Orleans residents:

> Yeah, I was the only poor black girl there. I was a project, I guess. It made all those white folks feel good knowing they were providing me with an education. What they didn't realize is that I already had an education. My parents had raised me right, actually I knew more academically than the girls I was studying with. However, when I would turn in papers I would receive failing marks because I wasn't using proper English. It didn't matter that what I was saying was right, or even that it was new and cool. What mattered was that I wasn't using the right voice, so I had no power. That's when I started resisting. I decided as a little girl in a stupid maroon colored uniform that I was going to play this part. And I got to be really good at it, so good that my college was paid for. Not because I was black and poor, but because I learned how to perform resistance, to harness my role, and to defeat my dystopia [19].

Coleman's decision to display her power by performing a role she could try on and cast off is representative of the times people currently live in. Modern people witness, and are constantly exposed to, performances of power frequently in today's media. In fact, Collins' novel, heavily impacted by the current trend of reality television, is situated perfectly in current culture which has been described by Janelle Reinhelt, a performance theorist, as "aggressively theatrical" (71). People living today are frequently exposed to performance through televised live events and spectacles. Reinhelt claims that events that impact the daily activities of an audience, attract significant media attention, appear ceremonial or ritualistic, and endorse nationalism are events that are inherently performative (74). In today's culture, events like breaking news announcements, presidential inaugurations, and even the singing of the National Anthem before a baseball game can all be thought of as performances that impact audiences.

The Hunger Games is perfectly suited for YAL because the nature of adolescence is that of rebellion and independence. At the same time, it is also appropriate for the composition classroom because of how it teaches people to perform identities to defeat controlling forces. Many young adults believe they are oppressed by the rules imposed upon them, either parental or institutional. In the beginning of the story Katniss is burdened with the role of both mother and father, and must behave as an adult in order to provide for her family; this leaves little time for teenage revelry. Although most adolescents cannot relate to Katniss's plight, they can admire her convictions and aspire to be as strong as her, making her an awe-inspiring heroine and role model.

Practical Considerations for the Composition Classroom

Teaching composition can be frustrating for some educators, even the most seasoned educator. For the most part, most English instructors at the college level have Master's degrees or a PhD; simply put, they are considered experts in their field; they are part of the academy and know what is expected of students. Yet, teaching students to write as a member of the academy is difficult. Collins' *The Hunger Games* series is an excellent teaching tool because unlike traditional textbooks, it provides students with real examples of successful role performance. Once students become aware of Katniss's role performance, it becomes possible to recognize it within their own lives. This allows for fruitful classroom conversation about code switching. People code switch multiple times in a day, which means they adjust their language for their audience. Someone speaking to an old friend will talk differently than they would to the president of a school. Becoming keenly aware of these roles, and how we switch in and out of them, helps students begin to understand how performance works in their daily lives, and how it can be applied in their writing.

To be sure, instructors could use *The Hunger Games* series in their classes to begin a discussion about role performance in fiction and real world. This discussion could then connect to a writing assignment exploring their own roles within their very real world, or an assignment where students rehearse and then perform their academic voice role. Students typically do not engage with textbooks, and the fast-paced present tense style of writing used by Collins in her novels is known for engaging young readers. Certainly, textbooks can be useful. However, historically they are the last thing that students want to read. On the contrary, educators seeking to engage students would be wise to use Collins' non-traditional text(s) as they are written in fast-paced present tense prose, gripping, and inspiring.

Designing a unit of study with *The Hunger Games* as a primary source focusing on identity performance is not the only way that instructors can employ Collins' series. In fact, an instructor could include the following within a unit of study: analysis of how audience affects tone; an exploration of argument by discussing how ethos, pathos, and logos are employed by President Snow, Cinna, Haymitch, and Katniss herself; and finally, word choice. Though Katniss is the heroine of the books, it can be argued that etymology is the champion, as the texts are masterful examples of how crafty language can be. An instructor could require a student to choose a term used in the texts and then provide a critical analysis of the use of this particular word within the story. A close inspection of the word "tribute" reveals that it was once used differently than it is today. In the mid-fourteenth century "tribute" meant "a stated sum of money or other valuable consideration paid by one ruler or country to another in acknowledgment of submission or as the price of peace or protection" (Online Etymology Dictionary). For those familiar with the story of original use of "tribute" is startling. Throughout the text there are etymological gems such as this that allow for heavy analysis in regard to word choice, and how important selection of words can be when writing. All of these areas of focus can be crafted neatly into singular units of study, or aligned with the notion of performing resistance that provides students the opportunity to become aware of performance in their own lives, and how to harness performative authority.

Conclusion

Indeed, performance is a powerful notion. It is a notion that is significantly present in the media driven culture that students live in today. Audiences witness characters performing on television and also in novels, where themes of body image, control, identity, and rebellion can be seen. YAL encourages readers to become a part of the epic theatre in that these texts serve to inspire adolescents to critically analyze the world around them and change what needs to be changed. They inspire to rebel against what is wrong and to create identities that allow for this performance. Literature is an art form and according to philosopher Herbert Marcuse, "Art cannot change the world, but it can contribute to changing the consciousness and drives of the men and women who could change the world" (33). Dystopian literature does just this. YA dystopian literature accomplishes this by featuring performances by characters who appear to be human. In his social issues blog "Presentation Zen," Garr Reynolds suggests that "what makes some of the best speeches or presentations so memorable is not that they are perfect or slick, or overly polished, but that they are human. And to be human is to be imperfect" (Reynolds). YAL provides its readers with characters who make do in unjust situations, are perfectly imperfect, and perform resistance in such a way that they appear human and relatable; thus, YAL dystopias can inspire readers to do as Marcuse suggests "change the world."

Students in a composition classroom who are given the chance to study Katniss and analyze her role performances, can become keenly aware of performance in their own lives. This opportunity can not only assist students in voice development and code switching, but it can also strengthen minority students who feel similar to Katniss in the Capitol: out of place and unimportant. As Coleman notes, "once I realized I just had to learn how to win my own Hunger Games (which was growing up in Louisiana) education was easy for me. I teach performance in the classroom because my students need to feel powerful, but what student doesn't." Though her experiences differ from most students, Coleman is absolutely on point. In these highly performative times, it is important to recognize how portraying a role can positively impact not only writing, but the life of the writer.

NOTES

1. Michel de Certeau coined the term "art of making do" in order to explain how people use tactics to overcome strategic maneuvers, or how they manipulate events in order to change them into opportunities.

2. The dramatic theater is the opposite of epic theatre in that it seeks to gain emotional connection with its viewers. Spectators of this type of theater often feel as if they can relate to the characters and the emotions these characters experience. Dramatic theater is not considered a platform for social change (like epic theatre is).

WORKS CITED

Baker, Deirdre. "Present Tensions, or It's All Happening Now." *Horn Book Magazine.* http://www.hbook.com/2011/12/opinion/present-tensions-or-its-all-happening-now/. Accessed 22 Oct. 2012.

Bell, Elizabeth. *Theories of Performance.* Thousand Oaks, CA: Sage, 2008.

Blasingame, James, and Suzanne Collins. "An Interview with Suzanne Collins." *Journal of Adolescent and Adult Literacy,* vol. 52, no. 8, 2009, pp. 726–727.

Brecht, Bertolt. *Brecht on Theatre—The Development of an Aesthetic.* Translated by John Willet. New York: Hill and Wang, 1964.

Coleman, Terri. Personal Interview. 27 Oct. 2016.

Collins, Suzanne. *Catching Fire.* New York: Scholastic, 2009. Print.

_____. *The Hunger Games.* New York: Scholastic, 2008.

De Certeau, Michel. *The Practice of Everyday Life.* Translated by Steven F. Rendall. Oakland: University of California Press, 1984.

Foucault, Michel. *The History of Sexuality: An Introduction.* Translated by Robert Hurley. New York: Random House, 1978.

Hintz, Carrie, and Elaine Ostry, eds. *Utopian and Dystopian Writing for Children and Young Adults.* Abingdon-on-Thames: Routledge, 2003.

Marcuse, Herbert. *The Aesthetic Dimension: Toward a Critique of Marxist Aesthetics.* Boston: Beacon Press, 1978.

"Online Etymology Dictionary." *Etymonline,* n.d. http://www.etymonline.com/index.php?term=tribute

Reinhelt, Janelle. "Toward a Poetics of Theatre and Public Events." *TDR: The Drama Review,* vol. 50, no. 3, 2006, pp. 69–87. *Project Muse.*

Reynolds, Garr. "Lessons in Engagement from Flight of the Conchords." *Presentation Zen.* http://www.presentationzen.com/presentationzen/2013/02/we-all-have-a-story-to-tell.html. Accessed 11 Feb. 2016.

Writing About Death

Young Adult Literature's Emphasis on Death and Its Place in the Composition Classroom

Matthew D. Fazio

Death is a common theme in young adult literature (YAL). More so than just a theme, death is so vital in many stories that it is inextricably tied to the texts themselves: without the death, these books would not exist. There are countless examples of death acting as the catalyst in YAL. *The Catcher in the Rye* (1951) has the narrator, Holden Caulfield, coping with the death of his younger brother, Allie. *The Book Thief* (2006) is riddled with death: Death is the narrator of the book, and the main character, Liesel Meminger, watches everyone around her die, including her brother, who dies at the beginning of the novel. Even *Harry Potter and the Philosopher's Stone* (1997) begins with the background of Harry Potter's parents being murdered by the evil Lord Voldemort. This begs the question: why is death so routinely represented in YAL?

To answer this question, there must be an appropriate understanding of the overarching goal of this project. This essay addresses three primary goals: to identify the prevalence of death in YAL, to attempt to understand why death holds such prominence in YAL, and to apply the findings to relevant assignments incorporating YAL in the undergraduate composition classroom.

The Prevalence of Death in Young Adult Literature

YAL is not the only type of literature where the theme of death is frequently used. From the "To be, or not to be" soliloquy in *Hamlet* to Arthur

Miller's *Death of a Salesman*, death is inescapable. Additionally, the theme of death is not even reserved for literature, as Socrates notes that the purpose of philosophy is to prepare us for death (Hakola, Kivisto, Pihlstorm vii).

This essay's purpose is not to assume that death has not been a part of literary and philosophical texts for centuries. Instead, this is simply an assertion that death is a common theme, especially in modern YAL. There will always be examples of texts that do not incorporate the theme of death; however, that does not negate the fact that many YA books are relying on the theme of death. Without researching the entire landscape of the YAL market, it would not be fair to determine that all of YAL uses the theme of death. A New York–like independent publisher, Blooming Twig, found that approximately 30,000 young adult novels are published each year (Kowalczyk). A comprehensive methodology would have to be constructed in order to sort through that type of data. Instead of a quantitative approach, this essay uses a qualitative methodology by looking at various sample lists and will produce a modest claim.

When reviewing YAL, it is readily apparent that death is often a major theme. The theme of death is so pervasive that there is even a section on the website *Goodreads* entitled "Popular Teen Death Books." In anticipation of books being released in 2015, one reviewer, Parkin, highlighted some trends in YAL and noted that "Dealing with Loss" was one of the most common themes. Specifically, she wrote that the stories often "deal with the loss of loved ones and how those left behind cope." Below is a small sample of recent YA texts with a short explanation of the type of death present within each text.

Gary D. Schmidt, two-time Newberry Honor-winning author and National Book Award Finalist, wrote *Orbiting Jupiter* (2015), a story about a 13-year-old boy who has a daughter of his own. Throughout the book, the theme and foreshadowing of death plays a major role in the unfolding of the story. Raziel Reid's *When Everything Feels Like the Movies* (2015) is a novel inspired by the "wretched murder of a 15-year-old" (Chilton). *Bullet Catcher* (2015) is a Western novel about Imma, who, after the loss of her parents, pursues her dream of joining a legendary band of outlaws who deflect bullets with their hands. Jennifer Niven's novel *All the Bright Places* (2015) centers on Theodore Finch's fascination of death. Although Theodore regularly thinks about ways he could kill himself, he stops each time something good happens in his life. Gayle Forman, #1 *New York Times* bestselling author, wrote *I Was Here* (2015) about a teen who has to endure life after her best friend commits suicide.

The theme of death can be seen, at times, as a rhetorical device wherein the author demands attention by shocking or scaring the reader. However, the theme of death in YAL goes far beyond a simple literary device. YAL authors may choose to write about death for myriad reasons including: a way to create an emotional bond between a reader and a text; elevating the impact of a work by promoting more serious and adult themes; and simply because the story being told requires death. The routine use of death in YAL does not mean that it is not used in other types of literature; nor does it negate the integrity of an author who chooses to use the theme. Many commercially successful and critically acclaimed YA books use the theme of death.

Some of the most successful YA books are series, many of which have become films. Five of the most success book series in recent years have been the *Harry Potter Series, The Hunger Games Series, The Twilight Saga, The Divergent Series,* and *The Maze Runner Series.* While death is most pronounced in *The Hunger Games Series,* it plays a vital role in each of these five series. However, it is not only the books that are being turned into movies that use death as a central theme. Many books that are awarded for outstanding writing also share the theme of death.

The Michael L. Printz Award is presented by the American Library Association as a literary award recognizing "the best book written for teens, based entirely on its literary merit." Each year, the committee nominates three to five books. In 2016, three books were nominated: *Bone Gap* (Winner), *Out of Darkness*, and *Ghosts of Heaven. Bone Gap* tells a story of a young girl, Roza, who goes missing and is presumed dead; *Out of Darkness* focuses on Naomi, a 15-year-old Mexican girl whose mother is dead; and *Ghosts of Heaven* has a number of different storylines, one of which, "The Easiest Room in Hell," is "the journal of a reforming young doctor mourning the death of his drowned wife" (Lacey). Once again, using a small sample, there seems to be the unifying theme of death.

Understanding that these examples are a small piece of the vast YAL market is important. However, research of various types of lists including critically acclaimed books and commercially successful series does seem to indicate, quite clearly, that death is pervasive in YAL. But that does not answer the question as to why the theme of death is pervasive. As stated earlier, there are many reasons why authors choose to include the theme of death in their writing. The next portion of this essay will attempt to make some conjectures as to why death is a common theme in so many YA novels.

Why Is the "Death" Theme Prevalent in Young Adult Literature?

Although looking at examples can prove the pervasiveness of death in YA novels, the reason why death is so routinely used seems harder to pin down. Attempting to enter the mind of a writer and claim to know why he/she used such a rhetorical device is not possible. However, this essay simply asserts that young adults gravitate toward stories with the theme of death; the fact that so many YA novels with death themes are being labeled as best-sellers shows that there is clearly a market for these types of stories. So rather than making a conjecture as to why authors write death into YA novels, this essay will explore why readers are inclined to read about death. Specifically, I will cover four potential reasons.

Coping Mechanism. For young readers who have had the misfortune of suffering a personal loss, death in a YA novel can serve as a coping mechanism. It is staggering to think of the number of children who are affected by death. *Childhood Grief: The Untold Burden* found that one in seven children deal with the loss of a parent or a sibling before age 20 ("Life with Grief Research"). Coping with the death of a loved one can be difficult for a person of any age, but the struggle is often deepened during adolescence. At a time when so much is changing for an individual, the loss of someone close can severely impact a young adult's life and development.

Many studies indicate a risk of ongoing mental issues that can occur after the loss of a loved one, especially for teens. A study published in *JAMA Psychiatry* entitled "Grief in Children and Adolescents Bereaved by Sudden Parental Death" concluded with the recommendation that "research regarding interventions designed to relieve the burden of grief in bereaved children and adolescents are needed" (Melhem, Porta, et. al.). The Childhood Well-being Research Centre published a study in 2014 noting: "Childhood bereavement may have both a short-term and longer-term impact on children's well-being, including their psychological health and educational achievement, yet there is little clarity about the kind of support that such children might need, nor the extent to which it is provided" (7). The unpredictable nature of children and young adults dealing with death shows that different methods may help with coping. Although literature should not be equated to seeing a psychologist, learning to cope with life's difficulties is a tremendous fringe benefit of reading YA novels. Reading about other young adults, albeit fictional, can help readers better understand how to cope if/when they have to endure loss. In an article entitled "Why Death Is So Important in YA Fiction," the author notes that current YAL uses a tone "with death woven as realistically into the lives of characters as it would be into our own, making the stories grittier and darker. This allows young adults to engage with the reality of dying through the safe act of reading" (Wallis). Experiencing death vicariously though characters in a story can help to create an emotional connection with a book and help those grieving to find a way to cope.

Taboo Subject. There are a number of topics that many people are uneasy talking about. However, there is often a need to talk about some of the awkward and difficult topics, especially to children and teens. There is significant research that shows the importance of talking to teens about sex education (Ginsburg & Kinsman; Berl; Kaufman). Additionally, there are many initiatives to raise awareness for teen suicides, depression, and other afflictions that today's young adults may be facing. Similarly, talking about death with children and teens could also help in their understanding as they mature. Despite knowing that these conversations are important, some topics, such as death, still seem to be taboo (Peacock).

In addition to being taboo, some adults, parents, guardians, and teachers alike, might not feel qualified to talk about death. Topics such as sex education may be awkward, but there are biological answers to the questions that may be asked. However, when fielding questions from children about death, many adults are not sure exactly what to say. The Center for Effective Parenting notes, "Many parents simply don't know how to explain death to their children" (Zolten & Long, 1). Regardless if it is a difficult subject, it is important for adults and parents to talk with children. A national poll of bereaved children and teenagers found that "71% said that adult(s) they live with gave help and support to them after (a) death" ("National Alliance for Grieving Children"). The importance of support begins with actually opening up a conversation about death.

One way to open up that conversation may be with a book. "There are many good … books about death, and reading these books … can be a great way to start a conversation with (a) child" (Ehmke). Despite not feeling qualified to talk about death the way a trained professional can, a text can offer common ground.

Novels allow young adults to wrestle with a topic like death. Movies and television shows dramatize death, adding music and manipulating camera angles to evoke specific emotions. However, when reading about death, a person has the ability to think while using the text as a companion. By using reading as an entrance in to a topic such as death, young adults have a new way to better understand one of life's most difficult challenges.

Understanding Death. Prior to the age of social media, some young adults could have been protected from the problems of the world. However, since the Columbine High School massacre in 1999, shootings have become more prevalent and so has the media coverage. Additionally, young adults who do not watch the news or read a newspaper still are aware of tragic fatalities, as most young adults are on some form of social media. Since the tragedy at Columbine, there have been 50 mass murders or attempted mass murders at schools (Pearle). Additionally, according to a Pew Research Center study recapping 2015, over 71 percent of teens use multiple social networks (Lenhart). With the increasing number of violent crimes in schools coupled with the immediacy of information traveling through social media, it is clear that students are more aware than ever of heinous crimes.

So, even young adults who do not have to experience the loss of a loved one firsthand are still confronted with the fear that fatal occurrences, like school shootings, are a very real possibility. Death, then, is something that young adults are thinking about even if they are incapable of talking about it. Thus, there is a need for a safe space for young adults to think and talk about death. YA novels provide a space to learn and understand death better.

It is important to remember that many deaths are accidents: the CDC (2016) lists accidents as the fourth leading cause of deaths. While cancer and heart disease, the two leading causes of death, are more prevalent, unnecessary deaths like shootings and terrorist attacks seem to affect people on a different level. A person may be able to cope with a disease because there is science to explain its existence. However, deaths that do not have a reason cause people to question life in general.

In spite of the fact that there is no singular answer as to why people die, literature provides an outlet to understand death in the confines of a book. And if for nothing else than trying to understand one of life's greatest mysteries, literature allows readers to think and contemplate issues such as death. Heinous acts of violence, such as school shootings, may affect young adults as they begin to think about their own mortality. Opening up lines of communication can act as an outlet for young adults who are struggling with complex feelings that are weighing on them.

Overcoming Circumstances. Finally, young adults gravitate toward death in YA novels because the main character most often overcomes the loss of others and continues to move forward. Another hallmark of YAL is that despite troubling topics, most have positive endings. Even though loved ones may perish, the main character finds a way to overcome obstacles and continue living life. This is particularly important for children who have already gone through loss.

Whether or not readers realize this, the common trope of resilience in the face of loss or challenge helps to give readers the confidence to overcome their own challenges. Perhaps that is why most stories begin with the tragedy; that way the main character can spend the entire novel overcoming challenges until the true resolution at the end.

In 1999, Gail Radley, author of 15 books for young people, wrote an article entitled "Coping with Death in Young Adult Literature." Using three books as examples, she found "adolescents struggling through the very typical reactions of shocked disbelief, anger, fear, sorrow, and isolation." Her assessment is that the realistic and plausible presentations of death make these books accessible for young adults. Additionally, her request was that "YA book(s) portray some aspect of the grieving process in a way that contributes to readers' understanding and growth."

Young adults need to feel connected to a book's characters and conflicts. Regardless if the book includes otherworldly features or science fiction, the reactions to the action must still feel real to the reader. In real life, if a parent dies, a child will have to live with that forever. However, finding ways to cope and ultimately moving forward is the goal for all who encounter death.

Practical Considerations for the Composition Classroom

The pervasiveness of death in YA novels may help to provide an entrance point of discussion in the undergraduate composition classroom. Positing that adolescents gravitate toward YAL and many YA novels include themes of death, there could be an opportunity for practical applications as those young adults enter the college classroom. Specifically, writing-based courses can allow students to explore more difficult and abstract ideas in a confined space. Additionally, in a study reported in *Psychology Today*, there were indications that writing about death repeatedly could lessen depression and even promote happiness (Heflick).

The Bureau of Labor Statistics stated in October of 2015 that 69.2 percent of 2015 high school graduates were enrolled in colleges or universities. Most high school graduates are 17 or 18 years old, the majority of whom end up going to college. "The term 'young adult' was coined by the Young Adult Library Services Association during the 1960s to represent the 12–18 age range" (Strickland). Using this logic, young adult readers begin near 4th grade and end near 12th grade, senior year. Although many YAL readers are actually adults (Rosenberg), their motives for engaging with those texts may be different.

Even though the number of non-traditional students is on the rise (Anderson), the majority of college freshmen are traditional students who come directly from high school. This means that there are opportunities for classes such as composition to use the fact that students are reading and engaging with YAL to benefit the overall learning process. Although these assignments are geared toward traditional students, they are also applicable to non-traditional students, as YAL is read by people of all ages. This portion of the essay will identify three applications of using YAL in composition classrooms.

Prior to reviewing each of the three applications, it should be noted that the core aim of a composition class does not change with a newfound emphasis on YAL. Composition should provide students with rhetorical foundations to prepare them for both academic and professional writing. The applications of YAL will help to engage traditional college students with texts they are familiar with and concepts worth discussing. However, good writing skills must always be the true foundation of a composition class. The assignment examples below are used to help with the creative part of the course without disturbing the organizational, grammatical, and fundamental aspects of writing.

Exploratory Essay

Students are often asked to write an exploratory essay in a composition course. Often, exploratory essays ask students to engage with something personal so they can write from their existing experiences.

Writing an exploratory essay on the meaning of death using literature as a framework will allow students to explore a deep topic early in their academic careers. Also, by using literature, there is a distance between the writer and the material; if asked to write about death in general, many students would likely write about their own personal experiences with death. This poses two problems: 1) Some students may not feel comfortable expressing ideas about personal loss in an essay; and 2) some students may become too personal, making it difficult for the instructor to separate the actual text from the writer.

In the first instance, writing about the death of a loved one may be a difficult task for anyone, but asking a novice writer to write about such a difficult topic could possibly have adverse effects. Some students may even wish not to submit an assignment. In the second instance, some students may want to express their stories through writing and may be too focused on the personal aspects that they do not write a quality, academic essay. A poignant consideration lies in the fact that it is difficult for instructors to be critical of personal essays, especially ones where the author is opening up about the death of a loved one. An instructor does not want to be seen as curbing a student's personal voice, but at the same time there are writing standards that must take precedence. Rose's article, "The Language of Exclusion: Writing Instruction at the University," deals with the difficulties of academic writing for those unaccustomed to its style; adding the challenge of balancing personal tragedies with formal writing makes it even more difficult for an instructor to champion writing's "rich relationship with inquiry (and insist) on the importance of craft and grace" (359).

Aligning the assignment with literature will allow the student to explore the themes while also using an external text as a framework. Students may feel more comfortable writing about how death is dealt with by characters in a book than how the students themselves would deal with such a profound loss. Also, opening up the assignment to any YAL instead of making specific reading requirements can encourage students to incorporate texts that have already impacted them.

For example, an instructor may ask students to choose a piece of YAL, identify the themes of death within the text, and then discuss whether or not the text accurately represented death. This would allow students to first perform a close text analysis of a work and also incorporate their existing thoughts about death while still maintaining the parameters of the assignment.

Comparative Analysis

Another typical assignment in a composition course is a traditional compare and contrast. A comparative analysis can weigh in on multiple perspectives of an issue or theme, helping students to understand varying perspectives.

Instead of simply asking students to submit a comparative analysis on two texts, students could be asked to incorporate YA novels that have a theme of death. Due to time limitations in a single undergraduate classroom, it may be difficult to ask students to read multiple novels for a single assignment. Instead, instructors could provide excerpts from multiple YA texts to use for the course. To give a good mix of different types of novels, it is recommended that instructors choose some novels where death is dealt with in a softer sense (such as *Harry Potter and the Philosopher's Stone*) and other texts where death is more detailed, such as *The Book Thief*. Also, it would be a good idea to include some excerpts of books that do not have film versions, as students who watch the film may have different views of the way in which death is handled.

A single student (or multiple students, depending on the size of the class) could be asked to be the class leader on each text. Students would then come to class prepared to talk about the excerpts from novels in the classroom or post responses on a discussion board. Each student would be responsible for a single text, and that student would give a brief overview of how death is portrayed in the book. This would include the emphasis on death (is death the major theme or does it play a smaller role), the type of death (accidental, murder, self-inflicted, medical, etc.), the scene of the death(s) (does the reader "witness" the person die or does the person die prior to the beginning of the text), and a whole host of other variances. By reporting back to the class on similar types of questions, students will have a better time grouping concepts and ideas for their comparative analysis essays.

Students would be asked to find similarities in different books to show that certain types of themes are common. Additionally, students would also be asked to find similar situations in books that have different outcomes. With all students contributing on the project, the class would be aware of a number of varying perspectives. This would allow for students to choose an appropriate match for a comparative analysis, too.

This assignment could work as a co-writing project, something that is very applicable for the marketplace, or it could also work as a traditional essay. Also, it may be worthwhile to include a presentation with this assignment. It may seem unorthodox to require a speaking component of a writing course; however, there is room for various forms of communication in a writing course, and talking about one's ideas from an essay may make for a good transition into speaking.

What's Different About Young Adult Novels?

In the final assignment, students would be asked to explore the differences between deaths in standard fiction and YA fiction. Although YAL deals with deep and complex topics like suicide, murder, terminal illness, and the loss of loved ones, the texts are clearly written differently than they are for adult readers of fiction. This is an important topic, especially for young adults on the precipice of adulthood.

Students could be asked to do a close text analysis of a YA novel where the theme of death is present in the text. Again, keeping the course workload in mind, student would only be asked to review a small portion of a text. Students would then write an essay about what the actual text is attempting to convey, and then make conjectures about what would be different if the book were written for adults.

Many people believe that the only fundamental difference between YA fiction and standard fiction is the age of the main character. However, one of the major differences is the way in which difficult subjects are written about.

For the traditional forms of literature, instructors could once again provide excerpts, if possible, to aid in the process for undergraduate students. This could also help shape the conversation for the class. Some of the texts chosen could be gruesome, others could be dramatic and emotional, and still others could show death in very realistic ways. Providing a varied number of options for the class could help to understand death in a broader context.

By engaging with this assignment, students will be compelled to think critically about coming-of-age novels and consider the ways in which audience determines the writing patterns. Many YA novels are less graphic about details, and instead focus on the emotional impact. This type of assignment will encourage in-depth text analysis and will ask students to consider the role of communication in death; after all, how death is communicated in fiction will ultimately frame how the audiences perceive death.

Concluding Remarks

As has been discussed in this essay, death plays a role in many modern YA novels. There is something appealing, in general, about YA novels, too.

In Pam Cole's text, *Young Adult Literature in the 21st Century*, there is a chapter specifically relating to the themes of YA literature: "Trends and Issues in Young Adult Literature." Cole writes:

> Young adult literature offers a window through which teens can examine their lives and the world in which they live. Unlike classical texts, young adult literature addresses modern-day issues—peer pressure, family relationships, sexuality, bigotry and racism, and it connects teens with the pop culture world in which they live. This connection with modern-day issues and culture piques interest and hooks at-risk readers and nonreaders. While classical texts may share similar themes (emotions are timeless), young adult literature is not bound by archaic language; teens can more easily navigate the text and enjoy pop culture references, themes, and so on, resulting in more reading pleasure and ultimately enhancing reading comprehension [61].

The idea that young adults can relate to and empathize with a text is one of the greatest benefits of YAL. Meeting young adults on their terms, using their language, and dealing with relevant problems helps to form strong bonds and connections between the texts and readers. Reading is an individual activity that helps young adults to quiet their lives in a very busy world.

As death is regularly brought to their social media news feeds without proper and planned modes for how to process these events, young adults have the opportunity to turn to literature in an attempt to better understand the world around them. Then, when those young adults become adults and walk into a composition classroom, they can begin to articulate how they understand death through writing.

WORKS CITED

Akerman, R., and Statham, J. "Bereavement in Childhood: The Impact of Psychological and Educational Outcomes and the Effectiveness of Support Services." Childhood Wellbeing Research Center, 2014.

Anderson, Lexi. "27 Is the New 18: Adult Students on the Rise." *Education Commission of the States*, 2016. http://www.ecs.org/27-is-the-new-18-adult-students-on-the-rise/. Accessed 2 January 2017.

Berl, Rachel Pomerance. "Teaching Your Kids About Sex: Do's and Don'ts." *US News*, 2012. http://health.usnews.com/health-news/articles/2012/08/03/teaching-your-kids-about-sex-dos-and-donts. http://www.ecs.org/27-is-the-new-18-adult-students-on-the-rise/. Accessed 2 January 2017.

Cole, Pam. *Young Adult Literature in the 21st Century*. New York: McGraw-Hill Humanities/Social Sciences/Languages, 2008.

"College Enrollment and Work Activity of 2015 High School Graduates." *Bureau of Labor Statistics*, 2016. http://www.bls.gov/news.release/hsgec.nr0.htm. Accessed 5 January 2017.

Ehmke, Rachel. "Helping Children Deal with Grief." *Child Mind Institute*, 2017. https://childmind.org/article/helping-children-deal-grief/. Accessed 5 January 2017.

Forman, Gayle. *I Was Here*. New York: Viking Books for Young Readers, 2015.

Ginsburg, K.R., and Kinsman, S.B. "Talking to Your Child About Sex." *Healthy Children*, 2015. https://www.healthychildren.org/English/ages-stages/gradeschool/puberty/Pages/Talking-to-Your-Child-About-Sex.aspx. Accessed 5 January 2017.

Hakola, O., Heinamaa, S., and Pihlström, Sami. Death and Mortality: From Individual to Communal Perspectives. Helsinki Collegium for Advanced Studies, 2015.

Heflick, Nathan. "Thinking About Death Can Make You Value Life More." *The Conversation*, 2014. http://theconversation.com/thinking-about-death-can-make-you-value-life-more-25505. Accessed 3 January 2017.

Kaufman, Miriam. "Sex Education for Children: Why Parents Should Talk to Their Kids About Sex." *About Kids Health*, 2011. http://www.aboutkidshealth.ca/En/HealthAZ/FamilyandPeerRelations/Sexuality/Pages/Sex-Education-for-Children-Why-Parents-Should-Talk-to-their-Kids-About-Sex.aspx. Accessed 2 January 2017.

"Kids Health." *The Nemours Foundation*, 2016. https://kidshealth.org/. Accessed 3 January 2017.

Kowalczyk, Piotr. "Young Adult Books—10 Most Interesting Infographics and Charts." *Ebook Friendly*. http://ebookfriendly.com/young-adult-fiction-infographics/. Accessed 3 January 2017.

Lacey, Josh. "The Ghost of Heaven by Marcus Sedgwick Review—Ambitious and Frustrating." *The Guardian*. https://www.theguardian.com/books/2015/jan/03/the-ghosts-of-heaven-marcus-sedgwick-review-childrens-teenagers-novel. Accessed 3 January 2017.

Lenhart, Amanda. "Teens, Social Media & Technology Overview 2015." *Pew Research Center*. http://www.pewinternet.org/2015/04/09/teens-social-media-technology-2015/. Accessed 3 January 2017.

"Life with Grief Research." *Comfort Zone Camp*. http://www.comfortzonecamp.org/news/childhood-bereavement-study-results. Accessed 5 January 2017.

Lowe, Joaquin. *Bullet Catcher*. London: Hot Key Books, 2015.

Melhem, N., Porta, G., et al. "The Course of Grief in Children Bereaved by Sudden Parental Death." Arch. Gen Psychiatry, 2011.

"The Michael L. Printz Award for Excellence in Young Adult Literature." *Young Adult Library Services Association*. http://www.ala.org/yalsa/printz. Accessed 3 January 2017.

Miller, Arthur. *Death of a Salesman*. New York: Penguin, 1996.

"National Poll of Bereaved Children & Teenagers." *National Alliance for Grieving Children*. https://childrengrieve.org/national-poll-bereaved-children-teenagers. Accessed 3 January 2017.

Niven, Jennifer. *All the Bright Places*. New York: Knopf Books for Young Readers, 2015.

"Number of Deaths for Leading Causes Of Death." *National Center for Health Statistics*. http://www.cdc.gov/nchs/fastats/leading-causes-of-death.htm. Accessed 3 January 2017.

Parkin, Lisa. "4 YA Book Trends to Look for in 2015." *The Huffington Post*. http://www.huffingtonpost.com/lisa-parkin/4-ya-book-trends-to-look-_b_5999458.html. Accessed 5 January 2017.

Peacock, Louisa. "The Real Reasons Why Death Is Still So Hard to Talk About with Your Loved Ones." *The Telegraph*. http://www.telegraph.co.uk/women/womens-life/10825710/The-real-reasons-why-death-is-still-so-taboo-hard-to-talk-about-with-your-loved-ones.html. Accessed 3 January 2017.

Pearle, Lauren. "School Shootings Since Columbine: By the Numbers." *ABC News*. http://abcnews.go.com/US/school-shootings-columbine-numbers/story?id=36833245. Accessed 3 January 2017.

Perez, Ashley H. *Out of Darkness*. Minneapolis: Carolrhoda Lab, 2015.

"Popular Teen Death Books." *Goodreads*. https://www.goodreads.com/shelf/show/teen-death. Accessed 9 January 2017.

Radley, Gail. "Coping with Death in Young Adult Literature." *The Alan Review*, vol. 27, no. 1, 1999, pp. 14–16.

Reid, Raziel. *When Everything Feels Like the Movies*. Vancouver: Arsenal Pulp Press, 2015.

Rose, Mike. "The Language of Exclusion: Writing Instruction at the University." *College English*, vol. 47, no. 4, 1985, pp. 341–59.

Rosenburg, Alyssa. "No, You Do Not Have to Be Ashamed of Reading Young Adult Fiction." *Washington Post*. https://www.washingtonpost.com/news/act-four/wp/2014/06/06/no-you-do-not-have-to-be-ashamed-of-reading-young-adult-fiction/?utm_term=.4eebf92bdbc4. Accessed 3 January 2017.

Rowlings, J.K. *Harry Potter and the Philosopher's Stone*. Richmond, British Columbia: Raincoast, 1997.

Ruby, Laura. *Bone Gap.* New York: Balzer & Bray, 2016.

Salinger, J.D. *The Catcher in the Rye.* New York: National Association for Visually Handi-capped, 1951.

Schmidt, Gary D. *Orbiting Jupiter.* Boston: Clarion Books, 2015.

Sedgwick, Marcus. *The Ghosts of Heaven.* London: Roaring Brook Press, 2015.

Shakespeare, William. *Hamlet.* Hauppauge, NY: Barron's, 1986.

Strickland, Ashley. "A Brief History of Young Adult Literature." *CNN.* http://www.cnn.com/2013/10/15/living/young-adult-fiction-evolution/. Accessed 3 January 2017.

Wallis, Rupert. "Why Death Is So Important in YA Fiction." *The Guardian.* https://www.theguardian.com/childrens-books-site/2014/aug/18/death-important-young-adult-fiction-rupert-wallis. Accessed 3 January 2017.

Zolten, K., and Long, N. "How to Talk to Children About Death." Center for Effective Parenting. http://www.parenting-ed.org/handouts/death.pdf. Accessed 3 January 2017.

Zusak, Markus. *The Book Thief.* New York: Alfred A. Knopf, 2006.

Curious Students in the Composition Classroom

The Impact of Neurology Ideology in Young Adult Literature

DANIELLE BROWNSBERGER

> Autists are the ultimate square pegs, and the problem with pounding a square peg into a round hole is not that the hammering is hard work. It's that you're destroying the peg.
> —Paul Collins, *Not Even Wrong: Adventures in Autism*

Introduction

With early identification and greater educational supports, students with autism have recently been able to make the difficult transition from high school to college for the first time. Composition instructors were among the first to note the distinct challenges presented by the new student group. Autism is a neurobiological disorder characterized by a triad of impairments in social interaction, pragmatic language skills, and communication—any one of which could have a significant impact on a student's writing (*DSM-III*). Perhaps more problematically, students with autism are challenged to come to voice when the mainstream ideological construction of their identity renders them as inevitably subordinated. Based on the theoretical frameworks posited by Louis Althusser and Michel Foucault, I argue that the problem of the autistic subject stems from a system that simultaneously privileges neurotypical writers, or those whose neurology most closely fits society's idea of "typical" or "normal," while marginalizing writers who fall outside of the ideal. Thus, the purpose of this essay is to examine: (1) the ideology of normalcy in representations of autism in young adult literature; (2) the impact of the ideology of normalcy on the identity-formation and subjectivity of autistic writers; and (3) pedagogical implications for the college composition classroom.

Representations of autism started appearing in the pages of young adult novels for the first time in the 1990s. The emergence of autistic characters in young adult literature occurred as a result of the publication of the third edition of the *Diagnostic and Statistical Manual of Mental Disorders*, which broadened the criteria and raised awareness of pervasive developmental disorders in 1987. The autism spectrum diagnosis became more and more common under the new definition, driving the estimated number of people living with the condition from one in five-hundred in the 1970s to about one in eighty-eight in 2006 (Blumberg et al. 1–7). Media sources as varied as the New York Times, Wired magazine, and the Huffington Post began speculating about the possibility of an "autism epidemic," and nearly every newspaper in the United States started considering the causal relationship between autism and vaccinations. The media attention and widespread public concern sparked a cultural fascination with autism. A flood of publications falling under the banner of "spectrum publishing" began arriving in the marketplace when savvy book publishers recognized the growing public appetite for autism narratives and sought out authors and works that could meet the demand (Murray 24–45).

As the appetite for books about autism has increased over the last thirty years, many young adult authors have jumped on the "autism bandwagon." A number of publications have even gone on to achieve high levels of critical and commercial success. For instance, *Al Capone Does My Shirts* by Gennifer Choldenko and *Rules* by Cynthia Lord were both recognized by the American Library Association as "outstanding books that portray emotional, mental, or physical disability experiences" in 2001 (Steelman 1–10). Another notable work, *Mockingbird* by Kathryn Erskine, was recognized with a number of awards in 2012 including the National Book Award for Young People's Literature, the International Reading Association Award, and the Dolly Gray Children's Literature Award. By far, the runaway best seller and most widely disseminated of these publications is *The Curious Incident of the Dog in the Night-Time*. Mark Haddon's young adult novel about an autistic child-detective has sold over twelve million copies worldwide and has been translated into thirty-six languages.

The influence of young adult novels featuring autistic characters is a concern of Composition Studies for a number of reasons. Through young adult literature, ideologies about neurological differences are passed down from one generation to the next. An ideology is a pattern of beliefs or ideas that guide the way members of a group interpret the world around them.

Multiple ideologies exist in any culture, though some are privileged over others. Dominant, or hegemonic, ideologies promote the cultural, economic, and political interests of groups that are in power. In order to maintain a position of dominance, hegemonic ideologies are continually renewed, reinforced, and defended in the discourse of the mainstream (Foss 11).

There are three main ways ideology is manifested in literature designed for young adults. First, ideology is present when writers deliberately attempt to impart their own social, political, or moral beliefs in order to influence young readers.

Through this kind of intentional surface ideology, authors of young adult literature promote a particular understanding of autism. Second, young adult literature is filled with unconscious ideologies that reflect the unexamined assumptions of authors. Unconscious ideologies in young adult novels are widely shared values that are taken for granted by integrated members of society. It is important to note that, unless these ideologies are pointed out and discussed, young readers are likely to take them for granted as well. Lastly, young adult literature contains ideologies that reflect the truths of the world in which they were written. Though writers may offer a vision of what could be possible, representations of autism disability are grounded in the realities of the world in which the author lives (Hollindale 10–15).

In the analysis that follows, I examine how the ideology of normalcy is deployed in young adult literature to marginalize individuals with neurological difference and reify the hegemonic position of neurotypicals in society. Representations of autism that draw from the ideology of normalcy adversely affect the subjectivity and identity-formation of autistic student writers. The impact and implications of a degraded autistic subject position are subsequently examined. Finally, a pedagogical approach is suggested that will help refashion the self-concept of autistic student writers in the Composition classroom.

The Ideology of Normalcy

The ideology of normalcy refers to ideas and beliefs surrounding what is considered "good" or "desirable" in society. As David Mitchell and Sharon Snyder explain, what society considers normal—Whiteness, affluence, ability, and so on—does not need to be defined. What needs to be defined and delineated are the identity categories that lie outside of the norm—the people of color, the impoverished, the individuals with autism. Any deviation from normalcy, then, is equated with deficit, disorder, or disease by mainstream society. Emphasis is placed on curing or eradicating abnormality, or, failing that, rehabilitating abnormal individuals as much as possible to conform to some "normal" standard.

In the words of Foucault, the ideology of normalcy is constructed upon the societal belief that "if you are not like everybody else, then you are abnormal, if you are abnormal, then you are sick." Foucault writes that these three categories—not being like everybody else, not being normal, and being sick—are "in fact very different but have been reduced to the same thing" (95). In young adult literature, the conflation of the abnormal with the sick can indeed take on the appearance of objectivity and absoluteness. The "cult of objectivity" that attends cognitive science extends to fictional texts that adopt the same language and theoretical understandings as the state-of-the-art in research (Sandler and Apple 326). However, it is important to remember that "normal" is a social construction that is historically and contextually situated.

Before the Industrial Revolution, there was no concept of normalcy in Western society. The prevailing paradigm for measuring human qualities was the "ideal." When measured against the ideal, everyone fell short of the standard and, thus, could be categorized by varying degrees of imperfection. By the latter half of the nineteenth century, the measurement of the ideal was cast aside as governments and other institutions began applying a statistical distribution of measurements to categorize and account for differences among citizens. Populations were divided into standard and nonstandard subpopulations; quickly thereafter, states began looking for ways to normalize the nonstandard group (Davis 24–30).

"Normalization" therapies began as a way to integrate disabled groups with the goal of helping individuals with disabilities acquire social value. By learning how to think and behave in the ways expected by "normal" people, the normalization theory suggested, individuals with disabilities would be able to integrate more successfully into society (Wolfensberger 1–258). O.I. Lavaas's Applied Behavior Analysis (ABA) therapy was one of the most rigid—and most popular—normalization programs adopted in the United States. Autistic individuals were taught how to "act normal" in functional skills lessons that lasted up to forty hours per week (Bumiller 976).

The legacy of normalization therapy has had an enduring impact on the societal understanding and treatment of autistic individuals. By identifying "uniquely autistic" attributes and targeting those qualities for elimination, researchers, educators, parents and other caretakers who administered normalization programs created a strong association between autistic abnormality and monstrosity. The conflation of autistic identity with monstrosity has made the labeling and segregation of autistic citizens from the rest of the population seem natural and legitimate. Autistic individuals have been labeled defective, excluded from educational opportunities, and segregated from society more than any other minority group, as a result (Longmore 13–412).

Narrative and the "Normate"

Young adult stories employ the ideology of normalcy through the treatment of autism as a challenge or threat to the traditional nuclear family. The strength of the family unit is a central concern in stories like *Al Capone Does My Shirts*, *Rules*, and *Mockingbird*. By incorporating autism within the family structure, the "otherness" that attends autism is reinforced and made more familiar to readers. In these texts, neurological difference is treated as just another element (in the same way crime, divorce, or drug addiction are deployed) to be characterized and thematized as part of an industry effort to create normative narratives of social relations.

In young adult narratives about autism, there is often an important relationship between the autistic character and a sibling that can be identified—in Rosemarie Garland-Thomson's terms—a "normate." A normate is a person whose ways of being, communicating, and knowing represent what society thinks of as the epitome of normal. In the novel *Al Capone Does My Shirts*, the autistic character, Natalie, is the sister of the first-person narrator, Moose Flannigan. The narrative focuses on the impact of autism on Moose and the other neurotypical members of the family, while Natalie's experiences and point-of- view are treated as secondary considerations. Catherine, the first-person narrator of *Rules*, also occupies the role of neurotypical sibling whose point-of-view is central in the characterization of a sibling with autism. In the novel *Mockingbird*, on the other hand, Caitlin is an autistic narrator who enjoys a supportive relationship with her neurotypical brother, Devon.

In young adult stories that take on the subject of autism, the focus of the narratives is on the impact of autism on the neurotypical family members rather than on the autistic individual themselves. For example, both Catherine and Moose are met with obstacles that result, either directly or indirectly, from their sibling relationship with an autistic individual. They experience (1) frustration at the unresponsiveness of the autistic sibling character, (2) humiliation at the hands of a bully; (3) jealous feelings elicited from the parental attention and time devoted to the autistic sibling character; and (4) anxiety over their parents' constant stress and grief. As a result of these obstacles, Moose and Catherine struggle to reconcile their feelings of frustration, injustice, and guilt that accompanies their siblings' autism.

Because autistic individuals are characterized as problems rather than problem-solvers, narratives often turn to curing or rehabilitating autistic characters. In all three of the books in the *Al Capone Does My Shirts* series, for example, the plot is driven by various efforts to cure Natalie's autism. From the treatments offered by mainstream medical science to faith healing and voodoo, Natalie's mother exhausts every possible resource in finding a cure for her, daughter's condition. The elimination of any deviation and difference—such as Natalie's speech, her eye contact, and fixations—is the overarching concern of the series. Finally, the family determines that the only way to cure Natalie is to send her to The Esther P. Marinoff School, a mental institution. The failure to conform to neurotypical standards results in Natalie's banishment from society.

In *Mockingbird*, attempts to cure Caitlin's autism become a community-wide effort. Caitlin's neurotypical father is incapable of coping with her eccentricities and finds her behavior too emotionally draining, particularly during a time of grieving initiated by the death of Caitlin's mother. When he comes to terms with the fact that he cannot, alone, change Caitlin, he enlists the help of family, friends, and a school counselor to assist in the rehabilitation effort. In an author's note included in the novel, Erskine provides further evidence that *Mockingbird* is part of the literary tradition responsible for perpetuating the normalization story. She explains that "[u]nderstanding people's difficulties and—just as crucial—helping people understand their own difficulties *and* teaching them concrete ways to help themselves" is a mutually beneficial exercise that helps deviant individuals "better deal with their own lives and, in turn, ours."

The singular focus by neurotypical family members to eliminate difference and deviance is reflected in *Rules*, as well. In order to put an end to her autistic brother's "embarrassing behaviors," Catherine spends years instructing David in neurotypical rules for behavior. Catherine creates a list of rules to help David appear "more normal" in society. The rules include:

1. Chew with your mouth closed.
2. Say "thank you" when someone gives you a present (even if you don't like it).
3. If someone says "hi" you say "hi" back.
4. When you want to get out of answering something distract the questioner with another question.
5. Not everything worth keeping has to be useful.
6. If the bathroom door is closed, knock (especially if Catherine has friends over!).
7. Sometimes people laugh because they like you. But sometimes they laugh to hurt you.
8. No toys in the fish tank.

The specificity and literal-mindedness of the rules also help establish the symptomology that attends David's manifestation of autism. These differences mediate a refractive comparison between David and Catherine that invites readers to look upon autism as an object of fascination based on difference.

Through the "othering" of an autistic character, *Al Capone Does My Shirts*, *Rules*, and *Mockingbird* work to reinforce the hegemonic position of neurotypical individuals in society, or those who have the ideal "normal" mind and the right cultural capital. By placing an autistic character in relation to a sibling with typical neurological behavior, the idea of humanity is mediated through a refractive comparison between the two. Ultimately, *Al Capone Does My Shirts, Rules,* and *Mockingbird* reflect the realities and concerns of the non-autistic world rather than the autistic. The ideology of normalcy operates in these texts to marginalize autistic individuals through their differences.

Normalization and Communication

In young adult literature, the ideology of normalcy is propagated when neurological difference is the main—and, at times, the only—personality trait of a character with autism. For example, in *The Curious Incident of the Dog in the Night-Time*, the protagonist is an autistic teenager named Christopher John Francis Boone who seems to have jumped right out of the pages of autism research. Though Christopher's diagnosis is not explicitly stated, a blurb on the side of the book confirms that he is a high-functioning individual on the autism spectrum.

Indeed, Christopher displays all of the communication difficulties ascribed to individuals with autism. Like many of the real-life autistic subjects studied in the neurological research of Uta Frith and Kathy Thiemann-Bourque, Christopher struggles to use appropriate social greetings, initiate conversations, and stay on topic. Christopher refuses to use social niceties in a conversation with Mrs. Alexander, because, he explains, it is illogical: "Mrs. Alexander was doing what is called chatting where people say things to each other which aren't questions and answers and aren't connected" (67). Christopher says "thank you" but clearly out of a matter of repetition and instruction rather than genuine sentiment.

Christopher explains that *The Curious Incident of the Night-Time* will not be a funny book because of his difficulty with abstract language: "I cannot tell jokes," he writes, "because I do not understand them" (8). Idioms such as "I laughed my socks off" and "He was the apple of her eye" confound the autistic protagonist (15). Christopher is over-literal and struggles with metaphorical language, even when interpreting everyday directions:

> People often say "Be quiet," but they don't tell you how long to be quiet for. Or you see a sign which says **KEEP OFF THE GRASS** but It should say **KEEP OFF THE GRASS AROUND THIS SIGN** or **KEEP OFF ALL THE GRASS IN THIS PARK** because there is lots of grass you are allowed to walk on [59.3–4].

Far from being a peculiarity of a distinct, fully-developed character, Christopher's difficulty with idioms is reminiscent of an observation from Simon

Baron-Cohen's research. Autistic study participants, Baron-Cohen quipped, would ask earnestly for glue when told "stick your coat over there'" (98).

Many of Christopher's idiosyncrasies in *The Curious Incident of the Dog in the Night-Time* can be attributed to the research of Baron-Cohen. According to his study *Understanding Other Minds: Perspectives from Autism*, autistic individuals are inattentive to the interests and expectations of individuals outside of themselves. The deficit, Baron-Cohen writes, is a result of an impaired ability to "attribute mental states (such as beliefs, desires, and intentions) to themselves and other people, as a way of making sense of and predicting behavior" (3). Without the ability to theorize about the minds of others, writers with autism cannot predict the expectations or interests of their readers (Jurecic 7).

An inattentiveness to readers' expectations—and genre conventions, at large—is evident in the macrostructure of *The Curious Incident of the Night-time*, which is disjointed and defies the rules of form prescribed in any composition manual or rule book. Rather than number chapters as a neurotypical reader would expect, Christopher chooses to order his chapters by prime numbers (2, 3, 5, 7, and so on). The prime numbered chapter headings mark dramatic shifts in narrative that are unexpected and, at times, perplexing. For example, in chapter 149, Christopher discovers secret letters from his mother in a box in his father's room. In the following chapter, however, the narrative shifts inexplicably away from this surprise revelation to another, unrelated mystery over the ghost of a Franciscan friar.

Likewise, Christopher's descriptions of people and events are oddly specific at times, and they are oddly vague at other times. The autistic narrator provides details such as "60 tiny circular holes" (5) adorn Mr. Jeavons shoes, yet he fails to identify exactly who Mr. Jeavons is until nineteen pages later when we learn he is the school psychologist. Throughout the text, Christopher shares extraneous information with the reader such as Mrs. Shears wears a T-shirt that has "Windsurf" and "Corfu" written on it and that he beat her at Scrabble 247 points to 134 (28). Similarly, Christopher lists all of the items in his pockets when he was searched by police:

1. A Swiss Army knife with 13 attachments including a wire stripper and a saw and a toothpick and tweezers.
2. A piece of string.
3. A piece of wooden puzzle.
4. 3 pellets of rat food for Toby, my rat.
5. £1.47 (this was made up a £1 coin, a 20p coin, two 10p coins, a 5p coin and a 2p coin).
6. A red paper clip.
7. A key for the front door [13].

Despite the pains Christopher takes in cataloguing the contents of his pockets for the reader, the nature and description of the items are unnecessary to the narrative. Nevertheless, the items are unnecessarily catalogued for the reader again when Christopher retrieves his property before leaving the police station.

While neurotypical teenage narrators in YAL are perhaps unrealistically cogent and coherent as compared with their real-life counterparts, Christopher's narrative is fraught with consistency issues and technical errors. Despite the fact that Christopher's teacher Siobhan is helping him revise and edit his book, the text is marked by long, rambling run-on sentences:

> But if I say that I actually had Shreddies and a mug of tea I start thinking about Coco Pops and lemonade and porridge and Dr. Pepper and how I wasn't eating my breakfast in Egypt and there wasn't a rhinoceros in the room and Father wasn't wearing a diving suit and so on and even writing this makes me feel shaky and scared, like I do when I'm standing on the top of a very tall building and there are thousands of houses and cars and people below me and my head is so full of all these things that I'm afraid I'm going to forget to stand up straight and hang on to the rail and I'm going to fall over and be killed [19].

However, there are numerous footnotes throughout the text that are suggested by Siobhan, an editor who would remain mostly invisible if it were not for the recurring and conspicuous superscripted numbers and attendant annotations that appear at the bottom of most pages. While Haddon explains, through the voice of Christopher, that the notes are meant to clarify points of confusion in the narrative, they really serve as a device to illustrate and underscore Christopher's shortcomings as a storyteller. Like the unedited run-on sentences, the footnotes suggest that Christopher either cannot—or will not—write in ways that will make him appear well-expressed to a neurotypical audience.

In the end, Christopher conforms to the stereotypical idea of the autistic individual who has an extraordinary aptitude in a subject like math but cannot write a coherent essay on the same topic. Christopher is yet another incarnation of the "Rain Man" stereotype, able to calculate quadratic equations in his head but entirely lost when it comes to negotiating the social world around him. By depicting an autistic main character as excessively anti-social, uncommunicative, and unempathetic, *The Curious Incident of the Dog in the Night-Time* contributes to the widespread assumption that real-life autistic people lack the necessary skills to speak and write for themselves.

Autistic Subjectivity and Identity-Formation

Representations of autism in mainstream cultural texts have had a significant impact on the identity-formation and subjectivity of individuals on the autism spectrum. As this essay has demonstrated, autistic individuals are marginalized through their differences and portrayed as excessively anti-social, uncommunicative, and un-empathetic in young adult literature. These notions of autism have a significant impact on the way autistic student writers are perceived and treated on college campuses.

In *Aquamarine Blue 5: Personal Stories of College Students With Autism,* Dawn Prince-Hughes writes from personal experience that the public at large seems to hold "in its collective consciousness a certain manifestation of classic autism." Autistic people, she writes, are treated as "one dimensional and made from a single template mold" as prescribed by Kanner and other influential autism researchers. The template assumes that all autistic people exhibit "impairments in the use of nonverbal, expressive gestures … that all people with autism are by definition incapable of communicating, that they do not experience emotions, and that they cannot care about other people or the world around them" (28).

Writing from the perspective an autistic composition teacher at the post-secondary level, Melanie Yergau writes of the ethos-damaging effects of "typical autism essays" and how they work to marginalize autistic voices like her own. In attempting to enter the conversation and pen her own autism essay, Yergau anticipates how the genre conventions of the "typical autism essay" have already undermined her rhetorical authority:

I am not "low-functioning"; I despise functioning labels, and I'm an adult woman. Three strikes against me trying to pen the typical autism essay right there—although, if I were considered "low-functioning," I suppose I'd have four strikes. I was unofficially diagnosed as a teenager and officially diagnosed as a young adult—two more ethos-damaging strikes. (I'm also not a big fan or user of transition statements—and I teach college writing, the horror! More strikes?) I know lots of spectrumites in real life and through the interwebs—verbal and nonverbal and semi-verbal and who-cares-if-I'm-verbal-I-can-still-communicate. But my voice doesn't count and my ethos doesn't register, according to the typical autism essay (21).

Yergau identifies an *ethos* problem that has been identified and decried by a number of autistic speakers and writers over the years. Autistic individuals have historically been excluded from the conversations that concern them. Indeed, neurotypical parents, teachers, and caregivers have always held all of the cards in the autism discourse community (Blume 6).

The autistic subject is undermined by a predominant cultural script of deviation and defectiveness in young adult literature. The "subject," as the term is posited in the theoretical frameworks of Alhusser and Foucault, denotes the individual, or the unique consciousness, that exists as a result of ideological construction. The problem of the autistic subject stems from a system that simultaneously privileges neurotypical writers, or those whose neurology most closely fits society's idea of "typical" or "normal," while marginalizing writers who fall outside of the ideal. Autistic subjectivity exists "always already" and is discovered through the interpellation process. Writers with autism, in other words, are challenged to come to voice when the mainstream ideological construction of their identity renders them as "always already" subordinated.

Stereotypical representations of autism not only shape societal understandings of autism—they also shape the way autistic individuals, themselves, perceive the condition. While there is certainly a biogenic component that contributes to the meaning of autism, it would be a mistake to overlook the important role social influences also play in shaping autistic identity. In *Constructing Autism: Unraveling the "Truth" and Understanding the Social*, Majia Holmer Nadesan explains:

The person with autism is a being who has mind or consciousness and

> was thrown into a social or physical environment—may have difficulty organizing his/her perceptions and responding to others' expectations—and yet this person stands as more than the sum of his or her genetic/ neurological/physiological 'defects.' The term 'autism' in fact misleads in this regard because through its etymology is presupposes that someone with autism exists locked in a solipsistic universe when, in reality, they are not. The social world imbues their being—their consciousness and bodily comportment—even while its order and significance may at times elude [185].

Nadesan emphasizes the importance of the social world in constructing and mediating ideas about how an autistic person is expected to think, behave, socialize, and communicate. The expression of autistic symptomology, Nadesan writes, emerges in response to social and environmental factors that call upon an autistic person to "comport himself in particular ways" (186).

Autistic individuals represent two distinct kinds of entities labeled or categorized through mainstream discourse—indifferent kinds and interactive kinds. Indifferent kinds of entities are unaware that they have been labeled, and therefore, are unaffected by discourse. In the words of Ian Hacking, "calling a quark a quark makes no difference to the quark" (105). Interactive kinds of entities, on the other hand, are aware of the labeling and alter their behavior in response. This creates a "looping effect" in which the altered behavior of interactive entities, in turn, impacts the way they are labeled. Autism is unusual because it is both indifferent and interactive. The neurological and physiological characteristics of autism are indifferent because they operate independently from discourse. Autism is also interactive because autistic people understand and change in response to the language used to describe themselves and their condition (Hacking 105–121).

On one hand, the definition of disability categories such as autism are fixed through the realities that attend cognitive difference. However, the meaning of autism is also shaped—in very material ways—through discourse. Discourse, of course, includes mainstream societal representations that label, define, and categorize autistic individuals. *Al Capone Does My Shirts, Rules, The Curious Incident of the Dog in the Night-Time,* and other Young Adult works play a significant role in determining what autism means and what it means to be an autistic writer.

Practical Considerations for the Composition Classroom

Through a careful selection of curricular texts in the composition classroom, instructors can help autistic students refashion their identity toward a more positive self-concept. Oral and written works by autistic writers, particularly those that reflect the ideological positions of the Autism Rights Movement, are recommended classroom adoptions. The Autism Rights Movement is a civil rights initiative in which autism activists campaign for more tolerance of neurological difference. Brain differences, activists in the Autism Rights Movement argue, should be accepted and embraced in the same way as physical differences in society. Rather than view autism as a deficit or disorder, they ask that autism instead be viewed as a variation in brain wiring (Harmon 1).

The ideological stance of the Neurodiversity Movement is in line with the feelings expressed by professional writers on the autism spectrum. Today, most autistic writers insist upon their diagnosis as a fundamental part of their identity rather than an obstacle to a full and normal life (Foss 11).

Most poignantly, many autistics affirm that it would be impossible to segregate the part of them that is autistic. To take away their autism is to take away their personhood. Despite our politically correct labeling, they are autistic; they don't have' autism any more than homosexuals have gayness or lesbianism. Like their predecessors in human rights, many autistics don't want to be cured; they want to be accepted. And like other predecessors in civil rights, many autistics don't want to be required to imitate the majority just to earn their rightful place in society (Gernsbacher 1).

While mainstream texts written by neurotypical authors are historically grounded in a "disability as defectiveness" ideology, autistic writers in the Neurodiversity Movement emphasize a counter-ideology: "disability as human variance and difference."

Through the publication of book-length autobiographical works, essays, articles, and other life writing, autistic self-advocates have started to garner more attention upon the world's stage than ever before thought possible. The spread of literacy has enabled autistic citizens to write and speak about self, other, and community relationships on a broader scale than is possible with only an oral tradition or elite literary class. As Lynn Hunt points in her book *Inventing Human Rights,* the proliferation of personal narrative gives traction to human rights causes like the Autism Rights Movement: "Learning to empathize open[s] the path to human rights." Reading, or even simply hearing, the lived account of another's experience teaches students to feel more empathy for each other as human equals.

It is not enough to simply choose texts that offer insight into the inner world of autism, however. Personal accounts of autism selected for the classroom should challenge harmful stereotypes and promote tolerance of neurological difference. Autistic authors such as Claire Sainsbury, Gunilla Gerland, Donna Williams, and Daniel Tammet all offer self-affirming insight into the inner world of autism through their personal accounts of living with the condition. Another extraordinary autistic writer, Tito Rajarshi Mukhopadhyay, challenges every societal notion about individuals problematically labeled "low-functioning" or "severe." The first nonverbal autistic author to articulate his thoughts and experiences through any medium, Mukhopadhyay creates a window into autism "such as the world has never seen" in *Beyond the Silence: My Life, the World and Autism, The Mind Tree: A Miraculous Child Breaks the Silence of Autism,* and *How Can I Talk If My Lips Don't Move? Inside My Autistic Mind.*

Jim Sinclair is the author of "Don't Mourn for Us," a touchstone essay of the Autism Rights Movement that has been featured in *The New York Times* as well as *New York Magazine.* Speaking directly to the parents of autistic children, Sinclair writes, "We need and deserve families who … value us for ourselves, not families whose vision of us is obscured by the ghosts of children who never lived. Grieve if you must, for your own lost dreams. But don't mourn for *us.* We are alive. We are real" (1). "Don't Mourn for Us" is a powerful repudiation of the idea that autistic children are burdens to their family members.

Ari Ne'eman, cofounder of the Autistic Self Advocacy Network, has, too, argued passionately for autistic rights in *New York Magazine, Newsweek,* and the *Wall Street Journal.* He has also made a number of television appearances on programs like *Good Morning America,* National Public Radio's *The Bryant Park Project,* and XM Satellite Radio. Bringing the message of neuro-equality to a broader national and international audience, Ne'eman has played an enormous role in furthering the causes of the Autism Rights Movement. "When one listens to or reads the words of Ne'eman, a brilliant and incredibly accomplished 21-year-old college student," Chris Foss writes, "it is hard not to be inspired…. It is hard not to support a movement the fundamental basis of which is an insistence upon the granting of what surely are fundamental civil and human rights" (11).

By adopting the written and oral works of activists in the Autism Rights

Movement, students on the autism spectrum will likewise become inspired to adopt a more positive self-concept. To choose a neurodiverse text is to affirm the validity of autistic ways of speaking, writing, being, and knowing in the world. Just as importantly, neurotypical students will be inspired to challenge their preconceived notions of autism and adopt a more inclusive attitude toward individuals with neurological difference.

Revolutionizing Composition Studies: A Conclusion and Call to Action

Like the activists in the Autism Rights Movement, autistic students on college campuses are also calling for equality in the treatment of neurological difference. They are calling for acceptance of their different ways of thinking and being, for their right to speak and write unusually, for greater appreciation of their cognitive strengths and weaknesses. In the field of Composition Studies, they are calling for nothing less than a revolution.

In a collection of essays detailing the pioneering spirit of the Conference on College Composition and Communication over its sixty year history, Geneva Smitherman reminds us in *Language Diversity in the Classroom* (2003) that compositionists have long been revolutionaries and rabble-rousers "baptized in the fire of social protest and street activism" (18). Through its language policies, the CCCC has defied Boards of Education, politicians, parents, and members of the community whenever they have insisted that "the values taught by the schools must reflect the prejudices held by the public" (20). Since 1949, the CCCC has adopted radical and unpopular stances on minority languages and dialects to benefit "blacks, browns, the poor, and others on the margins" in order to level the playing field and make it possible for non-traditional student groups to attend colleges and universities (29). "No romantic idealists," Smitherman recalls, "we knew the roadblocks and limitations involved in trying to effectuate change within the system ... but we also knew that without 'vision, the people perish.'" After all, she quips, "what else was we gon do while we was waiting for the Revolution to come?" (18).

The CCCC went to extraordinary measures to influence the issue of language diversity in the 1960s and 1970s, at a time when student demographics began changing in response to new open admission and desegregation policies in schools. Many of the nontraditional students—while intelligent—possessed only a weak command of standardized English, its grammar and conventions, and the language of the academe. The "cultural and linguistic mismatch" between teachers and the new student groups, Smitherman explains, created a crisis in university composition classrooms that called for pedagogical change (19). As scholars in the field of composition began to respond to "the charge of intellectual activists ... to struggle for the wider social legitimacy of all languages and dialects," the "Students' Right to Their Own Language" resolution was drafted and passed by the CCCC in 1974 (18). However, CCCC cannot rest on its past accomplishments when attacks on nontraditional students have continued into the twenty-first century (36).

Indeed, the communication differences of students with autism—the latest newcomers to post-secondary education—have made them just as vulnerable to "zero tolerance" language policies as the nontraditional students of Color and class that came before them. Their struggle to interpret the social and linguistic code of the university, however, is compounded by the social and communication differences that attend autism. Autistic students may be enrolling in college in record numbers—but they are failing out at an equally staggering rate.

"Much more needs to be done," the U.S. Autism and Asperger Association points out, "to assist these individuals who have the potential to graduate from college but often fail because their needs are unidentified and their talents are under-supported." If the situation for autistic students at the college level does not improve, their career prospects are bleak. Current employment rates for autistic professionals in the workforce today are shockingly low. Instead of finding gainful employment, citizens with autism are isolated from the public and denied access to the benefits and opportunities available to other, nondisabled people. The limitation of their economic and social potential is simply dismissed as an "inevitable consequence of the physical and mental differences imposed by disability" (Funk 7–30).

Like the "Students' Right" initiative of forty years ago, the Autism Rights Movement calls upon teachers to once again consider how we can embrace to our own end the identity politics—the perspectives on neurology, normalcy, and ability—inherent in language. Rather than resist language that does not conform to our idea of "correct" English, we can celebrate the richness of linguistic diversity. Rather than adhering strictly to canonical texts, we can affirm the validity of autistic differences by choosing texts written by neurodiverse authors. As the efforts of self-advocates in the Autism Rights Movement achieve slow and steady gains in society, we can fan the flames of their activism in the classroom. After all, what else are we gon do while we wait for the revolution to come?

WORKS CITED

Althusser, Louis. *Lenin and Philosophy*. Trans. Ben Brewster. New York: Monthly Review, 1971. Print.

American Psychiatric Association. *Diagnostic and Statistical Manual of Mental Disorders (DSM-3)*. Washington, D.C.: American Psychiatric Press, 1987.

Baron-Cohen, Simon, Helen Tager-Flusberg, and Donald J. Cohen. *Understanding Other Minds: Perspectives From Autism*. Oxford: Oxford University Press, 1993. Print.

Blumberg, Stephen J., et al. "Changes in Prevalence of Parent-Reported Autism Spectrum Disorder in School-Aged US Children: 2007 to 2011–2012." *National Health Statistics Reports* 65.20 (2013): 1–7.

Blume, Harvey. "Autistics, Freed from Face-to-Face Encounters, Are Communicating in Cyberspace." *The New York Times* 30 June 1997: 6. Academic Search Complete. Web. 5 Nov. 2011.

Bumiller, Kristen. "Quirky Citizens: Autism, Gender, and Reimagining Disability." *Disability and Society* 33.4 (2006): 967–91. JSTOR. Web. 5 Nov. 2011.

"Children's Books Select Bibliography." American Literature Association. N.p., 20 Feb. 2008. Web. 23 Mar. 2017.

Choldenko, Gennifer. *Al Capone Does My Shirts*. New York: Penguin, 2006.

Clifford, John. "The Subject in Discourse." *Contending with Words: Composition and Rhetoric in a Postmodern Age* (1991): 38–51.

Collins, Paul. *Not Even Wrong: Adventures in Autism*. Harrisonburg, VA: Vision, 2006.

Davis, Lennard J. *Enforcing Normalcy: Disability, Deafness, and the Body*. London: Verso, 1995. Print.

Draaisma, Douwe. "Stereotypes of Autism." *Philosophical Transactions of the Royal Society of London B: Biological Sciences* 364.1522 (2009): 1475–1480.

Erskine, Kathryn. *Mockingbird*. London: Usborne, 2012.

Foss, Chris. "Emerging from Emergence: Toward a Rethinking of the Recovery Story in Nine Contemporary Nonfiction Autism Narratives." *Disability Studies Quarterly* 29.2 (2009): 11. Web.

Foucault, Michel. *Archeology of Knowledge*. Abingdon-on-Thames: Routledge, 2010. Print.

_____. *Discipline and Punish: The Birth of the Prison*. New York: Vintage, 1979. Print.

_____. "Je Suis Un Artificier." *Michel Foucault: Entretiens*. Ed. Roger-Pol Droit. Paris: Jacob, 2004. Print.

Frith, Uta. "Confusions and Controversies About Asperger Syndrome." *Journal of Child Psychology and Psychiatry* 45 (2004): 672–86. Print.

Funk, R. "Disability Rights: From Caste to Class in the Context of Civil Rights." *Images of the Disabled, Disabling Images*. Ed. Alan Gartner. New York: Praeger, 1987. 7–30. Print.

Gerland, Gunilla. *A Real Person: Life on the Outside*. London: Souvenir, 2003. Print.

Gernsbacher, Morton Ann. "Autistics Need Acceptance, Not Cure." *Autistics.org: The REAL Voice of Autism*. N.p., 24 Apr. 2004. Web. 05 Nov. 2011.

Hacking, Ian. *The Social Construction of What?* Cambridge: Harvard University Press, 1999. Print.

Haddon, Mark. *The Curious Incident of the Dog in the Night-Time*. Washington, D.C.: National Geographic Books, 2007.

Hollindale, Peter. "Ideology and the Children's Book." *Signal* 55 (1988): 3.

Hunt, Lynn Avery. *Inventing Human Rights: A History*. New York: W.W. Norton, 2008. Print.

Jessum, Jeffrey E. *Diary of a Social Detective: Real-Life Tales of Mystery, Intrigue and Interpersonal Adventure*. Lenexa, KS: AAPC Publishing, 2011. Print.

Jurecic, Ann. "Mindblindness: Autism, Writing, and the Problem of Empathy." *Literature and Medicine* 25.1 (2006): 1–23.

Longmore, Paul K. *The New Disability History: American Perspectives*. New York: New York University Press, 2001. Print.

Lord, Cynthia. *Rules*. New York: Scholastic, 2013.

Miller, Susan. *Textual Carnivals: The Politics of Composition*. Carbondale: Southern Illinois University Press, 1993.

Mukhopadhyay, Tito Rajarshi. *Beyond the Silence: My Life, the World and Autism*. London: National Autistic Society, 2000. Print.

_____. *Gold of the Sunbeams: And Other Stories*. New York: W.W. Norton, 2011. Print.

_____. *How Can I Talk If My Lips Don't Move? Inside My Autistic Mind*. New York: Arcade, 2008. Print.

Murray, Stuart. "Autism and the Contemporary Sentimental: Fiction and the Narrative Fascination of the Present." *Literature and Medicine* 25.1 (2006): 24–45.

Nadesan, Majia Holmer. *Constructing Autism: Unravelling the "Truth" and Understanding the Social.* Abingdon-on-Thames: Routledge, 2011. Print.

Prince-Hughes, Dawn. *Aquamarine Blue 5: Personal Stories of College Students with Autism.* Athens, OH: Swallow Press, 2002. Print.

Sainsbury, Clare. *The Martian in the Playground: Understanding the Schoolchild with Asperger's Syndrome.* Thousand Oaks, CA: Sage, 2000. Print.

Sandler, Jen, and Michael M. Apple. "A Culture of Evidence, a Politics of Objectivity: The Evidence-Based Practices Movement in Educational Policy." *Handbook of Cultural Politics and Education.* Comp. Zeus Leonardo. Rotterdam, the Netherlands: Sense, 2010. 325–40. Print.

Sinclair, Jim. "Don't Mourn for Us. Our Voice." *Autism Network International* 1.3 (1993).

Smitherman, Geneva. "The Historical Struggle for Language Rights in CCCC." *Language Diversity in the Classroom: From Intention to Practice.* Ed. Geneva Smitherman and Victor Villanueva. Carbondale: Southern Illinois University Press, 2003. 7–39. Print.

Steelman, Patricia. *Select Bibliography of Children's Books about the Disability Experience.* American Library Association. 2009.www.ala.org/awardsgrants/sites/ala.org.awards grants/files/content/awardsrecords/schneideraward/2009_schneider_bio_children.pdf.

Stork, Francisco X. *Marcello in the Real World.* New York: Arthur A. Levine, 2010.

Tammet, Daniel. *Born on a Blue Day: Inside the Extraordinary Mind of an Autistic Savant.* New York: Free Press, 2007. Print.

Thiemann-Bourque, Kathy. "Navigating the Transition to Middle School: Peer Network Programming for Students With Autism." *ASHA Leader* 15.5 (2010): 12. Print.

Thomson, Rosemarie Garland. *Extraordinary Bodies: Figuring Physical Disability in American Culture and Literature.* New York: Columbia Univeristy Press, 1997. Print.

Williams, Donna. *Nobody Nowhere: The Remarkable Autobiography of an Autistic Girl.* London: Jessica Kingsley, 1999. Print.

Wolfensberger, Wolf. *The Principle of Normalization in Human Services.* Toronto: National Institute on Mental Retardation, 1972. Print.

Yergeau, Melanie. "Circle Wars: Reshaping the Typical Autism Essay." *Disability Studies Quarterly* 30.1 (2011): 21. Academic Search Complete. Web. 3 Sept. 2011.

Chinese Folklore
and Popular Culture
in Gene Luen Yang's
American Born Chinese

TIFFANY M.B. ANDERSON

What seems normal to a young person usually exists in the realm of his world and is oftentimes limited to the confines of his home, the halls of his school, and his engagements with playmates. To be certain, kids are normal in their minds. The world may tell them there is a typical way people identify difference—for instance, if one identifies as normal, then he juxtaposes everyone different from him as an abnormality, an Other. One way to avoid this othering is to increase the familiarity of diversity broadly and early in the lives of young people. Children and young adult literature (YAL) attempt to expose young people through diverse characters, home lives, ability, and more. However, not every child picks up a book, and not every book a child picks up triumphs diverse demographics. However, most young people are exposed to popular culture.

Gene Luen Yang suggests that popular culture is a powerful voice creating negative representations of racially and ethnically diverse people in his graphic novel *American Born Chinese* (2006). While demonstrating the prolific stereotypes created by popular culture, Yang simultaneously demonstrates the desire popular culture creates for ethnic and racial minorities to assimilate to mainstream American expectations of normalcy. While its take on the cultivation of identity for young people makes *American Born Chinese* a valuable text to read and analyze in a literature class, the combination of Yang's words and images introduce students to multitextual composition. At the beginning of this essay, I argue that while Chinese mythology, legends, and folklore preserve Chinese culture, American popular culture disseminates stereotypes of minorities to Americans while simultaneously pulling minorities into mainstream American culture. The latter portion of the essay considers how *American Born Chinese* expands the notion of texts to include graphic images and, consequently, introduces students to image analysis. *American Born Chinese* pairs nicely with graphic essay assignments.

Gene Luen Yang's graphic novel *American Born Chinese* focuses on three main characters: the Monkey King, Jin Wang, and Chin-kee, cousin to Danny, who all eventually exists in the same story although Yang initially presents them separately. The Monkey King is rejected at Heaven's gates from a dinner party for the gods, goddesses, spirits and demons because he is a monkey. The Monkey King, consequently, finds ways to physically beat those who rejected him while transforming himself into a more humanized version of his monkey-self. Jin Wang is a school-aged Chinese boy who leaves his comfortable home in Chinatown to a new neighborhood and school where he is one of only a handful of Asian American students. His classmates make fun of him, his teacher generalizes his name and origin, and he worries if he'll ever be "normal" enough to gain the affection of his first crush. Chin-kee, on the other hand, is an amalgamation of Chinese stereotypes. He visits his "normal" white American cousin Danny once a year embarrassing him so much that Danny often transfers schools at the end of Chin-kee's visits. These stories collide when we realize that Danny is an Americanized version of Jin Wang, and Chin-kee is the Monkey King serving as Jin Wang's "conscience—as a signpost to [Jin's] soul" (Yang 221). I will analyze these points later in the essay.

Mythology in Chinese Literature

Before assessing how popular culture affects American society, it is important to consider the cultural guidance Yang (2006) presents in *American Born Chinese*. He begins his novel with a dedication:

> To Ma,
> for her stories of the Monkey King
> And Ba,
> for his stories of Ah-Tong, the Taiwanese village boy [5].

Stories of Monkey King have been told for centuries. Wu Cheng'en published the 16th Century novel *Xiyou ji* (*Journey to the West*) ultimately standardizing the varied tales of the Monkey King named Sun Wukong. According to the novel, Sun Wukong was born from stone and rose to the rank of King of Flower-Fruit Mountain gaining powerful magical knowledge and wreaking havoc in all kingdoms of the world. Ultimately, Buddha restrains him under a rock mountain to prevent further damage of the Heavens. It is here that a

Buddhist monk finds Sun Wukong releasing him to serve as a devoted disciple to the monk (Pearson 2–3). Stephen Pearson argues that the Monkey King is leaving his print in American Literature citing examples from Gerald Vizenor's *Griever: An American Monkey King in China* (1987), Patricia Chao's *Monkey King* (1997), and Maxine Hong Kingston's *Tripmaster Monkey: His Fake Book* (1989). My interest in the prevalence of the Monkey King in ethnic literature, especially Chinese American literature, is the interconnectivity of mythology, legend, and contemporary storytelling.

Maxine Hong Kingston's *Woman Warrior: Memoirs of a Girlhood Among Ghosts* (1976) establishes the complex childhood in a culture where mythology and legend present life-lessons, reject adult dreams, and ultimately guide one's life. In her debut novel, Kingston writes the famed story of girl-warrior Fa Mulan as her own coming-of-age story. She begins, "When we Chinese girls listened to the adults talk-story, we learned that we failed if we grew up to be but wives and slaves" (Hong Kingston 23). Immediately, Kingston explains the purpose of the sharing of folklore. Here, the legend of Fa Mulan inspires Maxine to be more than a wife or slave opening up the possibilities for her and her friends to become "heroines, swordswomen" (23). The family legend of her aunt who gave birth to a child out of wedlock and who kills herself and the child serves as a cautionary tale when Maxine begins menstruation. Maxine's mother concludes the horrid story with, "Now that you have started to menstruate, what happened to her could happen to you. Don't humiliate us. […] The villagers are watchful" (5). The reader sees quite perfectly the reasons the folklore remains so interwoven into Chinese (American) child-rearing, but Maxine makes it plain: "Whenever she had to warn us about life, my mother told stories that ran like this one, a story to grow up on. […] Those of us in the first American generations have had to figure out how the invisible world the emigrants built around our childhoods fits in solid America" (5–6). It is as if the parents' experiences of Chinese culture cast a shadow on their children in the form of old-world folklore.

Kingston establishes the use of Chinese folklore in the Chinese (American) household as teaching tools, guides to Chinese culture despite American surroundings. All legend and mythology serve as cautionary tales or spiritual manifestos in some way or another, but, here, we have Chinese parents attempting to entrench Chinese culture in their strangely American children. In this way, Chinese folklore becomes the weapon against Americanization.

The Power of Storytelling

The concept of Chinese folklore serving as a cultural lesson plan exists in two ways in Yang's *American Born Chinese*: in the dedication and within the pages of the narrative. We know that Yang's parents shared with him the myth of the Monkey King and the legend of a village boy, in this case, named Ah-Tong. Yang himself experienced the transmittance of Chinese folklore from his Chinese immigrant parents. While the Monkey King's story initially exists in a vacuum, separate from the main narrative of Jin Wang, Jin's storyline begins with folklore as well. We see an image of young Jin with a tear rolling down his cheek. The narration begins, "My mother once told me an old Chinese Parable" (Yang 23). The mother tells a story of a mother and son who moves three times to find the perfect home. Here folklore is meant to comfort her son. The mother shares a parable with a child in the same scenario to show the commonplace of moving, the adaptability of children, and the concept that one can make any place home.

When Jin scores a date with his first crush, Amelia, he filters his cover up plans to deceive his mother with the very story she tells him to keep him from dating:

> My mother once explained to me why she chose to marry my father, "Of all the Ph.D. students at the university, he had the thickest glasses," she said. [...] "Thick glasses meant long hours of studying. Long hours of studying meant a strong work ethic [...] a strong work ethic meant a high salary. A high salary meant a good husband. [...] You concentrate on your studies now, Jin, later, you can have any girl you want" [163].

The image of Jin asking his friend to lie to Jin's mother juxtaposes Jin's mother's story of why she chose Jin's father in the first place, the very explanation to why Jin should wait to date, illustrates how American cultural dating rituals infiltrates the Chinese cultural storytelling. Although his mother's voice and story is in Jin's head, the desire to date like a typical American teenager drives his actions.

This Chinese cultural norm of dating is echoed by Jin's friend, Wei-Chen, and later by Jin's cousin representing a voice from his generation that is detached from the folklore but mimics the basic sentiment of his mother's intention. Wei-Chen laughs once he realizes Jin has a crush on Amelia saying, "In Taiwan, any boy who loves girls before he is eighteen, everybody laugh at him!" (89). Jin responds, "This isn't Taiwan, you doof! Stop acting like such an F.O.B. [fresh off the boat]" (89). Jin's reaction distances himself and Wei-Chen from the cultural notion of waiting to date by villainizing the very act of aligning with old-world culture as being "fresh off the boat," a negative term denoting the cultural difference of immigrants in America. We see here Jin's fear of being associated by that difference, and, perhaps, this fear emboldens him to ignore the cultural whisperings.

When Jin finally goes on his date, the wisdom and tales of his mother are silenced symbolically severing the cultural tradition she has tried to impart upon him. Instead, Jin's cousin's advice provides the backdrop of the setting of the date, and amounts to a warning: "Don't bother dating before you have your driver's license [...] it's totally lame" (164). And as the image captures Jin struggling to pedal his bicycle up a hill with Amelia riding atop the handlebars, Jin marks his own cousin as different from him, "Charlie had breath that smelled of old rice, a Bruce Lee haircut, and parents even stricter than my own," creating another "fresh off the boat" naysayer to American culture.

Although Jin wants to Americanize and avoid being labeled different, the stories that align him to Chinese culture are ubiquitous, so much so that out of Jin's three sections, two begin with his mother's stories. In his sections, we see a battle between the lingering voices of Chinese traditional cultures alive through stories and American culture championed by Jin's desire to fit in.

The Power of Popular Culture

If mythology, legend, and other variations of folklore preserve Chinese culture, then popular culture exists as the comparable force in American culture. Pre-school aged children engage Elmo on *Sesame Street* before learning to read while middle schoolers watch YouTube videos in place of doing homework. Music on the radio score drives to and from the grocery store, and memes on social media are more likely to create understanding of diverse populations than books. And, unfortunately, the depictions of ethnic and racial minorities in popular culture are often stereotypes that regrettably stand representative for an entire group of people. Antoine Dodson's instructions for people to "hide your kids, hide your wives, hide your husbands" did more good for bandana companies than it did for black, gay men ("Woman Wakes Up to Find Intruder"). Similarly, *American Idol* hopeful William Hung struck popular culture gold with his rendition of Ricky Martin's "She Bangs," solidifying a new image for Americans to add to a well-stocked stereotype of Asian immigrants ("William Hung Original *American Idol* Audition").

Yang builds his argument against the stereotypes of Asians generated in popular culture with the creation of Chin-Kee. The first section of Chin-Kee's story is heralded with a sit-com style introduction coupled with audience applause immediately striking commentary on the representation of Chinese (American) people on American sit-coms. The other images of Chin-Kee (a play on the derogative term Chink) explode from other limited viewpoints Americans have of Chinese culture and people including buck-teeth, Chinese take-out, simpleton behaviors, outstanding school performance, slits for eyes, subjectivity of women, yellow (actually yellow) skin, a decades-old joke about Coke, and a rendition of William Hung's rendition of Ricky Martin's "She Bangs."

As readers who know that this is the cousin of the Americanized version of Jin Wang, we must assume that Chin-Kee is a manifestation of Jin's fears of Chinese identity he imagines/feels is projected upon him as a Chinese American. Although the stereotypes obviously pervade Jin Wang's mind, we might assume that they occupy parts of his classmates' assumptions about Chinese (Americans) also. For instance, the author includes an exchange between Timmy, Timmy's mother, and Jin in which Timmy says, "My Momma says Chinese people eat dogs." Before Jin can respond, Timmy's mother clarifies, "Now be nice, Timmy. I'm sure Jin doesn't do that! In fact, Jin's family probably stopped that sort of thing as soon as they came to the United States" (31).

Earlier in the novel we encounter a teacher who generalizes Asian names, experiences, and nationalities. We see classmates worry about their dogs being eaten by Jin and his family. They assume that the Japanese girl (and only other Asian American in the class) is betrothed to Jin with a wedding date set for her thirteenth birthday. His classmates demonstrate early in their educational careers their opinion and assumed knowledge of him. Of course, we do not assume this information came from an encyclopedia rather the stereotypes disseminated through the all-powerful popular culture.

In their book *Immigration and American Popular Culture* (2007), Rachel Rubin and Jeffrey Melnick consider the questions, "what are immigrants going to 'do' to American culture? And what is American culture going to 'do' to immigrants? And also: what will American popular culture producers do 'about' immigrants?" (3). Rubin and Melnick begin their exploration of popular culture as the stage upon which America teases through racial, ethnic, and national identities by considering the significance blackface minstrelsy plays for other racial and ethnic minority groups in American. Specifically, "[b]lackface minstrelsy […] gave birth to a popular culture in the United States that has never been able to shrug off its responsibility to process racial (and later) ethnic identity as a central task" (5). While the popularity of blackface decreased post World War II, the concept of "masking" remained as "both a symptom of and a remedy for the injuries of racial and ethnic persecution in the United States" (5). So, while for a time period "blacking up" was a "masking" that perpetuated extreme ideas of blacks, the notion of "masking" is taken up as a protector against the very opinions stirred by the proliferation of minstrelsy. Rubin and Melnick argue, "Americans of the dominant culture and those in marginalized immigrant and ethnic groups wear masks as emblems, as weapons, [and] as apologies" (6). In the case of *American Born Chinese*, Chin-Kee serves as a version of Chinese minstrelsy while Danny serves as a protective mask that allows for Jin Wang to exist in America.

Yang demonstrates the authority of popular culture through the lasting impression it has on young people about children different from them. But Yang also demonstrates the influence popular culture has over children of immigrants to become more Americanized. After all, Chin-Kee haunts the Americanized Jin Wang. The stereotypes replicated in popular culture tell Jin what *not* to be. For children of immigrants, popular culture also serves as a distraction from the carefully cultivated folklore intended to keep children steeped in Chinese culture. What, for example, gave Jin Wang the idea to create a fully Americanized identity in the first place? Why, popular culture, of course.

Before he even felt pressured to assimilate by his classmates, Jin knew the options to transform that America offered. Even while living in Chinatown, Jin watched cartoons with other Chinese (American) boys his age. His exposure to American cartoons convinced him he was destined to become a Transformer, which is an occupational dream he tells an elder woman in a Chinese herbalist shop. She tells him quite simple, "It's easy to become anything you wish ... so long as you're willing to forfeit your soul" (29). When Jin becomes so frustrated with being Chinese in America, he imagines this elder magically granting him the transformation with the underlying truth that he has sold his soul to become an Americanized version of himself

Popular culture functions in two powerful ways in Yang's *American Born Chinese*. First, popular culture perpetuates stereotypes of ethnically diverse people on a large scale ultimately forcing individuals from those demographics to fight the stereotype to prove individual worth. Second, American popular culture permeates the cultivation of culture that immigrant parents create with folklore. In Jin's unique situation, popular culture also promotes an American ideology that encourages the transformation of self. Although this message of transformation is often received as empowering, for a child of an immigrant, it might require the forfeiture of one's soul.

Practical Considerations for
the Composition Classroom

American Born Chinese as a graphic novel is an interesting text for analysis before assigning graphic essays to students primarily because Yang's thesis, that Chinese American double-consciousness, although created by society, is affirmed and encouraged by American popular culture, cannot exist with this delicately nuanced presentation in prose alone. The dramatic irony that Yang capitalizes on revealing Danny's true identity as Jin is only achievable through graphic presentation. Yang visually signifies the inner desire to change one's identity through Jin's altered appearance. In other words, we see Jin as Danny because Jin's inner self wishes he could transform into a wholly white American boy. While words might capture the internal struggle of identity, only graphic images can create the layered narrative achieved in *American Born Chinese*. Without the visual of the transformation panel included in the text, Yang's shifting identities would feel shallow.

This is the gift of graphic novels. While we read novels without illustrations, we often create images in our mind to match the descriptive language. The author cannot entirely control these images we create. Additionally, graphics provide another layer of information that creates narrative opportunities that do not exist in prose alone forcing our brains to craft meaning between the images and the written text. Graphic novels also teach students to see more than the written language as text. They encourage the reader/viewer to value the images as text as well. For example, in *American Born Chinese*, Jin claims he feels a "jolt of confidence" which is paired with lightning bolts in the panel. The lightning bolts become a regular motif throughout the story that signals to the reader/viewer his increased confidence level. However, the bolts are attached to Jin's newly permed hair, his first attempt at undoing his Chinese identity. Yang's connection of Jin's confidence to the lightning bolt is an obvious detail, but the significance of this frail jolt of confidence connected to his shifting identity requires an attentive reader/viewer. However, the lightning bolts are details that deepen the analysis of the visual text and can be read seamlessly without acknowledging their existence. By pointing out the significance of these added images as paralleled to metaphors, motifs, and meaning in the written text, educators can demonstrate the wider categorization of texts and the importance to read all texts, graphic or words, with a critical eye.

Similar to how reading graphic novels require readers to create meaning between image and language, the graphic essay expects the writer/artist to consider ways language and images can demonstrate a thesis statement. The assignment of a graphic essay opens a new realm of critical thinking for students. Moreover, the graphic essay is a prime rhetoric genre for explorations of identity. The written language normalizes whiteness, heterosexuality, and abled-bodiness and requires an introduction of one's marginalized identity otherwise. Graphic essays avoid this compulsory expectation and allows those with marginalized identities a place to exist without the restriction of language.

There has been an increase in graphic essays since 2010 with publications in the New York Times and the Paris Review further validating the genre. Graphic essays like Gene Luen Yang's "Glare of Disdain" (2016) Christopher Noxon's "What the Civil Rights Movement Can Teach Us about Surviving Trump" (2017) and Lucy McKeon's "Stolen Glasses" (2016) explore how sharing stories can undo prejudices, connects the "moral clarity" of the civil rights movements to contemporary politics (Noxon), and present poor eyesight as an equalizer of people everywhere. For example, Noxon's essay replaces words that might come across as forced pathos with compelling drawings of Civil Rights activist's mugshots. Similarly, graphic essays allow students to think beyond trite phrasings with the use of fresh original images.

Here are two prompt examples for a graphic essay upon the completion of reading *American Born Chinese*:

- Gene Luen Yang has said, "I love the interplay between words and pictures. I love the fact that in comics, your pictures are acting like words, presenting themselves to be read." Create a graphic essay that demonstrates an interplay between words and images. How do words become pictures and pictures become words? How does this interplay affect the reader/viewer with meaning?
- Gene Luen Yang's American Born Chinese is a graphic novel chronicling the characters' reactions to rejection. Create an expository graphic essay about the first time someone rejected you. How did your identity shift because of this rejection? Did you ever return to who you were before, or did you remain forever changed?

These prompts demonstrate the wide range of graphic essays that might result in this *American Born Chinese* unit of study. Because the graphic novel introduces a reliance between image and words, students are already in a mode of considering the significance in the relationship between the two. In addition, the book feels remarkably intimate and invites a personal reflection of identity.

Yang's *American Born Chinese* doubles as a text worthy of literary analysis and as an example of how graphic images combined with words can communicate complicated concepts in ways that words alone cannot. In the classroom, teachers can ask students how the story of Jin changes without the images, how their understanding of his struggle with identity is fully realized in part due to the images, and how could their own stories of identity benefit from multitextual narratives. The connection between Yang's explorations in identity will undoubtedly lead students to connect to their personal identity stories while his style of storytelling with encourage them to conceptualize their stories in not simply words or images, but both.

Works Cited

Chao, Patricia. *The Monkey King: A Novel.* New York: Harper Perennial, 1997.
Kingston, Maxine Hong. *Tripmaster Monkey: His Fake Book.* New York: Vintage International, 1989.
Kingston, Maxine Hong. *The Woman Warrior: Memoirs of a Girlhood Among Ghosts.* New York: Vintage International, 1976.
McKeon, Lucy. "Stolen Glasses." *The Paris Review.* https://www.theparisreview.org/blog/2016/02/29/stolen-glasses/. Accessed 25 April 2017.
Noxon, Christopher. "What the Civil Rights Movement Can Teach Us About Surviving

Trump." *Fusion.* http://fusion.net/graphic-essay-what-the-civil-rights-movement-can-teach-1793858121. Accessed 25 April 2017.

Pearson, J. Stephen. "The Monkey King in the American Canon: Patricia Chao and Gerald Vizenor's Use of an Iconic Chinese Character." *Comparative Literature Studies,* vol. 43, no. 3, 2003, pp. 355–374.

Shu, Yuan. "Cultural Politics and Chinese-American Female Subjectivity: Rethinking Kingston's *Woman Warrior.*" *MELUS,* vol. 26, no. 2, 2001, pp. 199–223.

Vizenor, Gerald R. *Griever: An American Monkey King in China.* Minneapolis: University of Minnesota Press, 1987.

"William Hung original *American Idol* Audition." *YouTube.* https://www.youtube.com/watch?v=0d5eP0wWLQY. Accessed 25 April 2017.

"Woman Wakes Up to Find Intruder in Her Bed." *YouTube.* https://www.youtube.com/watch?v=vZKXAFqdlC4. Accessed 25 April 2017.

Yang, Gene Luen. *American Born Chinese.* New York: First Second Books, 2006.

_____. "Glare of Disdain." *The New York Times,* 23 Aug. 2016. https://www.nytimes.com/interactive/2016/04/01/books/review/28sketchbook-yang.html?ref=todayspaper. Accessed 25 April 2017.

About the Contributors

Melissa **Ames** is an associate professor of English at Eastern Illinois University, specializing in media studies, television scholarship, popular culture, feminist theory, and pedagogy. Her publications include *Women and Language, Time in Television Narrative*, and *How Pop Culture Shapes the Stages of a Woman's Life*.

Tiffany M.B. **Anderson** received her Ph.D. in U.S. ethnic literature at Ohio State University. She is director of Africana studies and assistant professor of English at Youngstown State University. She has published and presented on black masculinity, suicide as a tragic form of resistance, and disability and race.

Padma **Baliga** earned her Ph.D. in feminist theory and children's literature at Gandhigram Rural University. Her research and teaching interests include children's and young adult literature, women's studies, language pedagogy, Indian literature and Dalit writing. She co-translated *Alice in Wonderland* into Konkani.

Andrew **Bourelle** is an assistant professor of creative writing and rhetoric and writing at the University of New Mexico. He has written scholarly articles for numerous academic journals and has also published various stories, poems, and comics. His debut novel, *Heavy Metal*, won the 2016 Autumn House Fiction Prize.

Danielle **Brownsberger** is an assistant professor of English and coordinator of secondary English education at the University of North Carolina at Pembroke. She has seven years of experience teaching writing at the middle and high school levels, and her experience teaching students with autism has inspired her research.

Michele D. **Castleman** is an assistant professor of education at Heidelberg University in Tiffin, Ohio. She holds an MFA in creative writing from Chatham University and earned her Ph.D. in teaching and learning from the Ohio State University, focusing on young adult and children's literature.

Mary-Lynn **Chambers** earned her Ph.D. in technical and professional communication from East Carolina University. She teaches composition with a research focus in online education at Historically Black Colleges and Universities (HBCU). She aims to teach students how to write better, think more critically, and love literature.

Christi L. **Cook** is an assistant professor of language and literature at Southwestern Oklahoma State University. She earned her Ph.D. in English from the University of Texas at Arlington. Her dissertation and subsequent publications are comparative studies of gender and sexuality in recent Chicana and Anglo young adult literature.

Matthew D. **Fazio** is an adjunct faculty member at Robert Morris University and Point Park University where he teaches courses in communication, English, literature, and composition. He also acts as the marketing supervisor for an accounting and consulting firm. Hi research interests include online education, ethics, and literature.

Jenny **Ferguson** earned her Ph.D. in English at the University of South Dakota and is an activist and feminist. She writes fiction for adults and young adults as well as essays on rape culture, mental health, and Métis culture, as she attempts to reclaim their language, Michif.

Kelly F. **Franklin** is an English professor in Southern Iowa. She directs the Southwestern Community College drama club and is working on her EdD in curriculum and instruction. Her research interests include identity performance in virtual mediums and the composition classroom. She has published in collections about monsters in children's literature, bullying in popular culture, and poetry anthologies.

Tamara **Girardi** is an assistant professor of English at HACC, Central Pennsylvania's Community College. She writes young adult fiction and her research interests are online pedagogy, student engagement, young adult literature, creative writing studies, and unique approaches to teaching popularly anthologized literary works.

Kathleen B. **Gray** is the assistant academic dean at St. Francis College in New York. She earned her Ph.D. in sociology from the University of Pittsburgh. Her research interests include race and critical pedagogy. Her work focuses on making higher education accessible to underserved student populations.

Namrata **Harish** earned her MA in English at St. Joseph's College (Autonomous) in Bangalore, India, and teaches at her alma mater. Her teaching interests include women's studies, digital humanities, online networking and young adult literature.

Jenny L. **Howe** is a full-time lecturer at the University of Massachusetts, Dartmouth. She received her Ph.D. in English literature from Tufts University in Medford, Massachusetts. Her research interests include gender in children's literature, particularly in contemporary young adult fiction and fairy tales.

Mariam **Kushkaki** is an assistant professor of English at San Diego Mesa College. She received her Ph.D. from Arizona State University and her research interests include composition studies, popular culture, and culturally sustaining pedagogy.

Lacy **Marschalk** is a lecturer in English at the University of Alabama in Huntsville. She collaborated on a chapter for the *Purdue Information Literacy Handbook* series about co-creating an inquiry-based first-year experience curriculum to complement first-year writing courses.

Mary **McCulley** is an assistant professor of English at Cedarville University in Ohio. She teaches courses in composition, British literature, world literature, and children's/young adult literature. Her teaching includes creating interdisciplinary connections between literature, writing, the arts and sciences, and multimedia.

LeeAnn **Olivier** is an assistant professor of English at Tarrant County College Northwest Campus in Texas. Her poetry and creative nonfiction focuses on the feminist reinvention of myths and fairy tales. She has published in several literary journals, including *The Puritan* and *Hermeneutic Chaos*, among others.

Abigail G. **Scheg** is an associate dean of faculty for the School of Business at Northcentral University in Arizona. She researches and publishes on composition, creative writing, distance education, and popular culture. She is the author or editor of numerous texts, including *Bullying in Popular Culture* and *Heroes or Villains?*

Richard James **Whitehead** teaches in the biblical and religious studies department and the department of general education at Messiah College in Pennsylvania. He teaches first-year writing courses as well as religions of the world, Judaism and world mythology.

Tara Stillions **Whitehead** is an English professor at Harrisburg Area Community College in Pennsylvania. She received her MFA in creative writing from San Diego State University. Her work has appeared in *Chicago Review, Fiction International,* and *Texas Review,* among others. She received the Glimmer Train Award for New Writers.

Index